# THE BIBLE MINUTE
*Got A Minute? Get Inspired!*

One Year of Concise Bible Studies
*for*
*On the Go* Christians

Karin Syren

Copyright © 2010 by Karin S. Syren

*The Bible Minute*
by Karin S. Syren

Printed in the United States of America

ISBN 9781609573003

All rights reserved solely by the author. The author guarantees all contents are original and do not infringe upon the legal rights of any other person or work. No part of this book may be reproduced in any form without the permission of the author. The views expressed in this book are not necessarily those of the publisher.

Unless otherwise indicated, Bible quotations are taken from the *New American Standard Bible*. (NAS). Copyright © 1960, 1962, 1963, 1968, 1971, 1972, 1973, 1975, 1977, 1995 by The Lockman Foundation.

Scripture quotations marked (KJV) are taken from the *King James Version* of the Bible.

Some Scriptures are taken from the *Holy Bible, New International Version®*. (NIV®). Copyright © 1973, 1978, 1984 by the International Bible Society. Used by permission of Zondervan Bible Publishers.

Scripture quotations marked (NKJV) are taken from *The New King James Version*. Copyright © 1979, 1980, 1982 by Thomas Nelson, Inc.

Scripture quotations marked (AMP) are taken from *The Amplified Bible, Expanded Edition*. Copyright © 1987 by the Zondervan Corporation, and the Lockman Foundation

Scripture quotations marked (NLT) are taken from the *Holy Bible, New Living Translation*. Copyright © 1996, 2004 by Tyndale Charitable Trust. Used by permission of Tyndale House Publishers

www.xulonpress.com

Diary, to be a doer
continue to know that
of the Word, know it to
the watered over it to
perform it. James 1:22 to
Jeremiah 1:12
In Christ,
Lori Dyer

# *Dedication*

First and foremost, *The Bible Minute* is dedicated to the glory of God, in Whom, by Whom, and for Whom are all things.

And to my sister Vicky, who has not only continually encouraged me to keep writing but who has insisted that I compile these mini studies. Thank you for never giving up on me.

# *Acknowledgments*

I am obliged to numerous people who ultimately contributed to this book, directly or indirectly.

My family, as a whole, continues to play a huge role in everything I undertake. My sister Vicky has for 40 years consistently encouraged me to write. I am very grateful for the honesty of my children, who tell me the truth whenever I ask, even when it may be difficult to hear. I am forever in their debt for attempting to think of me in terms beyond "Mom."

My daughters Robin, Molly, and Heather, each from a different perspective, spent hours proofing the manuscript and offering remarkably thoughtful suggestions for clarification. Their support has been invaluable. I could not have completed this project without their assistance.

I am so grateful to my son Jonathan, a true man of God, who helped me to figure out what I wanted the cover art to communicate and then so beautifully executed it for me — on a moment's notice.

Finally, and most especially, there would be no book without the Holy Spirit, who not only inspires me but strengthens me to continue to put down what He gives me to say. When I am completely overwhelmed by what He asks of me, which is most of the time, He is there to remind me that He did not choose me for talent but for my awareness of my inability and therefore my complete dependence upon Him. Without Him I cannot rouse myself out of bed in the morning, much less do anything of value. With Him — anything He asks!

# *Introduction*

For several years, the Bible Minute went out as a devotional, initially to family members and then to a growing group of friends and internet acquaintances. As the number of messages grew and I learned that some recipients were creating binders of the messages, I began thinking about compiling them as a year-long Word study.

> *Study to show thyself approved unto God,*
> *A workman that needeth not to be ashamed,*
> *Rightly dividing the word of truth.*
> 2 Timothy 2:15 KJV

*Walking in a manner worthy of the Lord* (Colossians 1:10) is something each of us desires to do. In order to conduct our lives in this way, we must rely on something or someone other than our own puny wisdom and our own weak will. The Word of God is the answer and that is why you have joined a Bible study group or picked up this book as a personal study resource.

It is not necessary to use a devotional or become a member of a Bible study in order to make the Word more fruitful in your life, but many find it beneficial to put some degree of structure to their study. Working with another believer or group of believers brings with it the likelihood of ever-increasing revelation from the Word as each person offers input from the corporate anointing.

*The Bible Minute* is intended to enhance your current worship, never to replace it. There is nothing that can replace being planted in your own local church, experiencing the corporate anointing present in your church family and serving the kingdom alongside your brothers and sisters. It is meant to work well in any setting where the desire to better understand and personally apply the Word is present, either in your private or small group study time.

*The Bible Minute* has been designed for those whose heart is the Lord's but whose time is claimed by the many responsibilities of living diligently in the world. We need not abandon priceless time with our heavenly Father and His Word. Often all we need is a starter, a catalyst in order to set in motion hours of peaceful, fruitful meditation amid the chaos of our days. To that end the Bible Minute provides you with twice weekly studies for daily meditation.

I would suggest you keep a chronicle of your revelations in the Word, your answered prayers, and those precious words the Holy Spirit speaks to your heart, referring to it frequently. All too often, we miss answered prayers because we haven't been waiting and watching, expecting the answer. Likewise, if we don't record what the Holy Spirit has to say to us, we too often forget that He speaks and that we really do hear Him. If you have been listening and hearing all along, commit today to a deeper listening and a quick to do it response, and consider helping a brother or sister in the faith with what you have learned.

The majority of the messages in this volume were born of those most precious early morning hours, when, in the stillness before the day begins, I am most at the disposal of the Holy Spirit and hear best what He is speaking to me. Whatever I begin, whether it is prayer or reading the Word, I always keep a pen and notebook at the ready, for when He speaks, I do not want to miss a bit of it.

Each of these messages has taken me to a place I needed to go, at just the most perfect time in my life. I pray that they will touch a place in your heart that is thirsting for the Word as well!

*Karin Syren*
*May, 2010*

# How to Use The Bible Minute

The Bible Minute is a Bible study resource, designed as an aid to a richer, more personal experience with your heavenly Father, through a deeper relationship with His written Word. The 104 mini messages in *The Bible Minute,* each requiring one to five minutes reading time, are arranged for twice weekly study through one calendar year.

Each message has three levels of possible study, depending on the amount of time you wish you spend or depth of study you are seeking. If even deeper study is desired, you may choose to work on one study each week for two years instead of two per week for one year. Some messages are longer than others and some of the study suggestions require deeper thought and self-examination than others. Hopefully all of them will, in some way, entice you to a more meaningful and intimate relationship with the Father, through His Word.

Begin by familiarizing yourself with the titles. Note any that may be particularly pertinent to your personal journey. The messages are not arranged in a particular order, for the most part. Some are seasonal in flavor and have been spaced throughout the fifty-two weeks accordingly, but any of them can be considered at any time, as it works best for your personal Bible study.

As you begin each new message, read any Scriptures listed under the title. You may wish to write them out or print them from your Bible software or online Bible, using several different translations to enhance your understanding.

Then read the message straight through without stopping to reread or analyze at this point. Most can be read in under five minutes, depending on their length and your reading and comprehension speed. Now that you have the overview, reread the message, stopping to check Scriptures or make notes. At this point, you will begin to personalize the message, making it your own.

At the end of each message, take a few minutes to look back and ponder the principles addressed. Is this an area you have considered in the past? Does the message present a new viewpoint? Does it pose questions you are unsure about? Does it answer questions you have been asking? You may want to re-read the message several times throughout the day.

Following each message, there are three proposed action levels intended to personalize the principles presented. How deeply you go into each is completely your decision. If you have read the message alone, at this point you may find it helpful to involve a friend or family member. If you are working through *The Bible Minute* with your Bible study or small group, these action points will offer opportunities not only for personal growth but for lively group interactions as well.

***Confession*** is simply a personalized declaration of the biblical principle on which the message focuses. How deeply you are affected by your confession will depend on how personally you have received the principle. Confessions should always be made aloud, so you yourself can hear them. Remember that *faith cometh by hearing...* (Romans 10:17)

***Go Deeper*** lists all the Scriptures referenced within the message. In some instances additional Scriptures pertinent to the message are suggested, as well as the occasional Bible search exercise, to give you the opportunity to go directly to the Word. This level of study will give you the opportunity to begin cementing the principles for yourself using your favorite Bible translation.

***Minute by Minute*** offers suggestions for the direction you might take in applying the material to your own journey with the Word of God, in your own very real and personal world. Some suggest private exercises or self-examination, but most will give you an opportunity to work with other committed Christians, one-on-one or in small groups or Bible Studies. At this level, you will have the opportunity to apply most deeply and personally the biblical principles presented, not only to your relationship with God, but with the Church and reaching out into the world as well.

How deeply you go with each devotion is completely up to you and your needs. You may find that simply reading a message twice a week is exactly what you want. Perhaps you will read the messages with a friend over coffee. Then you might come to a message which you would like to share with a group and make it a full Bible study. *The Bible Minute* is set up to serve your changing needs for Word study during every season of your year.

The value of *The Bible Minute* is not intrinsic to the messages themselves but in their ability to capture your interest and take you more seriously into the Bible, deeply, personally and passionately connecting you to all God would speak to you through His awesome Word.

## *A Word About Translations*

There is no one translation of the Bible used throughout *The Bible Minute*, though I do tend toward the New American Standard when I am studying a passage deeply. There is great richness to be gained, in my opinion, from a variety of translations. When I write, I am generally surrounded by Bibles, as well as my Bible software which has the complete Strong's Concordance available. I would urge you, in your own study, to become acquainted with several translations, as well as personally studying the meanings of key words in the original languages. Rely on the Holy Spirit to guide you in your study. He will lead you to the right translation at the right moment in time, opening up the richness of God's message to you — right where you are!

I am so grateful that you have chosen *The Bible Minute* to deepen your study of God's Word for the coming year and I look forward, with great anticipation, to hearing from you about your personal journey with the Word of God!

# The Bible Minute

*While the earth remaineth, seedtime and harvest,
and cold and heat, and summer and winter,
and day and night shall not cease.*
Genesis 8:22 KJV

# *Winter*

*Thou hast set all the borders of the earth:
thou hast made summer and winter.*
Psalm 74:17 KJV

# Whose Plan?            Week 1

> *My purpose will be established,*
> *and I will accomplish all My good pleasure.*
>
> *Truly I have spoken; truly I will bring it to pass.*
> *I have planned, I will do it*
> Isaiah 46:10b, 11b NAS

As we face the end of some things and the beginning of others, let us ask ourselves whose plan we are pursuing. In our Scripture verse, God is very clear that it is *His* purpose (also translated as plan or design) which will be established, *His* good pleasure accomplished. Do you currently have a project or a plan that you believe God breathed into your heart? If that is the case, then the Word of God says it will be established.

He goes on to assure us that *He* accomplishes; *He* brings to pass, *all* His good pleasure. A close look at the Hebrew reveals that *good pleasure* means delights, wishes and desires, but also indicates matters, business and pursuits. God will bring His matters, His pursuits, and His business to pass. He tells us the same thing in two ways in one verse. Do you think He wants to make sure we get it? But do we really get it? He goes on to say I have spoken truly to you and then He reiterates — *I* plan it, *I* will do it and then He repeats it. It would take a great deal of effort *not* to understand this.

You may wonder if we actually have any part in this plan. Indeed we do! Our part is twofold. First, we must be in line with God's plan, God's business, His good pleasure, not our own. We must be in tune with His purpose for our lives, our families, our ministries, and our businesses. Then we must stand back and let God's will and work be done. Our part then is to believe, not doubt. After all, what else does a believer do? That's a tall enough order to keep us busy, without trying to do God's part as well!

*And this is His commandment, that we believe*
*in the name of His Son Jesus Christ,*
*and love one another, just as He commanded us.*
1 John 3:23 NAS

So as you face the completion of a year, a month, a week, or even just a day, I pray that your plans are big, bigger than you can dream alone and far bigger than you can hope to accomplish! I pray that in the upcoming day, or week or month or year, you are so in tune with the voice of the Holy Spirit that nothing can stop the working of God's plan through you.

At the juncture between the end of one cycle and the beginning of another, I would suggest a time of stillness, a time of listening, not for what *you* should do, but rather for how to best be prepared for what *God* wants to do *through* you. Take time to prepare yourself to be a vessel of greatness. Does that sound like a tall order — too tall perhaps?

*Truly, truly, I say to you, he who believes in Me,*
*the works that I do, he will do also;*
*and greater works than these he will do; because I go to the Father.*
*Whatever you ask in My name, that will I do,*
*so that the Father may be glorified in the Son.*
John 14:12-13 NAS

\*\*\*

*Confession:*
I am not called to be an achiever. I am called to be a believer, one through whom God's glory can be made known to the world!

***Go Deeper:***
Isaiah 46:10-11
1 John 3:23
John 14:12-13
1 Peter 2:2
Hebrews 5:14

***Minute by Minute:***
We have seen that God has plans to accomplish great things through us, but the plan must be His and we must take care to align ourselves with *His* plan, *His* good pleasure and *His* purpose. It is faith and availability that God requires of us.

To help you achieve a clearer focus, consider a daily time of personal stillness, of listening, not for what you should do, but for how best to be prepared for what God wants to do through you. Take time to prepare yourself to be a vessel of greatness. In order to fulfill John 14:12-13, the prerequisite is closeness, intimate fellowship with the person of the Holy Spirit.

For the next 30 days, plan your day around your time with the Lord, adjusting your schedule to accommodate it, if necessary. If you are truly serious, consider tithing your time during this period, perhaps dividing it into three "meals" a day, moving from the *sincere milk of the word* (1 Peter 2:2) to the *strong meat* of the Word (Hebrews 5:14). Chronicle and share your experience with your prayer and accountability partner. You will be amazed how God will work through your life!

# *Proper Goodbyes*                            *Week 1*

> *Proper good-byes lead to*
> *Productive beginnings.*
> Sarah Bowling (Marilyn Hickey Ministries)[1]

When I first heard Sarah Bowling's observation I was struck by the simple truth of it. But as time went on and I continued to think about it, I realized that the depth of this truth was far beyond what I had initially grasped.

Then, many months later, with this observation rolling around the back of my mind, I caught a small piece of an interview on a morning talk show with the popular radio talk show personality Dr. Laura Schlesinger, in which she observed,

> *You can't be on your mission*
> *If you're on your history.*
> Dr. Laura Schlesinger[2]

The impact of these two observations, taken together, fit comfortably right into my pocket and tied together some of the pieces of a program I had been developing, which became *Mission Accomplished — Strategic Life Planning*.[3]

> ***Purpose*** is why you were created.
> ***Mission*** is what you are meant to do about it.
> ***Visions*** are the evidence, and
> ***Goals*** are the means of achievement.

We each have a Mission to fulfill, a reason we were dispatched into this earthly realm. More often than not, when we discover what that Mission is, we have a choice to make before we can move forward, a choice very often involving goodbyes.

Isaiah answered God's call with, *Here I am, send me.* (Isaiah 6:8). How different from the invited disciple in Luke 9:59, who said, *Lord, first let me go and bury my father*. How frequently do we bargain with God in this same way? How often do we want to continue on our history, hesitating at the fork in the road between our past, our own plans and God's future for us? Jesus' response to this fellow was, *allow the dead to bury their own dead.* (Luke 9:60)

Abram was called out by God and told, *Go forth from your country and from your relatives and from your father's house to the land which I will show you.* (Genesis 12:2) In order to go with God's plan he was forced to leave his history and depend on a Vision as yet unrevealed, a call to faith.

Jesus made it abundantly clear for us, spelling it out in great big letters, *No one who puts his hand to the plow and looks back is fit for service in the kingdom of God.* (Luke 9:62)

What is your Mission? Why were you specifically sent, for a season, to earth? Surely it was not merely to test your ability to survive the running of the race and then, exhausted and defeated, to limp into heaven, pleased only to have made it home. Spend some time alone with your heavenly Father if you are not sure. Then look closely at those things that require a farewell. What history must you leave where it belongs, in the past, in order to passionately move forward in God's great plan for you? (See Jeremiah 29:11) What follows is the promise.

*And I will make you a great nation, And I will bless you,*
*And make your name great; And so you shall be a blessing;*
Genesis 12:2 NAS

\*\*\*

## Confession:

I make a quality decision to lay down my past, to turn back no longer, whether in fear, regret or nostalgia. As I place my trust in God's Word, I become daily more determined to live in *His* plan for me. I say good-bye to my history, failures and successes, and I move confidently into productive beginnings. As I focus on His glory in all things, I walk in hope and my Mission is being daily revealed to me and my future is assured!

***Go Deeper:***
Isaiah 6:8
Luke 9:59-60, 62
Genesis 12:2, 3
Jeremiah 29:1
Exodus 20:5

***Minute by Minute:***

What is God's plan for you? If you have no idea, perhaps you have missed the critical step of truly turning away from your past. God is a jealous God. He will settle for nothing less than all of you. (See Exodus 20:5) That means giving up the past.

What areas of your past are holding you back? Are you bound by the pain of your childhood, the scars of damaging relationships, or are you locked into past successes, the faded glories of better days?

Is your future planned around running from the past or even on regaining the past? Jesus says this makes you unfit for the kingdom and which of us does not long for a kingdom future? Set aside some quality time and take honest stock of how often your past is the basis for your present dealings and future plans. Then share it with a trusted friend or a prayer/accountability partner.

# *Dream As Big As God!*          *Week 2*

> *And it shall come to pass in the last days, God declares,*
> *that I will pour out of My Spirit upon all mankind,*
> *and your sons and your daughters shall prophesy*
> *[telling forth the divine counsels]*
> *and your young men shall see visions*
> *(divinely granted appearances),*
> *and your old men shall dream [divinely suggested] dreams.*
> Acts 2:17 AMP

This surely sounds like a tall order! I think you will see, however, that it is no more than what we are expected to do. But you might say, *I've tried that and it didn't work. I'm still sitting in the same place I was. Maybe it's not God's will for me to dream big.*

God formed man, the crown of His creation, to dream God-sized dreams. If we are indeed created in His image and likeness, according to Genesis 1:26, then we are capable of dreaming on a grand scale. (See Psalm 37:4, 5) Let's walk through some suggestions to move you to that exhilarating place of anticipating God's best.

## *Clear The Path*

Start by taking stock of what might be blocking your way. With the guidance of the Holy Spirit, begin to identify any areas that may be holding you back. God wants every one of us to receive all that He has for us, so we can be assured that He will be faithful to identify these areas for us — if we are quite clear within ourselves that we really want to know.

Next, ask for the necessary change in the areas you have identified. (James 4:2) Then, either make the changes the Holy Spirit indicates, or submit yourself to the change that He Himself will make for you. This will become clear as you spend time in the Word and in prayer. Consider daily communion and perhaps a period of fasting and prayer.

Finally, receive the manifestation of change.

Now you are ready to…

### *Change Your Perspective*

Stop thinking from the viewpoint of your current circumstances. Move your thinking out of your situation and into the dream. That's one of the attributes that sets man apart from the rest of God's creation, not only the gift of dreaming, but the ability to step *into* the dream, and in so doing, producing vision.

Do not confuse this with goal setting. A goal is a stepping stone, an interim position along the way, while a vision is a point of reference from which you are actually able to operate before you get there in reality, a God-given gift enabling earthbound man to see with heavenly perspective. Your perspective must not only be from within the specific vision, but must be even bigger than the vision. Adopt a godly perspective. After all, you are seated with Him in heavenly places (Ephesians 2:6).

### *Know Your Expectation*

Now, you must expect from God, and you must expect BIG! Know Who it is you are petitioning and expect accordingly. Do not ask until you are truly ready to expect! Anything less is an insult to God. Sound harsh? When what you are asking is for His glory, according to His will as outlined in His word, He will not fail you. It is really quite simple — He is either God or He is not.

How do you accomplish this kind of expectation? It is possible only by receiving a revelation of God's love for you on a *personal* basis. Once you get hold of this, along with an understanding of covenant, you are ready for expectation to do its job and make room for the expected blessing.

A few years ago, I was gifted with a new bedroom set, a huge sleigh bed, a dresser and a nightstand. I arranged with the furniture store for a delivery date, but of course I had to remove the old furniture from the room first. How silly it would have been for me to wait and see if they would actually deliver the furniture before taking steps to make a space for it.

I expected them to make good on their word, and even if something delayed delivery a day or so, I knew it was coming. I even painted the bedroom while I was waiting! If I can rely on a furniture company with that level of expectation, how much more the God

Who stepped off His throne and saved and delivered me and assured me of eternity in His presence?

We know what it looks like, this kind if expectation. It is the very atmosphere of receiving, and true expecting is solid faith, the kind in Hebrews 11:1 and it always makes room for the dream to become a reality.

Expectation lovingly names every animal on the face of the earth while anticipating at any moment the perfect helpmate to appear (Genesis 2:18-23). Expectation builds an ark, even when no one has ever seen rain and the neighbors are taunting (Genesis 6:11-7:13). Expectation bubbles over with joy into laughter at the very thought of a baby in the arms of a nonagenarian (Genesis 21:6).

Expectation boldly speaks the Gospel of the risen Lord to a crowd of thousands who would like to think you are drunk on wine at 9:00 in the morning (Acts 2:13-41). Expectation takes the hand of a crippled beggar at the gate Beautiful and boldly instructs him to stand for the first time since birth (Acts 3:6, 7).

Expectation takes God at His Word, and not only holds Him to it, but holds to that Word of promise, regardless of the circumstances. Expectation is the atmosphere for miracles; it opens the door of the supernatural into the natural.

Be like Paul in Philippians 1:20, and *eagerly expect and hope* that God is a god of His Word and if He said it, He is also able to perform it beyond your wildest dreams. (See Ephesians 3:20) Don't slam the door on your manifestation. Dream as big as God and then *expect* as big as God!

\*\*\*

*Confession:*
In these last days, I will see visions and dream dreams, looking at life from His perspective, expecting God to show up as I step out on His promises.

*Go Deeper:*
Acts 2:17; Joel 2:28
Genesis 1:26

Psalm 37:4, 5
James 4:2
Ephesians 2:6
Hebrews 11:1
Genesis 6:11-7:13
Genesis 21:6
Genesis 2:18-23
Acts 2:13-41
Acts 3:6, 7
Philippians 1:20
Ephesians 3:20

***Minute by Minute:***
    The miraculous always occurs in an atmosphere of expectancy. Jesus frequently told people that it was their faith that had activated their miracle. Faith believes and therefore expects what it believes. Reread the final paragraphs and determine what expectation looks like, or *could* look like, if put to work, in your own life.

# *Birthing Your Dream*            *Week 2*

> *Delight yourself in the Lord;*
> *And He will give you the desires of your heart.*
> *Commit your way to the Lord,*
> *Trust also in Him, and He will do it.*
> Psalm 37:4-5 NAS

Are you hoping to birth a dream but are not at all sure how to go about it? Are you wondering if you are stepping out too far this time? Is God in it, or is it only you? And does that even make a difference? Will God bless your dream, or is He the author of it? Consider a pregnant woman. Whether you are a woman or not, whether you have ever been pregnant or not, you have surely had an opportunity to observe the process.

A pregnant woman knows that the dream growing inside her will be released into the world according to plan, though she may wonder about the process. There is an established birth process and unless an interruption is allowed to interfere, it will take place. She need not aid the process in any way until the very end, when indeed she is urgently prompted. Her job is to provide the right internal atmosphere for growth and then, as the time approaches, to set the stage, preparing the external atmosphere for the arrival. What does this process involve? And what is the dream birther's role at each stage?

1. *Conception.* Shortly after conception a woman begins to become aware of changes in her, subtle at first, becoming more pronounced with time. In her heart she knows her course has changed, though she sees *nothing* and her daily routine is little altered. Her vision expands to make room for the knowledge of what is almost imperceptibly occurring inside her.
2. *Growth.* Major internal changes are taking place from the first moment, though no one around her is aware of anything but perhaps a change in demeanor, a slightly rosier complexion, or a faraway look. She *knows* though she doesn't *see*. Could this be faith?

3. **Naming**. At some point before the dream is birthed, in most cases, the dream is named and begins to be called by the chosen name. The name is chosen by what the dream represents, though *nothing* is yet visible. Knowing that a name is meant to relate characteristics of the named individual, the parents of this dream use faith once again to call this dream according to what they want it to become. They are calling things that are not yet seen as though they were now visible. (Romans 4:17)
4. **Birth**. As the process of transferring the dream from internal (invisible) to external (visible) begins, the mother may be uncertain how a dream of this size can possibly manifest in the outside world. Though she may be weary and discouraged at the length of time and energy involved, yet she is trusting it will go according to plan. She may occasionally become uncertain of her own ability to carry it through to completion as exhaustion sets in.

    This is the point at which we often give up on our dreams, deciding they are too difficult. In the natural, the process will occur, regardless of the mother's fatigue and misgivings, though she may require additional assistance and encouragement to remain on track with the process.

    This is the point at which spiritual *dream birthers* often require some assistance, some coaching, to remain on track. Unlike the natural birth process, we ourselves *can* halt the birth of a dream at this point, if we do not stay encouraged in the promises of God, surrounding ourselves with people who understand dream birthing, who will coach and challenge us to press on. Surround yourself with strong coaches, who will speak the word of God to you, and continually encourage you to press in and deliver your dream

At no point, once the dream has begun to rearrange the life of its mother, expanding her body and her vision, changing her appetites and her needs, does she say *what if this isn't real? What if there is really nothing in there at all?* Absurd, of course, but often we do just that with the dreams we are carrying. Rather than nurture, we question. What if this wasn't God's idea after all? What if this was conceived of my own imagination? Does the process actually begin to work once conception occurs, regardless of the circumstances surrounding it?

God is a God of process, and the processes of the natural world mirror the processes of the spiritual. The Bible tells us in Romans 12:2, that we have three alternatives, the *good* will of God, the *acceptable* will of God and the *perfect* will of God.

1. **Perfect Will of God.** The dream is totally God's idea, so we know it is His perfect will.
2. **Acceptable Will of God.** It is an idea approved by God.
3. **Good Will of God.** It is your idea, not necessarily God's best for you, and perhaps you really haven't sought Him earnestly concerning it. In your heart, however, and in your life you desire to honor Him.

Will He bless all three? Almost certainly, if you are operating according to Godly principles and your character is strong and your integrity is sound. But there is one more possibility we have not mentioned, but which I am sure you have considered.

4. **Contrary to God's Will.** This dream is *not* God's will. But what is it then? Sin, sorrow, grief, self-glorification, etc. are all contrary to God's will. If you have conceived your dream based on these or in reaction to them, you are surely not concerning yourself with God's desires.

So, you are pregnant — congratulations! What do you do now? Nurture your dream by seeking God, staying in close contact with Him through prayer and time in the Word. Commit your dream to God; He is the author of the process.

Are you pregnant? We are *all* called, men and women both, to parenthood of our dreams. Do you think you have conceived a dream? Make room for it, make provision for it, nurture it and commit it to the Lord. I'll see you in the Delivery Room!

*Confession:*
I vow this day to become a dream birther, seeking God's plan by delighting in Him and in His Word and nurturing the dreams I am given. (See Psalm 37:4-5)

*Go Deeper:*
Psalm 37:4, 5
Isaiah 46:11b
Isaiah 54:2, 3
Ephesians 3:20, 21
Genesis 6

*Minute by Minute:*
If you have determined that you are pregnant with one or more dreams, good prenatal care is the next step. Nurture your dream by daily seeking God, staying in close contact with Him through prayer and time in the Word. Make this a priority, not something you fit in where you can. Order your time and activities around this life-giving time of nourishment.

Then nurture it and commit your dream to the Lord. Determine if this dream is the good, the acceptable or the perfect will of God. And then know that He is the author of the process. Actively delight yourself in Him, as the Psalm exhorts.

Now begin to make room for the dream, making provision for it, even before you can see it. Invest time in developing a vision. With dream birthing, what you cannot envision, you probably will never birth. Just as you would prepare a space for a baby before its birth, make room for the manifestation of your dream. If you never make time, at this point, you risk birthing an underdeveloped dream, unable to survive.

Finally, don't worry about what others think or say. Noah didn't! Joseph didn't! Moses didn't! I'll see you in the Delivery Room!

# *Fundamentals of Big Dreams*                  Week 3

> *And it shall come to pass afterward, that I will pour out my spirit upon all flesh; and your sons and your daughters shall prophesy, your old men shall dream dreams, your young men shall see visions:*
> Joel 2:28 KJV

Bible scholars and students of prophecy tell us we are in the last days and nearing the times spoken of by Joel. But God has *always* made His Spirit available to those who would receive Him. And into these hearts He has always planted Big Dreams and Visions. It is these dreamers of Big Dreams who have and will continue to cradle and nurture God's plan.

There is great significance in being a dreamer of Big Dreams. *Noah* took hold of God's Vision, making it his own (Genesis 6), and acted on it, seeing it through as the focus for a large part of his life, despite the fact that he had no concept of rain and was undoubtedly building his ark in the midst of dry land and mocking neighbors.

*Abraham* is truly the father of our faith. In obedience, as Abram, he packed up his entire household and left all that he knew to follow a Big Dream, though all God told him was that he would be a great nation and a great name and highly blessed for a purpose (Genesis 12).

He believed God that he was the father of many nations (Genesis 15), despite the obvious circumstances of advanced age and lifelong infertility and it was accounted to him as righteousness (Genesis 15:6). And to prove it, he even accepted God's new name for him, Abraham (Genesis 17:5), thereby declaring what must have been reckoned as foolishness by all who knew him.

*Moses* had some difficulty making God's Vision his own at the outset (Exodus 3 & 4). In his dialogue with God, we can almost hear his tone of voice as he objects, his "buts," his "what ifs," and his protestations of heaviness of tongue (Exodus 4:10). And yet God gave him far more detail of what is to come than he initially gave to Abraham. I personally find it very easy to identify with Moses — *but God, are you sure you mean me?*

*Joseph* was already wildly unpopular with his large and complex family, but he intensified the animosity by flaunting his prophetic dream of superiority. (Genesis 37:8) Nonetheless, Joseph became firmly bound to the dreams, the Vision for his future. So much so that he spoke openly about them, against what we might consider better judgment.

Perhaps you are in the process of nurturing a Big Dream God has planted in your heart. If so, you have probably found that acceptance of the dream and all that implies, though often overwhelming, is only the beginning of your journey.

As the Body of Christ, we are in the midst of exciting times and not one of us is here by accident. We were chosen to be here (Psalm 139) at this time and like Esther, we each have a *for such a time as this* to fulfill (Esther 4:14).

You may already be well on the road to walking out the Big Dream God has given you. But whether you are already in the process of nurturing the dream, or do not yet know what God has for you, it is important to recognize there are certain elements common to all Big Dreams.

If we are really honest with ourselves, wouldn't it be wonderful if God would just touch us once and we could see instant manifestation of His dreams for us. But time and again, we are reminded that God is a god of process and we are required to fall in line if we are to be and do all that He has for us.

Here then are seven fundamentals of Big Dreams. Some of them may already be very familiar to you. Others you have yet to discover. Whatever your point on the journey, know that God has seen it all beforehand and He will never let you go. He will be with you to the end. (Matthew 28:20)

Though this is not a definitive list, it is a beginning and each is born out in Scripture. Add others to your own list as you go and be prepared to share them with those who follow after you.

*The Bible Minute*

1. People often scoff at Big Dreams and those who dream them. Learn to turn a deaf ear.
2. Big Dreams are sustaining through periods of positioning.
3. Big Dreams call for strong character.
4. Big Dreams necessitate future thinking, present excellence, and letting go of the past.
5. Big Dreams require knowing when to *flow* and when to *go*.
6. Big Dreams demand divine focus.
7. Big Dreams require faith in the blessing of the Giver of Big Dreams.

*And his brethren said to him, Shalt thou indeed reign over us? or shalt thou indeed have dominion over us? And they hated him yet the more for his dreams, and for his words.*
Genesis 37:8 KJV

\*\*\*

### *Confession:*
For my part, I will delight myself in the Lord, with the assurance that He will give me the desires of my heart. (Psalm 37:4) They will be the Big Dreams He has planned for me, and with my focus turned to Him, I will see them come to fruition.

### *Go Deeper:*
Joel 2:28
Genesis 12
Genesis 15:6
Genesis 17:5
Psalm 139
Esther 4:14
Matthew 28:20
Genesis 37:8
Psalm 37:4
Psalm 37:7

***Minute by Minute:***

Has God planted Big Dreams in your heart? (Psalm 27:4) Can you identify with Noah, Abraham, Moses and Joseph, all of whom were asked to nurture dreams way beyond their capacity? Have you tried to talk God out of it as Moses did, trying to convince Him of your inability?

Have you waited and waited and waited as Abraham did, wondering if you were meant to help the dream along with your own Hagar? Or perhaps, like Joseph, and Noah, you have enthusiastically shared your dream and been laughed at, snubbed or even rejected in the process.

Reread the fundamentals of Big Dreams and be encouraged and then exhorted. You have been chosen just as surely as any of the well known Big Dreamers of the Bible. Work your way through each of the fundamentals listed, and any others the Holy Spirit shows you.

Make sure to record the dream as God unfolds it to you. Allow God to make whatever changes are necessary in you to prepare for the manifestation of His plan. And then, keeping your eyes on Him at all times, go with the flow of His perfect plan. (Jeremiah 29:11)

# *A Peaceful Life*                      *Week 3*

> *These things I have spoken to you,*
> *That in Me you may have peace.*
> *In the world you have tribulation;*
> *But take courage,*
> *I have overcome the world.*
> John 16:33 NAS

Can any of us say we are not seeking peace? The Greek word for peace used in this verse expresses a state of untroubled, undisturbed well-being. The Greek Lexicon goes on to say that this kind of peace comes only from "accomplished reconciliation." It is a peace that is the fruit of knowing the need has already been met, the desire fulfilled.

Brother Lawrence, a 17th century French Carmelite lay brother laid hold of this peace and made it his own. The fact that he was crippled as a young man and in constant pain in no way disturbed the peace and joy he daily experienced working as a cook and sandal maker in his religious community.

In the small book, *The Practice of the Presence of God*,[4] through conversations and letters, his simple secrets are shared. Well worth reading and rereading, this small book speaks volumes. Consideration of a few of the principles by which he ordered his life will start us toward attaining the same transcendent peace.

1. Establish a sense of God's presence by means of a simple ongoing conversation with Him. Make no differentiation between set times of prayer and devotion and the ordinary hours of your day by praising and loving Him continually (1 Thessalonians 5:17).
2. Free yourself from concern about sin by doing all for the love of God, even the seemingly simplest and most insignificant daily tasks. Such unbroken love is not a reflection of the size of the work, or its worldly importance, but of the size of the love behind it. Sin after all is not a separate institution, but simply the result of a break in this flow of love. (Matthew 22:37, 38)

3. Reject useless thoughts, which become the "spoilers." It is the little foxes that spoil the vine (Song of Solomon 2:15), those seemingly simple, harmless diversions that start us down the slippery slope. (1 Corinthians 10:23)
4. Acknowledge failures and your inability, in your own strength, to do otherwise. Then move forward, not dwelling on them. If you miss the mark, which is what the Greek word implies, aim higher next time, but don't park on failure. Repairing the break in continual communion with God that fostered the failure must be your focus. Keep your eyes on God rather than self.
5. Forsake penances and religious exercises as a means of entering into the presence of God. Practicing continual communion, simple all-inclusive constant conversation with your heavenly Father, which after all is the desired end of all religious exercise, will enliven those very practices and exercises. Practice His presence first — the rest will follow.
6. Live in His grace at all times, knowing that nothing you will ever do can earn His presence. It is His gift to you out of His great and abiding love for you. You have but to receive it and bask in it to begin to truly practice His presence in every corner of your life.

You will quickly find that God's presence and His peace go hand in hand, that all other roads are useless rabbit trails. In the foundation scripture today, Jesus Himself makes it clear, *that in Me you may have peace.* There is no other way.

\*\*\*

*Confession:*
"*O my God, since Thou art with me, and I must now, in obedience to Thy commands, apply my mind to these outward things, I beseech Thee to grant me the grace to continue in Thy Presence; and to this end do Thou prosper me with Thy assistance. Receive all my works, and possess all my affections.*" Brother Lawrence

***Go Deeper:***
John 16:33
1 Thessalonians 5:17
Matthew 22:37, 38
Song of Solomon 2:15
1 Corinthians 10:23

***Minute by Minute:***
    Using the six principles above as a basis, create a chronicle of your own personal journey to a peaceful life in the continual presence of the Lord. Consider working with a friend or prayer partner, or your Bible study group to encourage one another in this pursuit.

# *Judge Not*                        Week 4

> *Judge not, and ye shall not be judged:*
> *condemn not, and ye shall not be condemned*
> Luke 6:37a KJV

*That's not me*, you may be saying. *No, this message is definitely not about me. I never presume to judge another. But oh boy, my neighbor (sister/husband/friend), now that's another story!* Let's take a closer look at what the Scripture is really saying and see if it just might be directed at us after all.

According to Webster, to judge is to form an estimate or evaluation of; especially a negative opinion and judgment is a formal utterance of an authoritative opinion. Clearly, a careful judgment requires a thorough collecting of information. Do we always have *all* the information before handing down our opinions? When were any of us last inside another's heart? After all, that is the only place where we will find all the information needed for a fair judgment.

And what if we actually do have all the necessary information? Jesus' words don't change because we are well informed. Judgment is His province (Deuteronomy 1:17; Romans 12:19), not ours. Is there one among us who believes he can do a better job of it? But in order to better keep ourselves in check, we should know what actually constitutes judgment. Are there ways, perhaps, in which we are unknowingly judging one another daily?

How about **disapproval**? I am sure each one of us can pull from the not too distant past an instance of our disapproval of another. The word simply reeks of judgment. It assumes that what we cannot approve of must be wrong.

What about **opinion**? How often do we offer ours — unsolicited? The dictionary says this is *a view, judgment, or appraisal formed in the mind*.

And then there is the ever popular scapegoat when it comes to judging — **interpretation**. *Well, you know, that's just my own interpretation of the matter*. But in the process we have managed to inter-ject our two cents on the subject, and often without being asked.

As we leave the first month of a new year, let us resolve to become more sensitive to our tendencies to be judgmental and to replace them instead with a tendency toward forgiveness. If we can tend toward the one, then we can surely tend toward the other.

> *Forgive, and ye shall be forgiven:*
> Luke 6:37 (KJV)

The last part of our verse gives us the positive side of the exhortation. Those whom we quickly forgive, we simply cannot judge — the two are at opposite ends of the spectrum.

\*\*\*

### *Confession:*
I set my intention this day to relieve myself of the burden of judgment. I will leave that to the Lord and occupy myself with forgiveness!

### *Go Deeper:*
Luke 6:37a
Deuteronomy 1:17; Romans 12:19
Luke 6:37

### *Minute by Minute:*
*Disapproval, opinion* and *interpretation*. These are words we may not readily associate with judgment, but we sometimes use them to cover a judgmental spirit. As you move through the next several days, be aware of the number of times you employ these and in what circumstances. Have you been asked to offer your thoughts or are you making judgments? Ask for guidance from the Holy Spirit in moving from judgment to understanding to forgiveness.

# Complete Transfusion                     Week 4

> *There was then only one remedy for SIN: sinless blood;*
> *and only one could supply this, even the sinless Son of God.*
> M.R. DeHaan, M.D., <u>The Chemistry of the Blood</u>[5]

Have you ever felt as though you needed a fresh start; an opportunity to go back to square one and just start all over again, and maybe get it really right this time? There is an old expression that was often used when a situation began to go stale. Someone would say, *What we need is some fresh blood!* Well, I have some good news for you! Not only is our spirit forever brand new, *born again* (see John 3), but we have been given a total transfusion as well, complete replacement of our tainted, genetically flawed blood, carrying every type of sin, sickness and disease.

That old blood contains in it the capacity for *every* type of sin, beyond our wildest imaginations, and is merely waiting for the right catalyst to awaken it into deadly manifestation. Every conceivable anguish is inherent in its composition, waiting like a sleeping giant in each individual for the spark that will ignite it and propel that person to certain doom, both now and in the hereafter, on into eternity.

But God Himself stepped from His eternal throne into the envelope of time, manifesting His own nature, which is Divine Blood poured into human flesh as Jesus Christ, and forever altered the ancestry of those who, by an act of the will, choose total exchange of their tainted, deadly blood for His abundant life (*Zoë*) carrying blood. (See Leviticus 17:11 and John 10:10.)

Ephesians 2:13 reminds us that, *now in Christ Jesus ye who sometimes were far off are made nigh by the blood of Christ*. If you have submitted yourself to this exchange, the same Divine Blood that flowed in Jesus' veins now runs through you, cleansing all it touches, bringing healing and restoration to every area, and removing all residual effects of the deadly blood it has replaced.

Life must be conducted from the inside to the outside to experience the manifestation of this transformation. The power of your words now becomes vital to the visible manifestation of what has taken place. Take care not to hang on to the old ways, the old sins, the old infirmities, weaknesses, inadequacies, sicknesses, and deformities. Allow the blood to work.

> *Work hard to show the results of your salvation,*
> *obeying God with deep reverence and fear.*
> *For God is working in you, giving you the desire*
> *and the power to do what pleases him.*
> Philippians 2:12b-13 NLT

God will not force Himself on anyone. Everything with God is *always* a choice. He never forces us to come to Him and He will never force us to submit to the Blood in any area. We must open the doors of our souls, our bodies, our past, and expose them to the Blood. The Blood does not condemn; it only washes and renews, destroying the deadly, pulverizing and disintegrating anything of darkness it touches. Now that's Good News!

\*\*\*

*Confession:*
The life is in the blood (Leviticus 17:11) and I choose this day to be cleansed by the life-giving blood of Jesus Christ.

*Go Deeper:*
John 3
Leviticus 17:11; John 10:10
Ephesians 2:13
Philippians 2:12b-13
Romans 12:2

*Minute by Minute:*
We are three part beings, comprised of spirit, soul and body. The soul (mind, will and emotions), the fleshly area, is ever at odds with the spirit. If you are born again, you can be assured that your spirit has been completely regenerated, born anew. But the flesh is not directly impacted by this New Birth and must be subdued and

brought under submission by an act of the will. Romans 12:2 tells us we must renew our minds and the Word of God is the way. Paul exhorts us in Philippians 2 to work out our salvation. He is saying, *you are saved, now what?*

Are you saved but living like the world? Are you born again but still struggling with sickness, infirmity, depression, lack and addiction? If so, the answer is to start living from your reborn spirit by strengthening the influence of your spirit man. Begin with Paul's encouragement to the Romans. Renew your mind *daily* with the Word of God and you will see the completion of your transformation, spirit, soul and body. Consider starting a regular Bible study with like-minded family and friends and hold each other accountable each day for following through individually on what you receive together.

> *And so dear brothers and sisters,*
> *I plead with you to give your bodies to God*
> *because of all he has done for you.*
> *Let them be a living and holy sacrifice —*
> *the kind he will find acceptable.*
> *This is truly the way to worship him.*
> *Don't copy the behavior and customs of this world,*
> *but let God transform you into a new person*
> *by changing the way you think.*
> *Then you will learn to know God's will for you,*
> *which is good and pleasing and perfect.*
> Romans 12:1-2 NLT

# *Fruit of the Presence*            *Week 5*

> *And whatever you do in word or deed,*
> *Do all in the name of the Lord Jesus,*
> *Giving thanks to God the Father through Him.*
> Colossians 3:17 NKJV

We have looked together at the simple way in which Brother Lawrence, a 17$^{th}$ century Carmelite lay brother lived his life in perpetual conversation and close communion with God. (See *A Peaceful Life*) The third chapter of Colossians tells us something of how such a lifestyle will manifest in the world.

While Paul is definitely admonishing the church at Colossae to behave in a particular way, to *walk worthy of the Lord* (Colossians 3:10), without the practice of the presence of God such a walk will scarcely be conceivable and certainly not attainable.

As we become daily more fully focused *on things above, not on things of the earth* (Colossians 3:2), sowing our time and focus as a seed, increasing in our communion with the Father, praying without ceasing (1 Thessalonians 5:17), we will come to that worthy walk certain of the harvest.

The end result is a walk in love, which Paul calls *the bond of perfection.* (Colossians 3:14) We tend to avoid any admonition to perfection, but if we read on, we see that our part in attaining this state is simply to get out of the way. Verses 15 and 16 tell us to *let* the peace of God rule and to *let* the Word of God dwell in us. Step back and allow God's Word and His Spirit to ascend and accomplish that worthy walk.

Continue to practice the presence of God today and, as you fellowship with Him, simply and continually, you will daily look and act more and more like Him. The result must be that whatever you do, you will *do it heartily as to the Lord and not to men...* (verse 23).

***Confession:***
As I set my intention to do *all things* in the name of the Lord Jesus, giving thanks to the Father through Him, my works cannot fail to reflect His image to the world.

***Go Deeper:***
Colossians 3:2-17, 23
1 Thessalonians 5:17
1 Corinthians 13:4-8
Galatians 5:22-23
1 John 4:8

***Minute by Minute:***
Love will always be the ultimate Fruit of His Presence. (1 John 4:8) Consider 30 days of the Love Exercise based on 1 Corinthians 13:4-8, as explained in the message *Without Love*. In your prayer journal, chronicle the changes you observe in your personal Christian walk. Be careful to record changes in the way those around you are responding to you as well.

## *Releasing the Power*   Week 5

> *Now He could do no mighty work there,*
> *except that He laid His hands*
> *on a few sick people and healed them.*
> Mark 6:5 NKJV

How often have you grown weary waiting for the power of God to show up in your situation? Disheartenment begins to creep in and then discouragement, closely followed by doubt and ultimately unbelief. Possibly God has ceased caring about your situation. Perhaps you are not worthy of His attention. Or maybe the day of His miracle intervention has passed completely.

Mark 6 gives us the real truth about the miracle working power of God, a simple underlying principle of godly intervention, over which we ourselves exert the influence.

In Mark 6:1-6, Jesus is in His home town and his neighbors are having difficulty considering Him in any capacity but that of Mary's son, the carpenter. As a result of this "who do you think you are" mentality, they have become offended at this hometown boy passing Himself off as a rabbi.

The very nature of offense is to hinder, to deter, and to cause to stumble and it has done all of these very effectively in this instance. Offense walked the citizenry of Nazareth right into unbelief, literally meaning *without faith,* in the Greek.

Numerous Gospel instances make it clear that faith is the key to experiencing God's promises. God cannot work His will in your situation when the faith connection is broken by doubt and unbelief (yes, that's right, He *cannot* — read Mark 6:5 again).

God is unchanging and unchangeable (Hebrews 6:18; Hebrews 13:8), so we know the power is still there; but we need to tap into it. So, if you are not seeing the *dunamis* power of God manifest in your life and circumstances, the question is how to restore the broken faith connection. Following are a few scriptural suggestions.

1. ***Begin by repenting for your lack of faith.***
   Hebrews 11:6 tells us that we simply cannot please God without faith. Have you ever wondered about that Scripture — I have. Without faith we lose that vital connection to the power of God in our lives, the avenue by which He not only blesses us, but the world through us as well. (Genesis 12:2) God is love and love is always disposed to giving and cannot be fulfilled (or pleased) any other way.
2. ***Renew your mind by filling it with the Word of God.*** (Romans 12:2, Romans 10:17)
   Rid your mind of sometimes useless and often dangerous information by washing with water through the Word. (Ephesians 5:26) Fill yourself with the Word just as Jesus ordered the water pots filled in John 2, fully expecting the Word to transform you and your output as well. As you continue to fill yourself, your faith and expectation of the arrival of God's power will increase.
3. ***Consciously open the gates and expect the promised rivers of living water to flow from your innermost being.*** (John 7:38)
   There are two elements to this step. First you must *allow* the flow and then you must *expect* it. There are those who don't believe God could work through them and there are those who are actually afraid that He will! Allow it, release it and expect it.
4. ***Step out in faith.***
   You will never know for sure what God can and will do in your life until you are willing to open yourself to His power. And you will never open yourself to His power by waiting for assurances. The assurance follows the leap. True faith must act on the Word. (James 1:22)

> *Now faith is the substance*
> *of things hoped for, the evidence of things not seen.*
> Hebrews 11:1 KJV

The Amplified translation says that faith is *the assurance (the confirmation, the title deed)*. When you hold a deed, you may not have seen the property, but you know it belongs to you!

You will get no more than that on the front end. But *expect the power* and oh what wonders await you on the other side!

*\*\*\**

*Confession:*
I hold the key to the dunamis power of God in and through my life. My faith is the connector. Romans 12:3 assures me that I have faith because everyone has been given a measure and I know how to keep it coming and growing by feeding myself daily on the Word of God. (Romans 10:17) The manifest power of God will follow!

*Go Deeper:*
Mark 6:1-6
Hebrews 6:18; Hebrews 13:8
Hebrews 11:6
Genesis 12:2
Romans 12:2, 3; Romans 10:17
Ephesians 5:26
John 2
John 7:38
James 1:22
Hebrews 11:1
Romans 12:3
Romans 10:17

*Minute by Minute:*
If you are really serious about experiencing the release of God's power in and through your life, begin by following the suggestions above. Keep in mind that the release of God's power cannot be reduced to a formula. However, since these suggestions are all Scripture based, you cannot go wrong. As you work your way through them, your journey will become a unique and personal one.

# Without Love                                     Week 6

> *Love bears up under anything and everything that comes,*
> *is ever ready to believe the best of every person,*
> *its hopes are fadeless under all circumstances,*
> *and it endures everything [without weakening].*
> *Love never fails [never fades out or becomes*
> *obsolete or comes to an end]*
> 1 Corinthians 13:4-8 AMP

Throughout the Old Testament, we are witness to the constant struggle of God's own chosen ones, the Israelites, to keep faith with Jehovah God, to maintain the special relationship He Himself initiated and into which he invited them.

The Law, beginning in Exodus 20, was given to them for this very purpose. Observance was intended to keep them holy, to sanctify them and set them apart from all others as God's own, in familial relationship with Him. Full observance served to brand them, not only as His *peculiar treasure*, His *precious possession* (Psalm 135:4; Deuteronomy 26:18; Malachi 3:17), but as righteous in His sight. As we well know, they never did arrive at full observance. Though righteousness eluded them and they were certainly less than loyal, Jehovah remained faithful.

In the New Testament, we are introduced to a *new Way* to achieve this righteous standard of the Law, not removed *from the Law*, but removed *from the letter of the Law to the heart*, the very spirit of the Law (see Matthew 5-7).

Put it all together and it still seems like more than we can manage. That's because it is! Even the Apostle Paul admitted as much, *in my flesh, I can will what is right, but I cannot perform it.* (Romans 7:18). Until we see for ourselves that the Law, in its entirety, as presented in the Old and New Covenants, is the Law of Love, we cannot hope to achieve, much less *be* the Righteousness of God. Our only hope is to know that God is Love (1 John 4:8, 16) and Love is the key.

This Love is no mere human emotion, but the God kind of Love, *Hesed* in the Old Covenant and *Agape* in the New Covenant.

What's more, this Love is within every Christian (Romans 5:5) and we are meant to evidence this to the world (Matthew 5:13-16; John 13:35; Romans 2:13). The fruit, the evidence to the world, is the visibility of the Law of Love in action. (Matthew 22:37; Mark 12:30 and Luke 10:27)

We have a detailed guide to recognizing this Love and to checking our own daily Love walk in 1 Corinthians 13. Read chapters 12 through 14 in their entirety for the full context, and then concentrate on the picture painted by chapter 13. It still seems impossible, until we realize we already have all that we need to do all that the Law requires of us.

Try this very simple, very effective exercise for 30 days and watch your capacity for Agape Love grow. Each day, read chapter 13:4-8 three times aloud, as a confession, in the following way. This is particularly effective when read from the Amplified Bible translation.

1. Read the verses first right from the text, exactly as translated.
2. Next, since God is Love and, therefore Love is God, the second time you read it, replace the word *Love* (or *Charity* in the King James) with *God*.
3. If you are a Christian, you have God living inside your spirit, in the form of the Holy Spirit (1Corinthians 3:16, 17; 1 Corinthians 6:19). You already have the God kind of Love available in your heart (Galatians 5:22) and you are empowered to walk in it. The third time you read the passage, begin by saying *therefore* and substitute your own name, or *I*, whichever you prefer as you read.

There is no mystery or magic in this exercise. It is simply a statement of what the Bible says is true, and a reminder that we were never meant to walk in the Law of Love in our own strength and power. This is the evidence that though God asks the impossible of us, He has already given us what we need to do it. Hallelujah!

\*\*\*

*Confession:*
I am an ambassador of the Law of Love to the world, filled with Hesed/Agape. I will let my light so shine before men that they, seeing my good works, will glorify my Father, the God who IS Love. (See Matthew 5:16 KJV)

*Go Deeper:*
1 Corinthians 13:4-8
Exodus 20
Psalm 135:4
Deuteronomy 26:18
Malachi 3:17
Romans 5:5
Matthew 5:13-16
John 13:35
Romans 2:13
Matthew 22:37
Mark 12:30
Luke 10:27
1 Corinthians 13:4-8
1Corinthians 3:16, 17
1 Corinthians 6:19
Galatians 5:22
1 John 4:8, 16

*Minute by Minute:*
1 John 4 tells us that God and Love are one and the same. Therefore, an understanding of Love throughout the Bible will reveal to us the nature and character of God Himself. *Hesed*, often translated as mercy or lovingkindness, appears 250 times in the Old Testament and *Agape*, translated as love or charity appears 116 times in the New Testament. Clearly understanding Scriptural Love is critical to the believer. At the same time you are doing the Love exercise suggested above, embark on a study of *Hesed* and *Agape*, using a good concordance and your Bible software or an online Bible resource. You will be blessed and amazed at what is revealed to you about the heart of God and your role in making it known to the world at large.

# *Be Encouraged — Believe the Love*        Week 6

*For I am convinced, that neither death, nor life,*
*nor angels, nor principalities,*
*nor things present, nor things to come,*
*nor powers, nor height, nor depth*
*nor any other created thing,*
*shall be able to separate us*
*from the love of God,*
*which is in Christ Jesus our Lord.*
Romans 8:38, 39 KJV

*Now if you will obey me and keep my covenant,*
*you will be my own special treasure*
*from among all the peoples on earth;*
*for all the earth belongs to me.*
Exodus 19:5 NLT

*For thus saith the L*ORD *of hosts;*
*After the glory hath he sent me*
*unto the nations which spoiled you:*
*for he that toucheth you*
*toucheth the apple of His eye.*
Zechariah 2:8 KJV

*In this is love, not that we loved God,*
*but He loved us and sent His Son*
*to be the propitiation for our sins.*
1 John 4:10 NAS

*As the Father hath loved me,*
*So have I loved you:*
*Continue ye in my love.*
John 15:9 KJV

Read these scriptures several times, from your own Bible, in your own favorite translation, and then from other translations, if they are available to you. Allow them to sink deeply into your heart. Each one tells us something of the character of God, since it tells us about the Love of God.

God cannot be separated from Love because His nature is Love itself, and that Love is directed toward us! This is the essence of Scripture. The volume we loosely refer to as the Bible is, in reality, one lengthy Love Letter to each one of us. If one book or letter, verse or phrase, proverb or single word does not sink into your spirit, bringing you that life-giving revelation of His total passion for you, He has provided thousands more from which to choose.

He has expressed His Love toward each one of us in everything He has ever said or done. His creation, from the majestic expanse of the universe to the unique intricacy of a single snowflake, to the awesome wonder of these bodies in which He has housed us, is an expression of His Love for us. Every Word He has spoken is an expression of this Love. In truth, since God and His Word are one (John 1:1), every word He has spoken *is* His Love.

Jesus is the Love in flesh. He came to be seen, to be heard, to be known with the senses. God loves us so completely that He left nothing to chance. He surrounded us with it, to the point that we must actively run from it, purposely avoid it, in order to attempt living life without it. Even then, we cannot escape the Love. It is there, at all times, in all places, under all circumstances whether we choose to acknowledge it or not. Believe the Love.

Now, that's encouraging!

***

*Confession:*
If I have not felt God's passionate love for me, I will stop running this day and surrender. I will quiet all the sounds of life and determine to allow Him to capture me with His love.

*Go Deeper:*
Romans 8:38, 39
Exodus 19:5
Zechariah 2:8
1 John 4:10
John 15:9
John 1:1

*Minute by Minute:*

The nature of fire is to burn and give off warmth. Anyone who comes close to a campfire will be warmed by it. The fire knows no distinction, not deciding who will be warmed and who will not. If you draw near, you will benefit and if you are not warm, it is because you have wandered off into the chill of the surrounding darkness.

The nature of love is to give. Anything else, though calling itself love, is a perversion, a wolf in sheep's clothing. Those among us who seem unable to receive God's Love have likely experienced a counterfeit love and, having been deeply hurt and perhaps even shamed by it, have turned away. If that describes you, begin this day to know the truth of Jesus' statement of His earthly mission that He came to seek and save that which was lost. (See Luke 19:10 and Luke 15.)

Any change of course, though fueled by a desire of the heart, is begun with a conscious, quality decision to move in a specific direction. Make a decision this day to turn toward the Love, not allowing your past, your present or your feelings to make the decision for you. Then begin to learn the nature and the character of the Love, which is God Himself by digging into His word and finding out for yourself what He says about you and what He has done for the love of you. Begin with the writings of John, including his gospel account and his three letters.

# The Survey Shows...                                   Week 7

> *I am come that they might have life,
> and that they might have it more abundantly.*
> John 10:10b KJV

A Gallup poll taken in 2006 indicates that 73% of the population is convinced that God exists and only 3% that He does not, with the rest of the sampling distinguished by their degree of conviction. 43% purport to be evangelical or *born again*. Twenty-eight percent believe the Bible is the actual Word of God and 49% believe it to be the inspired Word of God.

A brief piece in an issue of *Christian Counseling Connection* (2005, Issue 1)[6], a publication of the American Association of Christian Counselors (AACC), reported that according to a Newsweek poll, 78% of Americans believe Jesus physically rose from the dead. Seventy-five percent believe He came to absolve mankind of their sin.

In the same issue, George Barna is quoted as observing that *"...about half of all born again adults do not share their faith with any non-believers..."* Those who actually share their faith do so infrequently.

There appears to be a disconnect here. If we believe that God exists and His Word is true; if we believe in Jesus Christ as the Son of God and in His purpose for us, why would we not share it? If we believe that our own sin is washed away and we will share eternity with a loving God in a paradise He created for us, why would we not shout it from the housetops?

If you are already liberally sharing the Good News, great. But if you, like many, are shy and reticent, perhaps one or more of these concerns will be familiar.

### Fear of ridicule.

You don't want to be known as a fanatic, a Bible nut, one of *those*? It's a valid concern. Jesus was clear that ridicule would come (John 16:33). He never promised ease, but He promised us successes

(Mark 16:17-18) and He promised we would never be left alone (Matthew 28:20)!

### *Desire not to offend.*

You are concerned about being "PC," a valid concern. But ask yourself how politically correct it is to allow someone to go careening over the edge of a cliff to certain, unsuspecting death. It may be correct to hold your tongue but if the result is eternity separated from the love of God, isn't it worth the risk?

### *Inexperience.*

You may never have shared your faith because you simply do not know where to start. Most of us prefer not to be "sledgehammer Christians," beating people mercilessly about the head and shoulders until they succumb just to get us to back off! That's not witnessing; that's harassment!

### *Uncertainty of your calling.*

You may not be called to the evangelistic ministry or you may not yet be sure of your personal call from God. Nevertheless we are all called to be witnesses of the Gospel in and by our daily lives. (Matthew 5:13-14)

The Great Commission calls each of us. Mark 16:15 is a direct command from Jesus *Go ye into all the world, and preach the gospel to every creature.* It leaves no room for choice or excuse. But it also does not expect the believer to go it alone. We have been well-equipped with the *Word,* the *Name* and the *Blood,* with the *Holy Spirit* to guide us, all that we need in order to do all He asks of us.

Jesus said, in John 15:12, *This is my commandment, That ye love one another, as I have loved you.* Jesus' love for mankind was characterized, in His earthly ministry, by laying down His life, His flesh, for all. We are called to overcome our flesh to spread the Good News. Read through John's Gospel and his letters for a refresher.

Here are a few suggestions to get you started.

***Begin by loving the unlovely.***
Be a friend to that one person in your office who everyone else avoids. Respond to the angry with patience. Sow peace where there is conflict. These are also part of the Great Commission. People will undoubtedly be so confounded that they will come back for more.

***Share your personal testimony with friends and family.***
If you are a believer, you have a testimony. It is truly that simple. People may not want your opinions but they will always be interested in your story. It's a non-threatening approach, one you can be comfortable with. Sow it as seed and wait for it to germinate and sprout. Give it some time to grow and people will begin to come back with questions. In the meantime, keep them covered with Scripture based prayer.

***Trust the Word of God to do what it was sent to do. (Isaiah 55:11)***
Our part is to apply the Word of God faithfully and it is His part to cause it to come to pass. If we do our part, God will do His. Cast any concern about that onto Him (Psalm 55:22) and go forth joyfully and confidently proclaiming the love that has been so liberally poured into your life (Romans 5:5).

> *Then the Lord said to me,*
> *'you have seen well,*
> *for I am watching over my word*
> *to perform it.'*
> Jeremiah 1:12 NAS

\*\*\*

*Confession:*
I will step out of my comfort zone this day and reach out to at least one person. I know that I need not be an evangelist, just a witness of God's great love. This I can do!

***Go Deeper:***
John 10:10b
John 16:33
Mark 16:17-18
Matthew 28:20
Matthew 5:14
Mark 16:15
John 15:12
Isaiah 55:11
Mark 4:14-20; 1 Corinthians 3:6
Psalm 55:22
Romans 5:5
Jeremiah 1:12

***Minute by Minute:***
    If you are not currently sharing your faith with those around you, which of the concerns listed above most closely approximates your reason(s)? Know that if you are in the Word and prayer daily, you are fully equipped to carry out The Great Commission. (Mark 16:15) Choose one of the suggestions and step out of your comfort zone today (we have included some resources in the Appendix to help you get started). Record your decision in your prayer journal and at the end of the day record the results. Do your part and trust God to do His. You will be pleasantly surprised.

# Faith Catalog  Week 7

> *Jesus replied, 'I tell you the truth, if you have faith
> and do not doubt, not only can you do what was
> done to the fig tree, but also you can say to this
> mountain, 'Go, throw yourself into the sea,'
> and it will be done. If you believe, you will
> receive whatever you ask for in prayer.'*
> Matthew 21:21, 22 NIV

Have you ever taken a faith stand, found your scriptures, confessed them, spoken it to several people, and then somehow it got put on the back burner, along with all those other issues you are standing and believing for?

James tells us, *that the trying* (testing the character, determining its caliber) *of your faith worketh patience. But let patience have her perfect work, that ye may be perfect and entire, wanting nothing.* (James 1:3. 4). Obviously endurance plays an important role, patience in standing for what God has promised. It has been said that faith and patience are a powerful duo and must go hand in hand toward manifestation. Paul coaches us on the importance of this patient stance in.

> *And having done all [the crisis demands],
> to stand [firmly in your place].
> Stand therefore [hold your ground],*
> Ephesians 6:13, 14 AMP

We can bring some practical wisdom to the execution of our faith. God is a god of process, and since we are created in His image, we are also inherently process driven beings. Create for yourself a card file, using a recipe box, which holds 4x6 index cards. Use one card for each issue, including on it the following information:

1. ***The issue*** you are believing for, healing, salvation of a loved one, wisdom in a specific area, the perfect job, a financial breakthrough, a new home, etc.
2. ***Foundation scriptures***, which assure you that the issue is God's will for you. It is, after all, of no use to believe for something God has not willed for you. Back up your desires with the Word. Psalm 37:4 says that He gives us the desires of our hearts, but if we back up to verse 3, we see that we must delight ourselves in Him first. The Holy Spirit will never say anything to you which is not confirmed by the written Word of God.) So if God has spoken a word to you, you must find confirmation in the Scriptures.
3. Set down ***your statement of faith***, draw your faith line, and step across it. Make a quality decision, one from which there is no turning back, and then,
4. Seal it the next time you ***receive communion***. Record the date, and put God (and yourself) in remembrance of His covenant and His covenant promises.
5. ***Praise Him*** for his faithfulness, for being a covenant keeping God. The Bible tells us that we must take our petitions to God and give thanks at the time of asking. (Philippians 4:6) Envision your excitement at seeing what you have believed for, and put that into effect, *before* you actually see it.
6. Record ***the date of manifestation***, the date you receive into the physical realm what you have already received in the spirit. (Mark 11:23, 24)

Make it a practice to go through your cards on a regular basis. Update progress, fill in new dates, check those issues which require additional scriptures, etc. Decorate your card file and keep it next to your favorite chair, or in your prayer closet, wherever it will be readily visible on a daily basis. Use dividers to differentiate between those issues you are currently believing for, and those which have become your testimonies. Share your testimonies — often!

***

*Confession:*
I will be one who takes my stand of faith and who does not move until I see the manifestation and then I will be one who gives God the glory, shouting from the housetops His faithfulness to His Word!

*Go Deeper:*
Matthew 21:21, 22
James 1:3. 4
Ephesians 6:13, 14
Psalm 37:3, 4
Philippians 4:6
Mark 11:23, 24

*Minute by Minute:*
Working with a prayer and accountability partner, together follow the steps above to create your own faith catalogs. Share your victories with one another and encourage each other in the word and in prayer. Set aside regularly scheduled appointments in order to keep the process alive. One of my clients meets early every Saturday morning for coffee with her prayer/accountability partner and they encourage and keep one another on track. They are both seeing the manifestation of God's promises in their lives as never before. You will be amazed at how faithful God has been all along!

## *Be Still*                 *Week 8*
## *Achieving Stillness*

> *'Be still, and know that I am God:*
> *I will be exalted among the nations,*
> *I will be exalted in the earth.'*
>
> *The LORD Almighty is with us;*
> *the God of Jacob is our fortress. Selah.*
> Psalm 46:10, 11 NIV

Most of us have heard the Stephen Curtis Chapman rendition of "Be Still." There are tears on many cheeks and many hearts are touched. He is delivering a message from the heart of God that we all yearn to receive at the deepest level. It is a very powerful interpretation of the Psalm.

Let's take a closer look at these verses and determine why we are so touched. It is God Himself speaking to us in verse 10 and He begins by exhorting us to *Be Still.* The Hebrew word, *raphah*, means to cease, to give up all activity, making room for stillness and quiet, for purposeful inactivity to replace whatever has engaged you. Become receptive.

The root word also suggests curing and repairing, making whole. God is telling us to give up our striving, to put aside all frenetic activity in order to come to a place of quietness to experience the curative power, the wholeness of what He has to say next.

Have you ever tried to speak to a small child whose attention is short and wanders continually? Each of my children was a champion squirmer, almost surely holding squirming workshops when my back was turned. They were all very "busy" children who wanted to keep tabs on what was going on over their shoulder as I was talking to them. No matter what I had to say, by the time I was finished, I felt certain they hadn't heard a word — I didn't have their attention! *God is saying in verse 10, I have something of benefit to say to you, something from My heart of love - give me your whole attention.*

When I was in high school, I tried everything to convince my mother that I could study effectively with the radio or TV playing. She would have none of it, and would urge me to go to my room to study undisturbed. In those instances when I was sure I knew best, and attempted to take in the necessary information amidst the sensory overload, I ended up studying late into the night in order to grasp what I had missed.

If we are never still, never ceasing our own activity, we will never hear what God has to say to us. He loves us beyond our understanding and has much He wants to tell us. Will we *be still* and listen?

### *Confession:*
Father, I will consciously practice stillness this day, knowing that I am meant to hear your voice above all others.

### *Go Deeper:*
Psalm 46:10, 11
John 10:1-5

### *Minute by Minute:*
*God is telling us to give up our striving, to put aside all frenetic activity in order to come to a place of quietness to experience the curative power, the wholeness of what He has to say next.*

Achieving stillness comes by practicing stillness. Just as with anything else we would like to master, stillness comes with practice. Purposeful inactivity is not something that we are taught, nor is it a state that is prized in our culture. But it is this very type of stillness that creates an atmosphere conducive to repair and to wholeness, and, as we shall see, to *knowing* as well.

Condition yourself to stillness. By decision, actively remove distractions, both external and internal. Aside from turning down, tuning out or, better still, turning off the external chatter, take stock of the internal distractions that habitually keep you from stillness as well. Actively laying them down completely may be quite challenging at first. So begin by giving yourself permission to just set them aside for a predetermined period of time. Assure your worrisome side that you will pick them up again at the prearranged time.

Practice this faithfully each day during your *quiet time*. If you do not already have a quiet time, a time for the Word and prayer, this would be a perfect time to begin the practice. You will very soon be amazed at how effectively you are able to *be still*.

# Be Still
# Knowing
### Week 8

> *"Be still, and know that I am God:*
> *I will be exalted among the nations,*
> *I will be exalted in the earth."*
>
> *The LORD Almighty is with us;*
> *the God of Jacob is our fortress. Selah.*
> Psalm 46:10, 11 NIV

The next thing He tells us to do is *know*. Before we can address what God wants us to know, we must understand what it means to *know*. This is a practical kind of knowing. It means to discern, to recognize and to acknowledge. This kind of knowing assumes that if we will observe, we *will know*. Our stillness will be followed by knowing. If we are never still, never cease our constant activity, we will never *know*.

God tells us in Hosea 4:6, *My people perish for a lack of knowledge,* the harvest of not knowing. He is very specific, referring to us as *His* people, so the knowledge He is speaking of is specific to us. One translation says, *My people are destroyed, cut off, for a lack of knowledge.* We gain a deeper understanding when we see that the word for knowledge used here is from the same primary root word we see in Psalm 46. It means a lack of the "contemplative perception of a wise man." Wouldn't we all like to fit into that category?

There is very little as frustrating as attempting to impart something to a person who is certain they know everything! If you are in a position of leadership and must daily face an employee who simply cannot be told anything, you know what true challenge is! Often, such a person will cut you off in mid sentence, "I know, I know" when you feel certain they have no clue what you are trying to convey. We are often obliged to watch this individual slide into deep trouble, perhaps even danger because of their refusal to accept vital knowledge.

January 17, 1994, the Los Angeles area experienced the strongest earthquake in an urban area since the great quake of 1906. With an epicenter 20 miles WNW of LA, the quake measured 6.7 on the Richter Scale, killing 57 and displacing 20,000, and doing an estimated $20-40 billion of damage. The I-57/Antelope Valley Freeway interchange sustained major damage. An aerial view shows the raised roadway neatly split into 6 sections, cars tossed like toys about the splintered sections, as well as thrown into the gorge below. One photo shows a vehicle hanging precariously from the remaining strip of highway.

I wondered what became of the driver. Had he known what was coming, he certainly would not have set out in his car. What were his thoughts as he hung suspended? Did he wish he'd stayed in bed? Did he think at any point, "if only I'd known?" The quake occurred at 4:30 AM, so he did not even have the comfort of daylight to orient himself to his surroundings. Had he known, possessed precious knowledge, he could have made some decisions based on that knowledge. He could have avoided the possibility of perishing.

Let us make a quality decision that every time we are given an opportunity to know, we do not do as the know-it-all but take time to know what it has been given us to know and let us not perish for lack of it.

*Confession:*
Father, I set my intention this day to stop periodically and, in stillness, recognize and acknowledge You, knowing You as God, as Lord of My life.

**Go Deeper:**
Psalm 46:10, 11
Hosea 4:6

*Minute by Minute:*
Being still and knowing are closely connected. God knew we would need to accomplish the first in order to achieve the second.

*Know that I am God.* On the surface, this sounds so simple, doesn't it? After all, we all know that He is God don't we? But that is most often a knowing of the mind. There is a far deeper knowledge to be gained from achieving stillness! *Deep calls unto deep* (Psalm 42:7) as the Holy Spirit speaks to you in the hidden, most secret part of you. The knowing that results is experiential in the same way that a husband and wife know one another, physically, emotionally and spiritually. If you desire this, be assured that it is God's heart for you to know Him in this way.

Set aside a regular time when you are most free of outside distractions and purposefully lay down those thoughts and concerns that would rob you of this sweet communion. This will undoubtedly take practice, so do not become frustrated. The reward is great! There is so much that God would have you know of Him.

*Draw nigh to God, and he will draw nigh to you.*
James 4:8 KVJ

# Be Still
## I AM God

**Week 9**

As we have practiced stillness and we have become ready to know, we discover that God has a simple and yet life-transforming message for us.

> *"Be still, and know that I am God:*
> *I will be exalted among the nations,*
> *I will be exalted in the earth."*
>
> *The LORD Almighty is with us;*
> *the God of Jacob is our fortress. Selah.*
> Psalm 46:10, 11 NIV

With this new found stillness, our attention is no longer wandering, we realize that what we are asked to do is come to an understanding and we are ready for it. Then God tells us very simply, *I AM GOD*. Without knowledge of the *I AM GOD*, we are effectively cut off from Him and all that He IS. There is more to these 3 words than all the books in all the world have been able to reveal (John 21:25).

The entire Bible is about these three words, though it is actually one word, *Elohim*. But it is best translated as *I AM GOD*. One way God has revealed His many facets to us is through His names (Elohim, Elyon, El-Shaddai, and Jehovah, to list a few). If our minds were able to grasp all these names at once, we would understand Who He IS. But our minds cannot fully take hold of what is Almighty, Everlasting, Omnipotent, Omniscient, All Powerful, and All Love. Our brains are finite and cannot comprehend the infinite, like attempting to contain the oceans in a dropper.

As three part beings, spirit, soul, and body, if we have accepted Jesus' invitation to be Lord of our lives, we *can* grasp all of this, through our new spirit in which He has come to live. Yes, God's own Spirit has come to dwell in us, and for that reason, we *can* understand, we *can* grasp, in our spirits, what is not understood in the limited human mind.

He has given us a Name for Himself that encompasses all the others. When our spirit hears this name, it leaps for joy. He told Moses, *you shall say to the sons of Israel, I AM has sent you* (Exodus 3:14, 15). He says of Himself, I AM WHO I AM, which in Hebrew is the unpronounceable tetragrammaton, literally a word of four letters, that has come to be synonymous with *YHWH*. The Israelites were constrained from speaking the Name of God, which was considered much too holy for human utterance.

What does this mean to you and me? He wasn't talking to us in Psalm 46 after all, was He? When the changeless God reveals Himself, we can be sure He is today what He said He was yesterday. He is the I AM God for each of us. He says to you specifically, I AM whatever you need, I AM whatever you lack, and I AM the God who loves you no matter what. I AM the God who understands you better than you do yourself.

I AM your Healer, your Sanctifier, your Victory, your Peace, your Righteousness, your Shepherd and your Helper, Who will never leave you and never forsake you. I AM the God whose name is too awesome to be spoken, and My love is directed toward *you*. You are my beloved child, you are the apple of My eye, you are My peculiar treasure, and the center of my attention.

He stepped out of heaven, stepped into time and took on flesh and blood to be like you, so you could be like Him, so you could be with Him for all of eternity. Be still and know Him who loves you when you are unlovable, understands you when you don't understand yourself, and desires nothing more than to fellowship with you when you feel at your most worthless.

## *Confession:*

Father, I may not understand it all, but I will choose to trust the Love. I will seek you at all times, in all things, and accept that You ARE my All in All.

***Go Deeper:***
Psalm 46:10, 11
John 21:25
Exodus 3:14, 15

***Minute by Minute***:

> *My people are destroyed for lack of knowledge*
> Hosea 4:6 NKJV

Make the quality decision that every time you are given an opportunity to *know* that you will take the time to stop and to comprehend, on a deep level, what is being revealed to you and let yourself not perish for the lack of it. This will require a true awakening to the kind of *knowing* that the Holy Spirit will reveal to you, as we talked about in Part 2, and then a decision to assimilate what has been imparted to you. If you are willing to invest the time, God will reveal Himself to you!

# Be Still
# The Lord Almighty

Week 9

> *'Be still, and know that I am God:*
> *I will be exalted among the nations,*
> *I will be exalted in the earth.'*
>
> *The LORD Almighty is with us;*
> *the God of Jacob is our fortress. Selah.*
> Psalm 46:10, 11 NIV

Once God has our attention and we have heard His declaration, He follows up with an assurance. He makes a pledge, a guarantee. He adds weight to His declaration, I AM GOD, by assuring us that He WILL be exalted among the nations. It is as though He is saying to us, you have nothing to fear, I really AM God, and one proof of it will be that you will see Me lifted up, worshiped, exalted, and extolled by those who do not yet know Me or who have rejected Me.

> *That at the name of Jesus every knee should bow,*
> *of things in heaven, and things in earth,*
> *and things under the earth.*
> Philippians 2:10 KJV

The Hebrew for *nations* in Psalm 46 does not refer to countries and governments, but rather to foreigners, those alien to the strong Hebrew belief in God. Remember that they were the only ones who knew God at that time. Everyone else was a foreigner, a heathen. God is telling us that *Who He Is* is so powerful and so victorious that even the ungodly will exalt His Name.

He goes on to assure us that His Name will be exalted in the earth, which covers everything from the physical earth to the nations. He is driving His point home. He is telling us that He doesn't just *say* He is God, but we will *see it*, as well.

As if that isn't enough to keep us assured until He comes for us, the psalmist then tells us that He is Jehovah, the Lord of hosts. He has the full army of the heavenly host, all the angels of heaven, at His command, at His beck and call. All He needs to do is speak a word and they are dispatched to the scene. Psalm 103:20 tells us that *(the angels) are mighty in strength who perform His word, obeying the voice of His word.*

Then, once the extent of His power has been established for us, we are told that He is with us. Now we have arrived at the crux of the matter. This is a precursor to God as He is revealed to us in the New Testament, in the form of the Man Jesus, Emmanuel, the personification of God With Us. The Lord Almighty, the eternal, self-existent God, Lord of the entire army of heavenly beings has *chosen* to be with us. It is no accident. It is His desire, His purpose, to be with us. Truly we must be still in order to fully absorb this wonder of wonders.

### *Confession:*
The God of all creation, the Lord Almighty, the Lord of hosts, is the very personal God whose presence brings me victory in every area. I will see Him exalted above all. It is truly an awesome God I serve.

### **Go Deeper:**
Psalm 46:10, 11
Philippians 2:10 KJV
Psalm 103:2
John 14:7-9
Exodus 3:14-15
Deuteronomy 31:6, 8; Hebrews 13:5
John 14-18

### *Minute by Minute:*
Who is the Lord Almighty? Do you know Him? And more importantly, do you know Him as the I AM God? It encompasses the greatness and the splendor as well as the personal. For if you are to really know Him, you must know both. You must know His splendor, what He stepped from, in order to fully grasp the very individual love He bears you.

Consider a very personal study of the names of God,. They reflect only how He is disclosed to us in the Old Covenant. All that Jesus revealed of Himself is the I AM God as well (John 14:7-9).[7]

Then read John 14-18, noting each instance in which Jesus reveals Himself as the I AM God. Then put the entire picture together. What is God, who says, *I really AM God,* trying to say to you personally? What can you count on from the IAM God in your own life?

# Be Still
# Our Refuge

**Week 10**

> *"'Be still, and know that I am God:*
> *I will be exalted among the nations,*
> *I will be exalted in the earth.'*
>
> *The LORD of hosts is with us;*
> *the God of Jacob is our refuge. Selah."*
> Psalm 46:10, 11 KJV

Imagine you are standing in front of an impenetrable fortress, the ultimate bunker, built to withstand anything that comes against it — it's there, it's real, it's solid, it does all it's built to do. If you never turn and step inside, what can you expect? When the attack comes, and it surely will, you will be destroyed. Who would be so foolish? And yet many millions of people are doing just that every single day.

This is a hostile and unfriendly world. And while we each have a circle of what we consider to be security comprised of family, friends, home, job, etc., it is false security at best. So why would anyone rely on what is transitory, and collapsible?

We all know the nursery tale of Three Little Pigs and most have told it to the little ones in our circle. We know the moral of the story. Or do we? The first little pig built his house of straw, the second little pig built his house of sticks, and the third little pig built his house of bricks. Each had absolute confidence that the house he had built would withstand whatever came against it. Each was aware that there was a wolf in the world and that he was hostile to little pigs.

The first two little pigs finished building their houses very quickly, with plenty of time left over to do the things that were enjoyable. The third little pig put considerably more time and effort into building his house, and I suspect had to deal with blueprints that the other two did not. But when the wolf came, as he always does (John 16:33, 1 Peter 5:8), the first two were immediately left homeless and were grateful to escape with their lives. The third little pig was safe inside his impenetrable fortress.

Our refuge has already been built for us. Not only do we not need to build it, but we could never hope to build a fortress that is truly impenetrable to the wolf of this world. It is already in place according to our Scripture, right behind us, just waiting for us to run to it. Proverbs 18:10 says that the Name of the Lord is a strong tower.

Why are so many crushed by the attacks of the enemy? There are several reasons.

1. Either they never turn around so they don't know the fortress is there, or

2. They don't believe what they've been told about it, or

3. They think they can do better on their own, or most tragic of all,

4. They don't believe they are worthy. They don't believe they deserve this perfect refuge, this safe refuge, so they turn their back on it, denying its existence.

Whatever the reason, the end result is the same, unnecessary, but certain destruction, sooner or later. Not one of the above is a good reason to be overcome by the enemy. Turn around right now today and see the fortress, the stronghold, and run to it, knowing it is built out of great love for you, just as you are.

Be still, and cease your striving. Know Him intimately. He IS whatever you need. He IS the Lord of all the heavenly host and He will be exalted; all knees will bow to Him. He IS our ultimate refuge, our ultimate fortress.

Be speechless!

***

## *Confession:*

Lord God of Hosts, I will ponder this day the wonder of wonders that You have chosen to be with me. In Your great love for me, You have made Your presence with me as Your name, Emmanuel. Truly, at Your Name I will bow my knee with all of creation.

***Go Deeper:***
Psalm 46:10, 11
John 16:33
1 Peter 5:8
Proverbs 18:10
Psalm 35:2
Psalm 91:4
Psalm 5:12

***Minute by Minute:***

*These things I have spoken unto you, that in me ye might have peace.*
*In the world ye shall have tribulation:*
*but be of good cheer; I have overcome the world.*
John 16:33 KJV

Have you been crushed by the enemy? Are you even now besieged? Be encouraged that his attacks indicate that you are a threat to his plans! But does that mean you have to endure his attacks? Not at all. If you are under constant siege, unable even to defend yourself, consider the possibilities we suggested.

1. Perhaps you have been unaware that the refuge is right behind you, or
2. You don't believe the fortress is actually strong enough, or
3. You believe you can do better on their own, or most tragic of all,
4. You don't believe you are worthy. You don't believe you deserve this safe and perfect refuge, so you keep your back turned away from it.

Do any of these strike a chord with you? Search the Word and then know that God has already provided, but you must avail yourself. Turn around and see!

# Altered Sight                                           Week 10

> *And Saul said, 'Who are You, Lord?' And He said,
> 'I am Jesus, Whom you are persecuting. It is dangerous
> and it will turn out badly for you to keep kicking against the goad
> [to offer vain and perilous resistance].'
> Trembling and astonished he asked, 'Lord,
> what do You desire me to do?'
> The Lord said to him, 'But arise and go into the city,
> and you will be told what you must do.'*
> Acts 9:5-6 AMP

As many times as we may have read the account of Saul's incredible Damascus Road experience, have we ever looked at it closely enough to find the correlation it has with our own experience? But that was Paul, you might be saying. How could there be any parallels between Paul, who was not only responsible for writing sixty-six percent of the New Testament, but for spreading the Gospel of the Kingdom around the world?

Let's closely examine the elements of Saul's experience on the Damascus Road as well as immediately following, and we may be surprised at how closely we can apply it to our own experience.

Saul was on his own "righteous" mission, doing great things for God — *of his own choosing and in his own power*. He was arrested by a brilliant light from heaven — suddenly. He fell to the ground and heard *"Saul! Saul! Why are you persecuting Me?"* (Acts 9:4) He was given instruction and he obeyed.

When he arose, he was blinded to the world as he had created it, his plan, the road he had chosen for himself and his future. He could no longer look into the distance and see Damascus. He was left with only inward vision. He remained thus blinded for three days, abstaining from food and water during that time. Scripture does not reveal if he chose this, or if it was chosen for him, but as a Pharisee, he would have been well acquainted with fasting.

In any event, he was cut off from the natural world in several ways. With the exception of Acts 9:11, in which Ananias was told by the Lord that Saul was praying, we are told little else. But we can speculate, based on the final outcome and on what we know from Scripture concerning fasting.[8]

God remained with Saul throughout his three days of sanctification and He must have imparted much to Saul as He went about setting him apart from the world for His own purposes. We know Paul had a vision of Ananias coming to him.

The Lord approached Ananias, a godly man and a believer. In a vision, Ananias was charged was delivering a message to Saul. He was obedient, in spite of his knowledge of Saul's deadly reputation with Christians.

Upon his arrival, Ananias laid hands on Saul, and Saul received the infilling of the Holy Spirit and, as the scales fell from his eyes, new sight. He arose, was baptized, took nourishment and was strengthened.

Now let's see if we can draw the correlation with our own experience. Have we had a Damascus Road experience, perhaps without even realizing it?

When we were first arrested by the Holy Spirit, I know that each of us was on a path of our own choosing. In fact, we may still be on our own path, though we are convinced, much like Saul, that we are doing it for the Lord. But have we asked Him?

Jesus interrupted and intercepted each of us. How did He interrupt you? Where were you headed? What important business were you about when He knocked you from your horse? How did He get your attention and what followed your encounter with the Risen Lord?

We spent a period set apart, a kind of honeymoon period. Like Saul, we were, for a time, blinded to the world, fasting from the familiar, alone with God, a time of heightened listening, separated and set apart. Like Paul, we were forced to shift focus from our own plan. If you have never experienced this, may I suggest you take a few days, if possible, away from your normal activity and immerse yourself in His presence? See what it is He would say to you.

We received a Rhema Word, a Word from God specifically for us, in and about our own circumstances, but one that will always be confirmed by the written Word. He has a plan for each one of us, individual and special, unlike His plan for anyone else. If you have not yet given heed to that Word, choose now to make yourself available to receive it.

Then we received a renewed filling, just as the disciples were filled with the Holy Spirit and joy in Acts 13:52 and new sight was the result.

Saul was baptized before he did anything else. If you have not been baptized since your conversion, consider this scriptural next step. If you are from a denomination that baptizes infants, ask about renewing your baptismal vows. If baptism is regularly available to adults in your church, take the step, and peel off that old nature that would try to hang onto you.

Though we may not have been aware of it, we surely received the strength necessary for the road ahead. You can be assured that God never calls us to a destiny that He has not first prepared and equipped us to carry out. Don't make the mistake of trying it in your own strength. Be assured that whatever He has called you to, you will *not* be able to do it on your own. Lean on Him; depend on Him. Total dependence is the pathway to total victory.

Finally, we stepped out, but how many of us realized that we had *a new name*. Saul hit the ground as Saul, but after three days, he set out as a new man. His plan, his purpose, his passion, his direction, his destiny were all changed and so the new man was given a new name, Paul. Not totally new perhaps, but a name with a new direction.

Have you been following your own chosen path? Submit yourself to the process. Saul did. You may or may not be arrested as dramatically as he was, but you can be certain the Lord is speaking to you. Still the sounds of the world that deafen your ears to the Holy Spirit. Set yourself apart for a time. It need not be three entire days, though it certainly can be. Perhaps you will start with a time each day. Blind yourself to all but the Word. Spend time set apart, sanctifying yourself. You may want to fast during this time, further removing yourself from the things of the world and the flesh.

Make up your mind to surrender to God's plan of sanctification, setting you apart for His purposes in the world. Only when you submit to His will, His remolding can you hope to accomplish what is in your heart. (Isaiah 29:16, 45:9, 64:8). Only then can you know the peace and joy and satisfaction that Paul knew. (Romans 15:13).

## *Confession:*
I purpose to allow God to set me apart, to change my name, to alter my goals, and to redirect my path. I will begin by focusing on Him and His Word and, for a period of time, I will blind myself to the ways of the world.

## *Go Deeper:*
Acts 9
Acts 13:52
Acts 22
Acts 26: 12, 16-18
Isaiah 29:16
Isaiah 45:9
Isaiah 64:8
Romans 15:13

## *Minute by Minute:*
Has Jesus interrupted and intercepted you? If so, what was your experience? Where were you headed? What important business were you about when He knocked you from your horse? How did He get your attention and what followed your encounter with the Risen Lord?

Perhaps you have been following your own chosen path up until now, not having had an experience with the God's interruption. Submit yourself to the process, just as Saul did. You may not be arrested as dramatically as he was, but the Lord is speaking to you nonetheless. Set yourself apart for a time, away from the influence of the world as you have known it and listen for the voice of the Holy Spirit. Perhaps you will start with a time first thing each morning, a time during which you can dedicate yourself to Him, a time of sanctifying yourself.

# One Foot in Heaven                                   Week 11

> *Now there is in store for me the crown of righteousness,
> which the Lord, the righteous Judge, will award to me on that day—
> and not only to me, but also to all who have longed for his appearing.*
> 2 Timothy 4:8 NIV

I have been accused of living my life with one foot in Heaven, my eyes focused on another country, my ears cocked to hear the trump of God. (1 Thessalonians 4:16) My response must be, *I surely hope so!* I have taken seriously Paul's assurance to Timothy in 2 Timothy 4:8 and I daily long for His appearing.

As a result, I often feel I am in a strangely foreign environment, as though I had taken up life under the sea, far from equipped to exist in that alien atmosphere. I cannot take breath into my lungs as the natural inhabitants of the sea so easily can. I must get necessary oxygen through a tube from another realm. (John 8:23; John 15:19; John 17:14-18)

This should be no surprise since when we are reborn, we are recreated to breathe a rarified air, no longer able to survive the putrid atmosphere of the world, which is slowly destroying all who attempt to draw life from it, even those who are native to it.

Notwithstanding, I have never felt I was left on my own in this hostile environment. Instead, it has been clear to me that I am here for a reason, on a Mission and that when I am attentive and remain focused, I will be led every step of the way. Indeed, the Holy Spirit has communicated with me as often as I have been willing to provide an atmosphere conducive to hearing His voice.

I have kept each of these precious communications in my heart, some for years. Occasionally it has been clear to me that they were intended as the basis for a Bible Minute or to be used for the benefit of others in counseling or coaching situations. But for the most part, they have been treasured evidences that my heavenly Father desires to be closely involved in my life, not only on a "grand plan" scale, but on a day to day basis as well.

When hearing a personal Word from the Holy Spirit, with specific application to your life, it is vitally important to check it against the written Word. Because the Word and God are One (John 1:1), the Holy Spirit will *never* speak a personal message to you that is at cross purposes with the Word in any way. Were it possible, that would make God either schizophrenic or a liar! And we know, first of all, that if God were indeed schizophrenic, that would instantly become the norm. We know also that God is *not a man that He should lie.* (Numbers 23:19) Finally, we are assured that changing is not an option for Him. (Hebrews 13:8) From the beginning He has assured us that He is God and He changes not. (Malachi 3:6)

So take your confirmed Word from the Holy Spirit and confidently step out wherever it leads you and know that in so doing, He will never leave you nor forsake you. You are assured of living significantly according to His plan for you. Keep your eyes on Him, your ears attuned to His Word and one foot in that Heavenly country.

*** 

*Confession:*
I will long for the appearing of the Lord above all else and live daily to hear and heed what He speaks to me.

*Go Deeper:*
2 Timothy 4:8
1 Thessalonians 4:16
2 Timothy 4:8
John 8:23; John 15:19
John 1:1
Numbers 23:19
Hebrews 13:8
Malachi 3:6
John 17:14-18

***Minute by Minute:***
Do you ever feel as though this world is foreign to you, or do you find that you are fitting in quite comfortably? If you are becoming too content with the world and its ways, what daily steps might you implement to decrease your dependence on the atmosphere of the world and increase your dependence on a heavenly supply of rarified air? The more specific you are about this, the more remarkable will be your results.

# *Heaven* *Week 11*

> *Let not your heart be troubled:*
> *ye believe in God, believe also in me.*
> *In my Father's house are many mansions:*
> *if it were not so, I would have told you.*
> *I go to prepare a place for you.*
> *And if I go and prepare a place for you,*
> *I will come again, and receive you unto myself;*
> *that where I am, there ye may be also.*
> *And whither I go ye know, and the way ye know.*
> John 14:1-4 KJV

Many people have the dangerous impression that being "good" will get them into their desired heaven. Some believe Heaven is a state of mind, a personal creation of their own mind, whatever they desire most and perhaps have not attained on earth. Their impressions of Heaven, as well as the prerequisites for entrance, are all relative to standards and basic "truths" of their own fabrication. When asked, they usually begin with "*I believe* heaven is…" Some will suggest that Heaven is right here on earth and is or is not "heavenly," based on their perception of the quality of their own lifestyle.

According to Jesus, Heaven is a very real place and is no more a creation of the human mind than the earth, the moon or the stars. The only difference is that we can see these with our natural eyes.

John 14 actually gives us some description. Jesus' words in verse 2 tell us His Father's house has many mansions. The Greek word for house is *oikia* and it means residence, home, or abode. The word *mansion* translates also as abode, or residence, from a root word that indicates a place to stay. The rest of the verse means exactly what it says. Jesus tells us that if it were otherwise, He would have told us. Then He goes on to say that He is going ahead of us to make these residences ready for us, and will return to take us there, where we will be together always. This is a real place! It is not a state of mind, or Disney World for the well-behaved. But that being the case, how do we get there?

Very simply, we gain entrance into Heaven by acknowledging Jesus as the One and only Way (John 14:6), and receiving His sacrifice, the exchange of His righteousness for our sin nature — at a personal level. This is a heart acknowledgment, not a mental assent. And it is what qualifies us. The natural *result* of following Him closely is goodness. That is the connection between "being good" and going to Heaven. We aren't going to Heaven because we are good; we are good because we know Whose we are and part of that knowledge is the certainty of Heaven.

You might ask why we can't just work at it and be good enough for Heaven. Doesn't God love us enough to be merciful in that area? If someone has always been fair, law abiding, and loving, won't he assure himself a ticket? To be sure, *if* he has also believed in his heart and declared with his mouth that Jesus is Lord, crucified and raised for each of us. (Romans 10:9) Remember, Heaven was created for believers, those who have placed their entire faith in Jesus, not in their own abilities, those who have acknowledged Him as Lord of their lives.

Jesus illustrated the risk of self-sufficiency with a parable in Matthew 22. A king prepared a great wedding feast for his son, to which he invited many honored guests. When the invited guests found reasons not to attend, he sent his servants out into the streets. *They gathered together all they found, both evil and good, and the wedding hall was filled.* (Matthew 22:10)

Note the prerequisite was not their lifestyle, but their willingness to turn and follow into the kingdom. Each of these people was willing to leave their own agenda, unlike the guests who had initially been invited. What follows warrants our very close attention. Upon entering the room, the king notices one guest who is not dressed appropriately and questions him. The guest offers no answer and the king orders him bound *hand and foot and cast into utter darkness; in that place there shall be weeping and gnashing of teeth.* (Matthew 22:13)

For years I was distressed by this account, especially since we are told at the outset that this is a parable of the kingdom of God. But a bit of knowledge (remember Hosea 4:6) about the culture of Jesus' time will bring clarity. An invitation such as this one always arrived accompanied by the appropriate clothing; it was a part of the invitation! Imagine not needing to hunt through your closet to attend a major function.

The guest in this parable chose to disregard the robes provided him when he accepted the invitation and so he came in his street clothes. That's why he had no answer when he was questioned. He thought his own clothes good enough for royalty. He must have been stunned at the grandeur he walked into, dressed as he was. We can be sure his clothing was not appropriate for a kingdom feast. How much easier to have accepted the free gift!

Now compare this to our good man, who thinks his goodness ought to get him in the door of Heaven. At the cross, Jesus executed the Great Exchange. He took on our filthy clothes, our imperfect attempts at achieving God's standard of perfection. In return we were given His glorious robes of Righteousness. These are the robes we must wear to the feast, not the ones we have created for ourselves. The Bible tells us that the very best we could ever hope to create on our own is nothing more than filthy rags.

It is a free gift, this robe of Righteousness, the Exchange, the open door to Heaven. It has nothing to do with what we have done or who we are, but is strictly based upon Who we choose follow, Who we belong to, on *Who He is*. Cast aside your own imperfect attempts and accept what a loving God has provided for those who are *choice and precious in the sight of God*. (1 Peter 2:4)

*\*\*\**

*Confession:*
I know that I am precious to my Heavenly Father and I am the apple of His eye. I need not understand it, but I choose to accept it.

***Go Deeper:***
John 14:1-4
John 14:6
Romans 10:9
Matthew 22 (Parable of the Wedding Feast)
Hosea 4:6
1 Peter 2:4

***Minute by Minute:***
In what way have you been approaching the feast in your own clothes? List several practical ways in which accepting the clothes provided would change the way you live each day. Would dropping your own attempts to earn Heaven, to be good enough, change your behavior? Would you spend more time fellowshipping with your Father and less time trying to earn His favor by your *doing*? Would you be bolder in sharing your faith? Would your demeanor change? If so, how?

## Salty Christians
## White Gold

*Week 12*

> *You are the salt of the earth; but if the salt has become tasteless,*
> *how will it be made salty again?*
> *It is good for nothing anymore, except to be thrown out*
> *and trampled underfoot by men.*
> Matthew 5:13-14 NAS

> *And he said to them, Go into all the world,*
> *and preach the gospel to all creation.*
> *He who has believed and has been baptized shall be saved;*
> *but he who has disbelieved shall be condemned.*
> *And these signs will accompany those who have believed;*
> *in My name they will cast out demons; they shall speak with new*
> *tongues;*
> Mark 16:15-17 NAS

> *Salt is good for seasoning. But if it loses its flavor,*
> *how do you make it salty again?*
> *You must have the qualities of salt among yourselves*
> *and live in peace with each other.*
> Mark 9:50 NLT

In Mark 16 Jesus tells us what we are to *do*. We all know these familiar verses as the Great Commission. Our responsibility to the kingdom could not have been stated more clearly. But we are, after all, human *beings*, not human *doings* and the state of *who we are* is critical to how well we execute what we do.

In Matthew 5:13 and 14, Jesus addresses just that. He tells us who we are, speaking to His professed followers, not to those as yet undecided. If we have made the decision to follow Christ, then He is talking to us — about us.

He uses a very powerful analogy, which it is worth taking a few minutes to explore. He says we are the salt of the earth, an expression still used to describe a person who is well respected and loved.

Simply assuming it was a good thing to be, I had never looked closely at its meaning?

The very character of salt is meant to be the character of the Christian in the world. Salt, sometimes referred to as *white gold*, historically is known for seven characteristics:

### *Seasons/Flavors*

Cooking meat destroys the salt content, rendering it flavorless, and so ancient man began replacing salt. It is used to add and enhance the flavor of so many foods now that the resulting craving for salt has promoted serious consequences in the American diet, which is often out of balance.

### *Preserves*

For centuries, salt has been an essential food preservative. Before refrigeration was the norm, meat was preserved by *salting it down*, storing it buried in salt.

Salt was also an essential ingredient in the preservation technique we know as mummification, the highly effective process used by the ancient Egyptians to embalm their dead.

### *Heals*

Not only has salt historically been know to have healing properties, but it has also been linked with purity, and in several cultures is believed to have power against evil spirits. The ancient Jews sprinkled salt on their animal sacrifices.

### *Medium of Exchange*

Gram for gram, salt has often been exchanged for gold. The main road in ancient Rome was the *Salaria* (the Salt Route), and a Roman soldier's pay was issued in the *salarium* (literally *money to buy salt*). Do you recognize our modern term for compensation?

The Jews closed deals with a salt exchange, the *salt covenant*, linking the participants inextricably as partners, the binding of a contract.

The salt producing area of Bolivia even has a hotel constructed entirely of salt, a testament to its great value to the region.

### Causes Thirst

Aside from dehydration, which is the severe effect of an imbalance in the salt and fluid content of the body, the addition of excess salt to the diet is a major cause of thirst. Anyone who's ever consumed a bag of pretzels without a tall drink nearby knows what that is like!

### Melts Ice

Salt is still the medium of choice for keeping winter's icy roads passable. Alongside the major state highways one can see the salt igloos filled with that precious commodity which will keep people (and hence the economy) moving in January and February. And have you tried to keep your mail service flowing in those months without salting your sidewalk?

### Necessary Element of Life

The human body has about 4 ounces of salt in its composition, without which there is no life. If the level of salt in the system is out of balance, numerous physical upsets occur, in their simplest form, dehydration from low salt content, and bloating from excessive salt content. If prolonged, both can lead to serious organ damage.

Are you beginning to see the correlation between the value of salt and Jesus' vision of the value of the Christian in and to the world? Next, we will take a deeper look at the similarities.

*\*\*\**

### Confession:

I purpose to learn the value of salt as an earthly element and to be what Jesus intended for me, adding value to the world around me.

### Go Deeper:
Matthew 5:13-17
Mark 16:15-17
Mark 9:50

***Minute by Minute:***
*We are, after all, human beings, not human doings and the state of who we are is critical to how well we execute what we do.*

First, in light of the above statement, and without reading part two of this message, what correlations do you see between the natural properties of salt and Jesus' expectation for salty believers? Then, how would *being* a salty Christian impact what you are called to *do* as a believer.

# Salty Christians
# Flavoring the World

*Week 12*

*You are the salt of the earth; but if the salt has become tasteless,
how will it be made salty again?
It is good for nothing anymore, except to be thrown out
and trampled underfoot by men.*
Matthew 5:13-14 (NAS)

*Have salt in yourselves,
And be at peace with one another.*
Mark 9:50b NAS

We learned in Part 1 of our study what salt has meant down through the ages, but why did Jesus use this particular analogy to describe the Christian in the world? Look again, through different eyes, at the seven characteristics of salt we examined. We, as Christians, possess these same characteristics. The question is whether they are evident in our lives and our walk with the Lord?

### *Seasons, Flavors*

What a wonderful charge Jesus gives us in Matthew 5:13! We are meant to bring flavor to the world. We are to provide the zest, the excitement, the appeal. Merriam Webster defines flavor as *the blend of taste and smell sensations evoked by a substance in the mouth.*

Flavor is an enticing word, and generally suggests a pleasurable or at least interesting taste experience. When others observe us and see what we are and what is shining through us (see verse 14), they will be drawn to Him. Are we actively flavoring our world? Or do we look and taste like everything around us.

### *Preserves*

Salt is still a major preservative, attractive because it is a natural substance. What exactly does it preserve? It preserves flavor certainly, and it preserves freshness, vigor, vitality — life. Salt extends the usefulness, the essence of what it preserves. It is a rescuer of what would otherwise spoil, rot and go to waste. This characteristic of salt sends the Christian to a world sinking towards death, rapidly decaying in its ignorance, to bring the preserving, redeeming Good News of life.

### *Heals*

Salt has been recognized for its healing properties since ancient times. There are many kinds of healing we are called to bring to this diseased and hurting world. There are sick and broken bodies, troubled minds and emotions, souls in darkness, and spirits plummeting surely to eternal death, if we do not bring the healing words of God and apply them as balm.

Jeremiah 51:8 speaks of balm for the ease of pain, which then promotes healing. The healing required of us must first ease the pain and suffering, and then bring healing from the disease. If we are salt, we are equipped by our very nature, to do exactly that.

### *Medium of Exchange*

Salt has value, so much so that it is referred to as *white gold*. Gram for gram, it has been exchanged at the same rate of value as gold. Of what value are we to the world? When they look at us, do they see character and integrity, or do they see themselves mirrored in our faces?

We are called to be of great value, *pearl(s) of great price* (Matthew 13:45, 46). The world is well acquainted with the tarnished and the worthless, and is searching for something by which to measure *true value*. According to the words of Jesus, we must provide what they are looking for.

### *Causes Thirst*

This is perhaps one of the most interesting characteristics we are to display in the earth. Salt always causes thirst — the more salt, the more thirst. And if one consumes enough water in response, the system is flushed of any excess salt and balance is restored to the body.

Our very presence must cause those around us to thirst. Eleven times in the New Testament, thirst is mentioned, and in five of these, the reference is to lasting water (John 4:14). Water is equated with the word of God (Ephesians 5:26). Jesus, in John's account, refers to this water as living water (John 4:10-11; 7:38). Do we have the Word dwelling richly in us (Colossians 3:16), in order to offer it to this world, so dangerously dehydrated that it is unaware of its critical state?

### *Melts Ice*

How many icy hearts are there in your circle of influence? I suspect there are many, perhaps not visibly icy, but frozen in their pain, quietly freezing to death in their cold and passionless suffering. Others have become visibly hardened over time, difficult to approach and as hard to touch as dry ice, so cold that they burn anyone who comes too close.

We are not naturally drawn to such as these, but we cannot argue that it is our purpose. If not us, who then? As salt begins to melt immediately, so we have the quality necessary to immediately begin to melt the iciest heart. Frozen hearts are waiting, locked in ice, for us to bring our salty freedom to them.

### *Necessary Element of Life*

We cannot live without salt — it is a necessary element in the makeup of our system. Without it, the system craves it. With it, we thirst for life-giving water. Who but a loving Father could have devised such a system? Who but the Son, bringing the life-giving message, could have equated the sons and daughters with such a necessary element of life? We truly serve an awesome God. Are we serving Him as He has charged us? Are we bringing to this world, at this critical time, the necessary element for eternal life, or are we waiting for someone else to be the salty Christian? There is no one else but you for your world.

Let us determine to be flavorful and life-giving, of great value to the Kingdom, healing, seasoning, causing thirst for the life-giving message of the Word, melting icy hearts wherever we go, so we can one day hear the Father say, *Well done good and faithful servant* (Matthew 25:21). I yearn for that — how about you?

\*\*\*

*Confession:*
I determine this day to be what the Word says I am. Filled with the life-giving Word and continually led and empowered by the Holy Spirit, I will fulfill the charge to add life and flavor to the world around me by my very presence.

*Go Deeper:*
Matthew 5:13-17
Mark 9:50
Matthew 5:13, 14
Jeremiah 51:8
Matthew 13:45, 46
John 4:10-14; 7:38
Ephesians 5:26
Colossians 3:16
Matthew 25:21

*Minute by Minute:*
You are already the salt of the earth. The question becomes, how *salty* are you? Are you white gold? Being salty is not something you have been asked to do. It is not a challenge you may choose. It is what you are meant to *be*. You will either be salty or, filled with impurities, as the salt which came from the Dead Sea,.

Either way, you are the salt of the earth. How effectively do you draw people with your saltiness? Drawn to you, do they find value? Does your presence melt icy hearts, bringing with it flavor and healing, creating thirst for the living water of the Word?

Join with other committed Christians and encourage one another to be truly salty. Look closely at the impurities that may have crept in, keeping you from being of maximum value to the world around you, to those who are drawn to you. Then exhort one another, holding each other accountable for the impact you make on the world around you.

# *Journey to Promise*  *Week 13*
# *Wilderness Trek*

> *...in the wilderness*
> *where you saw how*
> *the Lord your God*
> *carried you...*
> Deuteronomy 1:31 NAS

How often are we like the shortsighted Israelites, who suffered from tunnel vision throughout their wilderness trek? They so frequently seemed capable of focusing only on their lack or their highly overrated sojourn in Egypt.

They left Egypt in haste, nonetheless laden with treasure. (Exodus 12:35, 36). God provided them with sweet water from bitter (Exodus 15:22) and bread from heaven. Yet they grumbled and complained, murmuring among themselves from the time they were miraculously and ceremoniously delivered from captivity in Egypt, a mirror of our own captivity and release from the world and its systems.

The food was better and more plentiful in Egypt (Numbers 11:5). They reminisced fondly about the *pots of meat* and eating *bread to the full* and accused Moses of bringing them out to *kill this whole assembly with hunger* (Exodus 16:3). Still God continued to supply what He knew to be their need, responding to their complaining and supplying some of their whiny wants as well (Numbers 11:6, 18-20). In this way, His chosen people continued until they arrived at the very threshold of the Promised Land.

How often is our behavior the same on our journey to God's ultimate promise for us? How often do we miss the miraculous provision by looking back wistfully or focusing on the length of the journey? Like children, we complain *Are we there yet? When are we gonna' be there?*

Make time today to take stock of your own attitude toward the journey. Look back long enough to see how God has provided for your every need along the way, even giving you quail when you have murmured.

Purpose this day to focus on God's faithful provision in your life, neither looking back, nor unduly focusing forward, for *this day* is the day the Lord has made and it is your choice to rejoice and be glad in it (Psalm 118:24).

***

*Confession:*
The Lord has made this day, filling it with opportunity and provision for me. I choose to rejoice and be glad in it. I will no longer look longingly at the past, through rose colored glasses. Rather I will focus on God's faithfulness and His promises for each day and I will not be anxious for tomorrow knowing that He has already been there. (Matthew 6:33)

*Go Deeper:*
Deuteronomy 1:31
Exodus 12:35, 36
Exodus 15:22
Numbers 11:5-6, 18-20
Psalm 118:24
Matthew 6:25-33

*Minute by Minute:*
Set aside time today to take stock of your attitude about the journey. The longer you put it off, the longer you may harbor risky misperceptions about your journey, producing needless discontent. Look back long enough to see how God has provided for your every need along the way, even providing quail when you have murmured. Record your remembrances of His goodness and provision. From this perspective, also include those times God provided what you needed, though perhaps not exactly what you desired.

Next, determine to focus on God's faithful provision in your life — today, neither looking back, nor focusing forward. Like so many we suggest, this exercise is straightforward and simple, but not necessarily easy. It is well worth the effort though, if it helps you to bring your perspective back in line.

# Journey to Promise
## Confined to the Wilderness

Week 13

> *...and we were in our own sight as grasshoppers,
> and so we were in their sight.*
> Numbers 13:33 KJV

The Israelites failed to see the faithful provision of the God they continually tested, and as a result, they were called an *evil generation* in Deuteronomy 1:35. They focused so intently on the poorly remembered provision of the past, and on their present circumstances, that they managed to lose sight of the promise before them.

They habitually believed God delayed too long and they succumbed to the temptation of the "quick fix." (See Exodus 30:32) As a result, they circled the mountain until God finally spoke and told them enough was enough. (Deuteronomy 2:3)

These children of a patient God failed to grasp the provision and certainly did not fully understand that the Lord's blessing comes *in* the land. (See Deuteronomy 28:8) If they had, they would not have turned away from the promise before them.

Only Caleb and Joshua understood that the land was already theirs for the taking. God had already given them the land but it was up to them to possess it. That required trust and they were once again found lacking. (Numbers 14:1-4) As a result, their generation never experienced the fulfillment of the promise. (Numbers 14:2-23) God never told them He would drop the Promised Land in their laps. He told them to go in and possess it, and everywhere they set their foot would be theirs. (Deuteronomy 11:24)

They allowed their own puny abilities to step out in front of the mighty power of God, trusting the circumstances instead of the promise. Step outside some sunny day, and closing one eye, hold a penny in front of the other — it blocks out the sun right? But we know the penny is not bigger than the sun; it is merely a trick of perception. So it was with the spies sent in to scout out the land, and what's more, they knew it. (Numbers 13:33)

Have we, as did the Israelites, gradually and unknowingly confined ourselves to our own spiritual wilderness, delaying our entrance into God's promise with our own faulty thinking? God has not reneged on His promises to us. He is *not a man that He should lie* (Numbers 23:19) and He has not changed His mind. (Malachi 3:6) Let us determine not to be part of a generation confined to the wilderness by our own doubt and unbelief!

I am preparing my possessing shoes and everywhere I place my foot I am going to stake my claim based on God's promises to me! Are you coming along?

\*\*\*

### *Confession:*

I purpose to put my own observations aside and say only what God says about my situation, seeing myself in relation to Him, and not in relation to my circumstances.

### *Go Deeper:*
Numbers 13:33
Deuteronomy 1:35
Exodus 30:3
Deuteronomy 2:3
Numbers 14:1-4
Numbers 14:2-23
Deuteronomy 11:24
Numbers 23:19
Malachi 3:6
2 Corinthians 5:7

### *Minute by Minute:*

First, identify any areas in which you might be suffering from flawed self-perception by searching the Word for evidence of how God sees you and who He means you to be. Begin with the New Testament Letters, written specifically to the church, for instances of *in Him*, *in Whom* and *in Christ*. Then, consciously bring your thinking in line with what the Word says, not with what you *see* or *feel*. (2 Corinthians 5:7)

Next, begin to identify what Promised Land you may be missing as a result of grasshopper thinking. Now step out and take the land God has promised you!

You will find this exercise is particularly revealing and most effective when completed with a trusted prayer and accountability partner.

# *Journey to Promise*           Week 14
# *Without a Vision*

> *Where there is no vision,*
> *the people are unrestrained.*
> Proverbs 29:18 NAS

As we take our final look at the Israelites' journey to the promise of God, let us pause and recognize the root cause of their lengthy sojourn in the wilderness. Very simply, they had the wrong vision. Their vision of the Land of Promise was one of unbeatable giants. Their vision of themselves was not only inadequate but puny in the extreme, mere insects in fact. (Numbers 13:33) Certainly, such a self-perception would hinder even the slightest forward movement. Such a vision expects quite literally to be squashed at any moment!

The Bible has a few very pointed statements to make about our vision. Our foundation Scripture sums it up. The Hebrew word for vision used here means *mental sight*. In other words, something we can visualize, that we can see clearly in our mind's eye. Solomon goes on to tell us that where such a mental sight is lacking, the people are unrestrained, (unruly, unbridled, lawless), out of control. Without a vision, life loses focus and begins to come apart at the seams.

Jeremiah 29:11, a familiar scripture, assures us that God has His own vision for our lives. He tells us He has plans (thoughts or imaginations). Our Heavenly Father has dreams for us, just as we have for our children. But we must take the time to explore these dreams.

1. Set aside time to sit alone with the Father and ask Him to fill your thoughts with His dreams for your life and future. Let your imagination grow bigger than you have ever dared, knowing that His dreams for us are bigger than anything we can conceive on our own, *exceeding abundantly beyond all we ask or think* (Ephesians 3:20). One translation says *beyond all we **can** ask or think*.

2. Then write it down. If you never write it down, the chances are you won't follow the dream. Habakkuk 2:2 tells *us to record the vision* (the KJV says *make it plain*), *and inscribe it on tablets, that the one who reads it may run.*

The KJV of our foundation scripture says *where there is no vision, the people perish.* Lack of restraint (NAS) is the first step toward perishing. If you cannot see it, the best you can hope for is that you just might stumble into it one day. God is a god of process. Follow the process and step into God's great plan for your life and dare to dream on His scale, not as a mere insect.

*Dreamers dream to escape reality.*
*Visionaries dream to change it.*
Mission Accomplished, A Handbook for Visionaries[9]

\*\*\*

## *Confession:*
This day I am going to put my puny dreams aside and link up with God's grand design for my life. I am going to dream as big as God, and I will see God's results.

## *Go Deeper:*
Proverbs 29:18
Numbers 13:33
Jeremiah 29:11
Ephesians 3:20
Habakkuk 2:2

## *Minute by Minute:*
The process to promise is not a complicated one. First, set aside time to sit alone with the Father and ask Him to fill your thoughts with His dreams for your life and future. Let your imagination grow bigger than you ever dared, knowing that His dreams for you are bigger than anything you can conceive. It will likely take many such sessions to fully grasp the enormity of what God has for you.

*The Bible Minute*

Then write it down. If you never write it down, chances are greater that you will ultimately abandon the dream. Habakkuk 2:2 tells us to record the vision (the KJV says *make it plain*), and *inscribe it on tablets, that the one who reads it may run.*

Now put in place the goals you must achieve in order to bring the dream from your heart and mind into manifestation.

## *Daddy, Do You Love Me?*              Week 14

*Fear not, little flock; for it is your Father's good pleasure
to give you the kingdom*
Luke 12:32 KJV

Many of us have experienced a less than loving, less than nurturing, less than satisfying relationship with our fathers. Our society has gradually lost touch with true fatherhood and largely to blame is the media's presentation of fathers as idiots and buffoons, weak and disinterested. Many of us have suffered deeply as a result, not the least of these being the fathers themselves, who have never been sure what their role is meant to be, beyond the biological.

How often does a child climb into his father's lap and say, *Daddy, do you love me?* Before you answer too quickly, really think about it. In a healthy parent/child relationship, you will not hear *Daddy, do you love me?* Instead you will hear the joyous declaration *Oh, Daddy, I love you!*

What's the difference, you say. After all, both are about the exchange of love between parent and child aren't they? Though the difference may appear to be insignificant, in truth, it is critical and directly reflects our understanding and experience with parental love and trust; and so also our capacity for faith in our heavenly Father.

*Daddy, do you love me?* speaks from a place of uncertainty, a place of experience with unfulfilled needs, a place of uncertain identity and what can be expected from the relationship. The very thought of a child needing to ask this question either brings back unpleasant scenes from our own childhood or is unsettling on a more universal level. But how many Christians are operating daily in just this same kind of insecurity and ambiguity?

Dare we expect anything from God if we are not good enough and how can we ever know for sure if we are or not? Perhaps we lack the necessary significance in the grand scheme and He will forget us in the greater world shuffle. Maybe we are actually on our own, after all, with God too far above us to be personally involved. How can we ever be sure that He loves us, really, deeply, truly, personally, day in and day out?

The season surrounding our observance of the Resurrection brings the answer home to us particularly well. Good Friday should be the most reassuring, affirming day in all of history when it comes to the question of love. It is the day that *greater love* was defined for us forever. (John 15:13) It is the day that God Himself, by force of His will, stepped into death for love of a world that was anything but good enough, anything but lovable.

When a child is born, its parents immediately experience a virtually overwhelming love, an intense desire to nourish, protect, and nurture, to shower this child of theirs with everything within their power to provide. Why? Surely it cannot be that the child has done anything to earn such deep devotion. The answer is simple; they love this helpless infant with passion and devotion *simply because it is theirs.*

Now try and conceive of a love yet deeper, more inexplicable even than that, a love that brought God from boundless heavenly realms of glory into this clod of earth to die for humanity — one at a time! These beings for which he took on flesh had not only done absolutely nothing to earn or deserve it, but most of them long ago had turned their backs on Him. Really allow the enormity of this to sweep over you and wash away your doubt.

Once the revelation hits you, you will surely never again ask, *Daddy, do you love me?* The only possible response to the kind of love He has offered us, the kind that positions us for Resurrection life, must be, *Oh, Daddy, I love you so!*

If your relationship with your natural father has left something to be desired, begin by acknowledging the inability of any human being to satisfy the deep need that only God can meet. Determine to see your earthly father through the eyes of your heavenly Father, and then turn the table and try loving him simply because he is yours.

\*\*\*

*Confession:*

This day I will receive the love of my heavenly Father and will see all others through the eyes of that love, in the absolute certainty that my *Abba Father* loves me — because I am His.

*Go Deeper:*
Luke 12:32
John 15:13
1 John 4:19
1 John 4:8
Romans 8:35

*Minute by Minute:*

There are several Greek words in the New Testament that are translated into English as *love*. Using your concordance or Bible software, study the distinctions. To begin your study, what is distinctive about the Greek word, *agape*, as used in the following verses, making it a love that inspires confidence?

> *We love Him because He first loved us* (1 John 4:19)
> *Greater love hath no man* (John 15:13)
> *God is love* (1 John 4:8)
> *Who will separate us from the love of Christ* (Romans 8:35)

# *Father, Forgive Them...*            Week 15

*Then said Jesus, Father, forgive them;*
*for they know not what they do.*
Luke 23:34a KJV

Historically, this verse is understood as referring to Jesus' assassins. But take a deeper look and make it very personal. Can you fully get your mind and heart around the implication of these words?

Can you grasp the forgiveness that spreads as a result of His absorbing all the world's sin from the beginning of time to the end, becoming sin-soaked, disease riddled, maimed and mangled by grief and sorrow, clearing the books for every person who ever lived or ever would? I know that while my spirit rests comfortably in the truth of it, my mind is simply not big enough to grasp it.

One reason we resist is because we are so completely helpless to repay, and we are left with feeling incomplete when we cannot pay something back, return the favor, or give as good as we get.

In 1999, Catherine Ryan Hyde's book, *Pay It Forward* hit the market and became wildly successful, generating a movie of the same name the following year.[10] The story revolves around a challenge given to a group of seventh grade students for each to think of a way to change the world and then put it in motion.

One student presents a simple premise, not easy mind you, but simple. *If someone did you a favor — something big, something you couldn't do on your own — and instead of paying it back, you paid it forward to three people... in two weeks that comes to 4,782,969 people.*[11]

What Jesus accomplished for us at Calvary we could never do for ourselves. He paid a price that we did not have and by it obtained forgiveness for us. The only way for us to appreciate the sacrifice of God Himself is first, to accept it. And second to pay it forward, since we can never hope to pay it back!

There is a *but* involved here. We cannot pay it forward until we accept it, because we cannot give something we do not ourselves have. Accept the forgiveness, accept the sacrifice, and acknowledge that you have need of it. Then pay it forward, as an act of your will, not of your emotion. Don't wait to feel it, just do it. Throughout John 14, Jesus equates obedience with love, *If ye love me, keep my commandments...* (John 14:15)

Jesus said forgive, so we it must be within our capabilities to do so. Receive your forgiveness, your salvation, and all that goes along with it. Then, in humble gratitude and with great joy, pay it forward.

*Forgiveness is the fragrance
a flower makes when it's trampled on.*
Unknown

\*\*\*

*Confession:*
Putting aside my feelings, I will accept His forgiveness and pass it along, understanding that, in this way, His saving love will cover the earth.

*Go Deeper:*
Luke 23:34a
John 14:15

*Minute by Minute:*
In light of your biblical understanding of forgiveness, what do you think Dr. Martin Luther King and Thomas á Kempis had in mind when they said the following? Consider discussing your thoughts with your Bible Study or small group. How do your observataions impact your own personal attitudes toward forgiveness?

*Forgiveness is not
an occasional act;
it is a permanent attitude.*
Martin Luther King Jr.

*Be assured that if you knew all, you would pardon all.*
Thomas á Kempis

# *The Aching Void*                                                     Week 15

> *Nature will not permit a vacuum.*
> *It will be filled with something.*
> *Human need is really a great spiritual vacuum*
> *which God seeks to fill...*
> George Washington Carver

We are all daily employed in filling the vacuums of human need. It drives us to fill our stomachs with food and drink, to fill our world with relationships, and our minds with a steady stream of information.

We seem compelled to continually fill the envelope of our time. We say we long for time to do nothing and yet the vacuum must be filled and alas, if we are not *doing* every minute, we believe we are wasting that commodity. How about drawers, pockets and purses? They never stay empty for long, no matter how often we purge them. They refill seemingly without our assistance!

We cannot tolerate a half-filled cup of coffee or tea. On the road, if we spot an open space in traffic up ahead, we maneuver our vehicle to fill it. Flower beds, bookshelves, cabinets and, most importantly, those empty spaces deep within us, all seem to call out to be filled. On and on it goes. What needs or desires in your life are you seeking to satisfy? What spaces are you longing to fill?

With all our striving to fill the emptiness, it is very interesting that our attempts at it are never enough. It seems we frequently only come close to the state of satisfaction when we experience the condition of abundance called overflow. It is in our nature not only to desire simple satisfaction, the simple gratification of desires and appetites, *ful-fill-ment*, but then to desire the next step — overflow. Perhaps because we have all experienced deep lack, gaping holes, in our lives, we feel we need of the extra security of over-fill.

Empty spaces are often referred to as aching voids. Ponder that term for a moment; it is rich in meaning. If you have ever had a tooth pulled and experienced the painful condition called dry-socket, you can fully grasp the meaning of the expression. Nature will not permit a vacuum. Consequently, the vacuum state is an exceedingly uncomfortable one at best — it is the state of being *un-ful-filled*.

Vessels want filling and we are all vessels, which explains our nature as desiring beings. Desire is simply a longing to be filled in one area or another. A synonym for desire is craving, which really takes it to the next level. Craving is an overpowering drive, often moving one to actions they would not consider under normal circumstances.

Why does it seem we are never satisfied, always seeking *over*-filling, *over*-abundance, *excess*. It has been suggested that perhaps we come closest to satisfaction in the pursuit itself and when we are actually filled, with what we thought was the answer, we become dissatisfied and so we begin the whole cycle of engaging in the pursuit all over again. Sounds like an apt definition of addiction, the constant filling that never fills. Relationships, gambling, food, sex, drugs, alcohol — the more we engage, the less we are filled, the hungrier we become.

Can you see how this double edged sword is the beginning of a cycle of misery which takes us to what James says about desire in his letter? This cycle leads to lust, which is nothing more than sickened, unhealthy desire, our attempts to fill the aching void.

And what do we provide ourselves through our pursuits? Only more emptiness! We attempt to satisfy spiritual hunger with carnal counterfeits which can never satisfy. And why do we feel we must provide for our own needs when the Bible gives us a better way? James 4 has some simple, piercing truths which begin to point us to the answer.

> *You do not have because you do not ask.*
> *You ask and you do not receive,*
> *because you ask with wrong motives*
> *so that you may spend it on your own pleasures.*
> James 4:2b-3 NAS

Too often, we look to the world to fill our empty spaces and then fall into the trap of *friendship with the world* which James identifies as *hostility toward God* (James 4:4). The Bible calls this adultery! That may sound way too strong, but it is what God has to say about it.

What then is the answer? It is found at the cross upon which Christ bore not only our every emptiness, but all our attempts at filling that void, the attempts that only separate us further from true and lasting satisfaction through the Blood of Jesus.

> *How much more, then, will the blood of Christ,*
> *who through the eternal Spirit offered himself unblemished to God,*
> *cleanse our consciences from acts that lead to death,*
> *so that we may serve the living God!*
> Hebrews 9:14 NIV

*Submit therefore to God. Resist the devil and he will flee from you.*
*Draw near to God and He will draw near to you.*
James 4:7-8 NAS

His word is always a promise and His word declares if we will draw near to God, He will surely draw near to us (James 4:8). If we will accept the sacrifice, then we can boldly draw near the throne of grace and our needs are filled. (Hebrews 4:16) Any time you are in the presence of God you *will* be filled. Note that the Bible tells us this drawing near is something we must do ourselves. God will not do this part for us. We must accept and we must draw near. So often we turn it around and expect this of God, and then busying ourselves doing those things that God has said He will do *for* us.

> *If you then, being evil,*
> *know how to give good gifts to your children,*
> *how much more will your heavenly Father*
> *give the Holy Spirit to those who ask Him?*
> Luke 11:13 NAS

This then is the filling that truly satisfies, nourishes, heals and empowers and that connects to the Father, then to the aching world, bringing ever increasing fulfillment. Steep your mind in the Word of God, renewing it to the only real and lasting satisfaction. Learn what is yours by the blood. Be filled with the Holy Spirit. Renew and make complete your whole self, spirit, soul and body (1 Thessalonians 5:23) by means of regular fellowship with your heavenly Father in prayer, praise and worship. As Psalm 46:10 exhorts, make time to be still and know Him, truly know Him. It is the only true fulfillment and it is what you were created for.

> *Man's chief and highest end is to glorify God,*
> *and fully to enjoy him forever.*
> Westminster Greater Catechism

When you understand what took place at the cross, the Great Exchange, and its eternal and very personal significance, you will reap infinitely greater benefits in quietly allowing yourself to be filled than in your frantic lifetime quest to fill yourself!

\*\*\*

## *Confession:*
I open up my deep lack, the gaping holes in my life to the God of fulfillment.

## *Go Deeper:*
James 4:2b-4
Hebrews 9:14
James 4:7-8
Hebrews 4:16
Luke 11:13
1 Thessalonians 5:23
Psalm 46:10
Proverbs 30:15-16
Matthew 6:8, 11; 7:11
Philippians 4:6-7

## *Minute by Minute:*
What needs or desires in your life are you seeking to satisfy? What spaces are you longing to fill? Begin by making a list of the

voids in your life, those cravings that seem to haunt you no matter where you go or what you do. Then, beside each one, note the ways in which you may be trying to fill that void yourself. Beside that, note how well it has worked.

Now, delve into the Word of God and see what He has to say about fulfilling your specific needs. Are these needs addressed? If so, they are provided for you by the blood of the New Covenant. Consider abandoning your own attempts and looking to the God who loves you enough to have offered Himself to fill your every aching void.

# *Hope Realized*                                *Week 16*

> *Be of good courage,*
> *and he shall strengthen your heart,*
> *all ye that hope in the LORD.*
> Psalm 31:24 KJV

God's goodness and lovingkindness has manifested in the birth of a new family member, one that the medical world decreed impossible.[12] Her middle name, Grace, reflects the nature of the gift she is to our family!

How many of us are standing, this very day, in the presence of blessings that the natural world said were not possible? And how many more are looking toward future blessings that seem quite impossible right now?

What is the key? It is rooted in our ability to *hope*. There are two ways to define hope, both correct, but not equally effective. Over time, the word has taken on a very wishy-washy connotation to most. "I sure hope so…" carries with it no expectation of fulfillment.

Bible hope on the other hand, is filled with anticipation. I have heard it described as neck-stretching expectation, the kind you feel when you are standing curbside waiting for a parade to appear. You begin to hear the sound of the cymbals in the distance, so you know it's coming. You step off the curb and crane your neck to see when (not *if*, but *when*). This hope comes as a result of knowing what the Word says about your situation and then acting on it.

This baby girl is the fulfillment of a hope that might have been dashed 10 years ago when her mother was given a bleak prognosis. But just as the original woman with the issue of blood in Mark 5, she latched onto the word of God for her situation and refused to let hope leave her.

She was prepared to reach out and grasp her deliverance. She stretched out her neck and listened intently for the sound of cymbals in the distance. Just as her sister did in Jesus' day, she said to herself, *if I can just take hold of the promise, I will be healed*. She would not allow her hope to be deferred, deterred or defeated.

*Hope deferred maketh the heart sick:*
*but when the desire cometh, it is a tree of life.*
Proverbs 13:12 KJV

And a tree of life it was! And so we have this wondrous baby girl, who we can surely say is the child of Hope. What are you waiting to birth that the world says is an impossibility? Go to the Word, not the world. Find what God has to say about it and then stick your neck out in expectation of the sound of cymbals in the distance — your parade is on the way.

Update: Lest you think this healing is a fluke, in July of 2008, we received this miracle child's baby sister — God is faithful!

\*\*\*

### *Confession:*
*I wait for the LORD, my soul doth wait, and in his word do I hope.* (Psalm 130:5)

### *Go Deeper:*
Psalm 31:24
Mark 5:25-34
Proverbs 13:12
Psalm 130:5

### *Minute by Minute:*
If God has placed a desire in your heart and a world full of naysayers is trying to "spare" you the pain of hoping in a lost cause, go to the Word. Begin by delighting yourself in the Lord, putting yourself in His hands, at His disposal — no matter what! (Psalm 37:4) Then, be sure your desire is a Godly one. Find every promise in Scripture that pertains to your hope. Then give the circumstances to God, the Author of all and the great Changer of circumstances. Now, receive the promise in the spirit *before* you ever see it in the natural. Do not share it with every well meaning dream-slayer and finally, stay connected to the Word and do not allow yourself to be shaken.

*The Bible Minute*

*I have the Lord
Continually before me;
Because He is at my right hand,
I will not be shaken.*
Psalm 16:8 NAS

*The Bible Minute*

## *Trust the Plan*             Week 16

> *But the Lord's plans stand forever;*
> *His intentions can never be shaken.*
> Psalm 33:11 NLT

> *'For I know the plans I have for you,' declares the LORD,*
> *'plans to prosper you and not to harm you,*
> *plans to give you hope and a future.*
> *Then you will call upon me and come and pray to me,*
> *and I will listen to you.'*
> Jeremiah 29:10-12 NIV

Jeremiah assures that God has a good plan for you! But can you really be certain? Let's examine the evidence.

His plan is His will. God and His will are inseparable. He *is* His will. His Word is His will and God is His Word. The purpose of His heart is Who He is. They are all so intertwined that they cannot be separated. His word, which is His will, is Who He is. And Jesus Christ is the very manifestation of His Word, His Being, into the flesh of a man. (John 1:1, 14)

His plan, according to His will, can *never* be shaken. Even Job, in his discourse with God, understood that God's plan was incapable of failure. Proverbs 21:30 says, *No plan...can succeed against the Lord* (i.e., no *anti*-plan).

> *I know that you can do all things;*
> *no plan of yours can be thwarted.*
> Job 42:2 NIV

Amos 3:7 assures us that He does nothing without revealing His plan, *Surely the Lord GOD will do nothing, but he revealeth his secret unto his servants the prophets.* In fact, scholars estimate that half to two-thirds of the Bible is prophecy, so it becomes very clear that God does not want us ignorant of His will or His plan to bring it about.

It is those who do not know the plan who are headed for disaster. Hosea 4:6 says, *My people are destroyed for lack of knowledge*. Note that it says, *My people perish*. He is talking about those acknowledged as His own. The Hebrew word translated *destroyed* or *perish* is the word *damah*, and it can also be translated as *cease to be, be cut off, brought to silence, utterly undone*. The connotation is very permanent.

The word translated as *plan*, comes from the Latin *planum*, to level ground as well as from the French word *planter*, to fix in place. It is a method for achieving an end; a formulation of a plan of action; an overall objective, design, blueprint, or strategy. Is it beginning to take shape for you? God's plan is solid and secure, unchangeable, and formed around His intentions, His purpose and His immovable pattern and system.

Let's look at some dramatic statements, logically.

**God's plan is God's will.** God's plan is His statement of His will and desire. It is the diagram, the blueprint, the means by which it will be brought to completion.

**God's will is God's Being.** In His perfection, there can be no disconnect between who He Is and what He desires to bring about. (Matthew 12:25; Mark 3:25)

**God's will is God's Word.** God's will is communicated to His people through His Word. In the first five books of the Old Testament, the Pentateuch, referred to as the Torah (the Law) not only to the Israelites, but the modern Jews as well, His will is clearly communicated as the commandments. This includes not only the 10 Commandments with which we are familiar, but a multitude of laws governing every area of daily living.

**God's Word is God's Being.** It only takes a rudimentary understanding of logic for us to see that it follows that if God's will reflects who He is and His will is His Word, then His Word is who He is, one and the same. If we had any doubt at all, John 1:1 removes any question.

**God's Word is Jesus Christ.** We needn't take time to figure this statement out, because the Word is very clear. (John 1:14)

**Jesus Christ is God.** Logically, scripturally, we have arrived at exactly what Jesus says of Himself in John 10:30 and John 14:9, just to name two. Since all Scripture supports all other Scripture, that should be no surprise.

He announced Himself to Moses as I AM WHO I AM (Exodus 3:14). All the way through the New Testament, we see Jesus announcing Himself to the world as I AM. Give particular attention to the gospel of John. Mark each place where Jesus says the words *I am* and then look closely to see what He is revealing about Himself and the reaction of His listeners and you will come to a greater understanding of why He identified Himself to Moses that way.

*But the plans of the LORD stand firm forever,*
*the purposes of his heart through all generations.*
*Psalm 33:11 (NIV)*

He is saying *I AM your salvation; I AM your healing; I AM your deliverance; I AM your restoration; I AM the Love; I AM whatever you need and are unable to supply in your own strength.* He is the Alpha and the Omega, the All in All. He is saying, I AM the Plan.

Let's put it together in a statement:

*The Lord's plans stand forever; His intentions can never be shaken and His unshakable plans, the purposes of His heart, are to prosper you and not to harm you, to give you hope and a future, and you know He can do all things; no plan of His can be thwarted.* (Psalm 33:11; Jeremiah 29:11; Job 42:2)

Now that's good news!

\*\*\*

***Confession:***
The Lord's plans for me stand forever; His intentions for me can never be shaken and His unshakable plans, the purposes of His heart, are to prosper me and not to harm me, to give me a hope and a future. I know He can do all things and no plan of His can be thwarted unless I refuse to yield to it.

***Go Deeper:***
Psalm 33:11
John 1:1, 14
Jeremiah 29:10-12
Proverbs 21:3
Job 42:2
Amos 3:7
Hosea 4:6
Matthew 12:25; Mark 3:25
John 10:30 and John 14:9
Exodus 3:14
Psalm 33:11
John
Note: A close reading of the entire book of John will bring revelation upon revelation not only of Who He IS, but of His great love for us and who we are in Him.

***Minute by Minute:***
After meditating on the supporting Scriptures, are you experiencing a revelation of who He IS and who He wants to be in your life, minute by minute? Pinpoint concrete evidence that His plan is not only at work in your life now, but has been from the beginning. Just as God patiently put his plan of redemption into motion as soon as Adam sinned, so He was affecting His plan for your life, long before you ever acknowledged Him. Are you able now to see His footprints?

# Saved — Now What? Week 17

> *Therefore, my dear friends, as you have always obeyed—
> not only in my presence, but now much more in my absence—
> continue to work out your salvation with fear and trembling.*
> Philippians 2:12 NIV

This verse used to be a puzzle to me, becoming one of those verses that I read quizzically and than passed over, knowing that one day I must face it and dig deeper. It was disturbing to me in light of my understanding of the true exchange at the cross.

Biblical scholars and theologians use the terminology *positional* and *progressive* sanctification in explaining this verse. This was no help to me as it sounded as though there were two varieties of consecration and I must make a choice. It is no wonder that it was also at odds with my heart's understanding of the cross.

Simply stated, these two terms convey, *now you are saved* and *what are you going to do about it?*

*Positional sanctification* addresses what you *are* — saved. The Greek word is *sozo* and indicates a present reality with future implications, covering both the temporal and spiritual realms. The work of sanctification was finished *for* us, not *by* us. It is nothing we could have accomplished on our own. Once we have received the gift of salvation, our part then becomes what we will do about it. And that depends largely on our understanding of what has taken place.

*Progressive sanctification* deals with what must follow, the visible changes that are a result of the change in position. Both are necessary to fulfill God's will, not only for our eternal future with Him, but for our present purpose as well. (See Mark 16:5; Matthew 28:19; John 20:21) Philippians 2:15-16 gives us a glimpse of our present purpose. We must know that we are equipped to shine as lights... *holding out* and *offering [to all men] the Word of Life* (AMP).

Consider the case of a child adopted at three or four years of age. Through adoption, he is *positionally* a full and complete son of the house with all rights and benefits of that estate. But this child will not yet have learned to behave as a son. Eventually, if all goes according to plan, the child progresses to a point at which his behavior is in line with his position. He will begin to use family expressions and modes of speech, honoring and reflecting family values in his choices. He is *progressively* setting himself apart (sanctification) to match what is already positionally his.

Some of this comes naturally as his revelation of sonship becomes more deeply rooted. Some of it he may actively imitate in his desire to please and to feel a part of the family, to be "like" them. But it is a role he plays until such time as his revelation is deeply rooted enough that it alone influences his actions.

Eventually he may even begin to resemble his adoptive family — more noticeable evidence brought about by the invisible, the positional, which is real only in the unseen and legal documents attesting to the truth of it. This belonging becomes observable as his behavior comes to reflect it more and more.

The firstborn son of a ruling monarch is immediately a prince and the future king. That is his positional sanctification; set apart from everyone else at the very moment of his birth. But he is no more outwardly ready to assume the role than any other infant. His position as future king does not exempt him from outward preparation, education and training, in other words, progressive sanctification.

If he becomes king as a child, before this preparation is complete, a regent will be appointed to rule on his behalf until he is fully prepared. Ideally, in the day he assumes the visible role of king, enthroned, he will not only *be* king, but he will have taken on the mantle of kingship for all to see. Both positional and progressive sanctification are necessary for his reign to be marked by excellence.

Can you now better understand, perhaps, the draw of religion? There is comfort in a set of rules and regulations, dos and don'ts, as a way to please God and gain His favor. Little thought is required other than will you adhere to the law or will you break it. On the other hand, relationship requires maturity and ongoing communication — effort.

Understanding that the rules have been fulfilled for all time highlights our actions, our works as the fruit of our position, not a mantle that we put on to gain the position. Too often we don the mantle as a way to attain the position. But there can be no true and lasting sanctification in human attempts at holiness.

But what about James 4:22, *as a result of works, faith was perfected?* If you go back and read verse 10 and then verses 14-26, you will see it is all the same. *Enduring works* are the fruit of position. Progressive sanctification is a continuation of the process begun when the position was established.

When my children began to move out into the world alone and with friends, my last words to them as they walked out the door were always, *remember who you are.* That was all well and good — if they knew who they were to begin with. If they were stable and fixed in their position (see Psalm 91:1 AMP), the words were a valuable reminder to continue to progressively reflect it in the world. If they were not grounded in that knowledge, you can imagine the pitfalls awaiting them.

Are you struggling with a Christianity that expects more of you than you feel you can ever live up to? Are you trying to work out your own salvation? Or do you know who you are, really know at your deepest core? If you cannot honestly answer that you do, it is time to get into the Word of God and find out. As you immerse yourself, revelation will come and, along with it, the faith to accept that what the Word says about you is the Truth (Romans 10:17).

***

## *Confession:*
Since I belong to the Lord by virtue of my acceptance of the free gift of salvation, I am all that I am meant to be, by faith. That awesome knowledge sets me apart and positions me to make choices in and with my life that make my position increasingly clearer day by day. Hallelujah!

## *Go Deeper:*
Philippians 2:12
Philippians 2:15-16
Mark 16:5
Matthew 28:19

John 20:21
James 4:22, 10, 14-16
Psalm 91 AMP
Romans 10:17

***Minute by Minute:***
In my Bible, next to Philippians 2:12, I have written, *you're saved — now what? Allow the salvation of your spirit to infect your mind, will, emotions and body, becoming outwardly visible — the difference between being saved and being changed.* In other words, now you are saved, what are you going to do about it?

While the work of salvation has been completed for the sinner, the manifestation of change is up to him. If you have a revelation of the enormity of what has been done on your behalf, once and for all:

1. How will your self-image change?
2. How will your behavior change?
3. Will you continue attempting to be worthy?
4. Will you continue to compare yourself with others?

The answers to these questions will undoubtedly be very revealing. Share them with an accountability partner, or work through them with your Bible study or small group. Encourage and hold one another accountable for progress in each area.

# *Greater Works than These*                               *Week 17*

> *Most assuredly, I say to you, he who believes in Me,*
> *the works that I do he will do also;*
> *and greater works than these he will do,*
> *because I go to My Father.*
> John 14:12 NKJV

How often have we read that verse and slipped right by it, perhaps stopping only briefly to consider its world altering implications? And what was the nature of these identifying works of Jesus' earthly ministry that He would have us consider in these words? What did He do that He assures us we will surpass?

First, it was His custom to be regularly in the house of the Lord (Luke 2:49). Have you declared that He is your personal Lord and Savior and then forsaken the gathering together (Hebrews 10:25) that was His custom? If we are to walk in His power, as He tells us, then we must not only consider, but emulate, His customs.

Second, Jesus began his three year ministry *full of and controlled by the Holy Spirit* (Luke 4:1 AMP). We can certainly be no less filled, if we are to accomplish even more. His promise was that because He was going to the Father, the Holy Spirit would be as near to each of us as our next breath. (John 14:16-18; 15:26; 16:7; 20:22)

We must recognize that, as it was with Jesus, being *full of and controlled by the Holy Spirit* does not keep temptation away but strengthens us to keep it at bay. It prepares and enables each of us to withstand every trial, just as it did Jesus in His wilderness time of testing. (Luke 4:1-13). It is worthy of note that Jesus was full of and *controlled* by the Holy Spirit when He entered the wilderness (Luke 4:1) and He emerged full of and *under the power* of the Holy Spirit (verse 14), having overcome. Temptation did not drain Him of the Spirit. If we are tired, beaten down by the battle, we are resisting in our own strength.

These then were Jesus' points of strength. Now what exactly was His earthly Mission that we are expected to not only carry on but to build upon? (John 14:12). Luke gives us Jesus' own words in John 4:18:

He was anointed to:

- *Preach the gospel to the poor* (see also Matthew 5:3),
- *Heal the brokenhearted,* literally, to heal the ones broken, crushed completely, shattered in heart (see also Isaiah 61:1),
- *Proclaim liberty to the captives,* denoting a captive of the enemy, a POW, a prisoner of war,
- *And recovery of sight to the blind,* denoting both physical and mental blindness,
- *To set at liberty those who are oppressed,* translated as downtrodden in the New American Standard translation,
- *To proclaim the acceptable year of the Lord.* The Amplified Bible clarifies this as *the day when salvation and the free favors of God profusely abound.*

Our only question then must be whether Jesus did these things. Did He fulfill that for which He was sent? A fresh reading of the four Gospel accounts of His life and ministry will give us the answer. And if He did indeed carry out His Mission, then we are to do likewise, at the very least, but in the sure and certain knowledge that we have been empowered to do so.

*Not by might, nor by power,*
*but by my Spirit, says the LORD of hosts.*
Zechariah 4:6 NAS

If you are overwhelmed by the prospect, that's excellent! It means you are in the right place to receive the anointing available to you to go forth in the Mission. It means that you will waste none of the precious time remaining in vain human attempts to do what can only be done by the divine. If you know the anointing as God's divine power and ability poured out upon human flesh to do what only God can do, then you will be in position to do nothing of yourself, but as you are led by the Holy Spirit, even as Jesus did. (John 8:28)

Perhaps this contradicts everything you have ever believed or been taught, but it is according to Scripture, God's own Word. It is helpful to understand that Jesus' earthly Mission had two parts to it. The first was His three year teaching, preaching and healing ministry, in which He set the example for us of how to carry on until He comes for us. It was very much a *ministry of example*.

The Crucifixion however, was a *ministry of exchange*, in which God did for us what we were incapable of doing for ourselves, salvation and deliverance, total redemption, the breaking down of all that separated us from union with God.

Too often, we reverse the two and shun the responsibility to *do greater works than these* and instead pick up the shame of the Cross, attempting to bear our own sin and guilt, paying the price, as though we could secure a better redemption for ourselves than God has secured for us. Let us then get our roles straight, embracing what has been done and provided for us, that we might go forth and do what has been set before us to do.

\*\*\*

*Confession:*
As foreign as the concept may feel to me, if Jesus said I will do greater works, then I am prepared from this moment forward to yield to the empowering and the guidance of the Holy Spirit. I will step out in faith.

*Go Deeper:*
John 14:12
Luke 2:49
Luke 4:1 AMP
John 14:16-18; 15:26; 16:7; 20:22
Luke 4:1-13, 14
John 4:18
Matthew 5:3
Zechariah 4:6
John 8:28

*Minute by Minute:*

Read once more the Gospel accounts of Jesus' earthly ministry. But this time, read them with fresh and very personal eyes. His earthly ministry was in two parts. From the time of His baptism by John until his delivery for crucifixion was a ministry of *example*. The events of the crucifixion were a ministry of *exchange*. Reread Isaiah 53 and give some consideration to whether you may have reversed the two.

# *Spring*

*For, lo, the winter is past, the rain is over and gone;*
*The flowers appear on the earth;*
*the time of the singing of birds is come,*
*and the voice of the turtle is heard in our land;*
Song of Songs 2:11-12

# *Immediately*                                            *Week 18*

> *While He was in one of the cities, behold,*
> *there was a man covered with leprosy;*
> *and when he saw Jesus, he fell on his face and implored Him,*
> *saying, 'Lord, if You are willing, You can make me clean.'*
> *And He stretched out His hand and touched him,*
> *saying, 'I am willing; be cleansed.'*
> *And immediately the leprosy left him.*
> Luke 5:12-13 NAS

Jesus stated His purpose straight from prophecy in Isaiah 61, to preach the gospel, proclaim release to captives, restore sight to the blind, and set free the downtrodden, and ultimately to declare the Jubilee year, the year of cancellation of *all* debts. He further commanded this practice to be continued. (Mark 16:17, 18 and Luke 10)

This great freedom is available to us today. He taught it and then He sealed it with His own eternal blood. The Covenant is very much for today. Isaiah's prophecy and Jesus' fulfillment is physical as well as spiritual. The translation of the Greek for miracles is *attesting works*. Jesus has a twofold purpose: out of God's great love for us, he makes healing available to us, and then out of His great love for the perishing world, He causes it to "attest" to His word, His promises, His power to fulfill TODAY and IMMEDIATELY, Isaiah's prophecy about Him.

What are you full of today that needs to leave immediately? Is there something blinding you, holding you in bondage, captive and downtrodden? (Luke 13:11-16) Then speak this Scripture out your mouth, filling in the blanks. Speak it until it becomes more real to you than your condition, causing it to become your confession.

> *"Behold, here I am a man/woman full of_____; and when I see Jesus, I fall on my face and implore Him, saying 'Lord, if You are willing, You can make me clean.' And He stretches out His hand, and touches me, saying, 'I am willing; be cleansed.' And immediately the _____ leaves me."*

## The Bible Minute

Remember, God is no respecter of persons; what He has done for others, He will do for you. He is unchanging. (Acts 10:34 and Hebrews 13:8) Follow the steps given us in this account.

1. Acknowledge what you are full of that needs to leave immediately. Be completely honest with yourself, listen to the Holy Spirit. Have you been hanging on to infirmity, habits, strongholds, unforgiveness, unfruitful relationships, fear, etc.?
2. See Jesus. The man full of leprosy would never have been set free had he not *seen* and *acknowledged* Jesus. Spend time with Him; spend time in His word, learning who He is and who He wants to be in your life. If you do not acknowledge who He is, you will never take the next step.
3. Fall on your face. The ultimate in surrender, supplication and trust is to prostrate yourself before Him, physically and spiritually.
4. Implore Him. The man in Luke's account had no doubt at all about Jesus' ability. His only uncertainty was concerning Jesus' willingness. We can have no such uncertainty. He had no current written word concerning Jesus to inform, exhort and encourage, only word of mouth. We have the complete Word as our foundation for faith.
5. Let Him touch you — He is willing.
6. Receive the healing in His touch. He won't force you, you must open yourself to it.

In Luke's account, Jesus tells the cleansed man not to spread the word but to go to the priest and make an offering — for a testimony. Following the precepts in the prescribed form would have been a greater testimony. Jesus was speaking to a Jew, who had certain obligations. Remember that Jesus came to fulfill the Law, not to destroy it. (Matthew 5:17) We are still under obligation to give our offerings to God, but we have no obligation to keep our freedom quiet. Spread the word!

\*\*\*

*Confession:*
   Behold, here I am a man/woman full of _____; and when I see Jesus, I fall on my face and implore Him, saying *Lord, if You are willing, You can make me clean.* And He stretches out His hand, and touches me, saying, 'I am willing; be cleansed.' And immediately the _____ leaves me.

*Go Deeper:*
Luke 5:12-13
Isaiah 61:1-2
Mark 16:17, 18; Luke 10
Luke 13:11-16
Acts 10:34
Hebrews 13:8
Matthew 5:17

*Minute by Minute:*
   If you confessed above that ours is a willing and immediate God, how will your life be impacted from minute to minute by completely believing and accepting the truth of your declaration? What will change? What have you been filled with that might be holding you back?

## *What Do You Have Faith For?*        Week 18

*For she said, If I may touch but his clothes, I shall be whole.
And straightway the fountain of her blood was dried up;
and she felt in her body that she was healed of that plague.*
Mark 5:28, 29 KJV

In Matthew 14, Peter had faith to step out of the boat, but his faith failed him when he focused on the circumstances. In Matthew 17, Jesus rebuked his disciples for their lack of faith to cast out a demon. He blamed it on their unbelief, not on a lack of available power. In Mark 4, once again Jesus rebuked his disciples for their lack of faith to calm the storm.

But in Mark 5, we are shown what sustained and focused faith can bring about. The woman with a twelve year issue of blood, which seems likely to have been endometriosis,[13] set her faith on healing. She was convinced, without a doubt, that all she needed to do was touch the healing fringe at the hem of Jesus' garment. She not only set her mind, *"I shall be made well,"* but she stepped out, acting on her faith. (James 1:22) She risked everything by venturing out into the crowd while ceremonially unclean.

What differentiates this woman from Peter on the water? Focus. Focus on Christ kept her free of doubt and ultimately brought her victory. Lack of focus caused Peter's faith to falter and ultimately to fail quickly.

I have shared with many the story of another woman with an issue of blood. Ten years ago, she was also a woman who *had endured much at the hands of many physicians.* (Mark 5:26) She had been given a bleak prognosis. Repeated surgeries, battling cancer and the inability to have children were her predicted future. But she stepped resolutely into a church service one Sunday morning, determined to be delivered from her affliction.

Her focus was on Jesus Christ, the Healer, not on her circumstances. She shut out all else but Him. That February morning God honored her faith and changed the course of the service and her entire future. The Holy Spirit moved, and in obedience to His prompting, the pastor altered his plan for that Sunday morning and held a healing service instead.

The power is always present, always available, but Jesus tells us again and again that it is activated by *our* faith. How do we get hold of that kind of power unleashing faith? Romans 10:17 answers us that *faith comes from hearing and hearing by the word of Christ.* Fill up on the Word and crowd out the circumstances. Focus on the promise, not the problem, on the Truth instead of the facts. Keep your eyes on Jesus.

What do you have faith for? If there is an area in your life where faith seems to fail you, fill up on the Word and watch the circumstances come in line. And what has become of this woman ten years later? I hold her two precious little daughters in my arms — I'm their Nana!

***

*Confession:*
I set my mind on the Word of God and step out in faith, as a doer of the Word. While the world may think I am risking everything, the risk is not mine. It was taken for me and I am reaping the benefits. And now I set my eyes on Jesus. According to Hebrews 12:2, He is the Author and finisher of my faith. Now I maintain my focus, not shifting it to the wind and waves. Victory is the harvest of my seeds of faith.

*Go Deeper:*
Mark 5:28, 29
Matthew 14
Matthew 17:20
Mark 5:25-34
James 1:22
Romans 10:17

*Minute by Minute:*
All of us have experienced disappointments at one time or another when we were so certain our faith was strong. Now that we

have explored the importance of maintaining focus in keeping our faith strong, what personal crisis of faith might have gone differently had your focus not shifted from faith to sight? What would you do differently today?

# *I Had My Oil Changed Today*          Week 19

> *Train up a child in the way he should go:*
> *And when he is old, he will not depart from it.*
> Proverbs 22:6 KJV

In itself, this is not particularly noteworthy, save for the fact that I don't enjoy oil changes and tend to procrastinate as the time approaches. I suspected it would be crowded on a Saturday, so I took some of my catch-up reading. It continually amazes me how wonderfully God displays our lessons, laying them out in the simplest of our daily routines.

Of all the people who waited with me during that hour, two parent/child pairs provided a stunning contrast for me of the fruit of our approaches with our children, and for that matter, with one another.

First to enter was a mother with a young son about seven years old. It was clear who was in charge from the moment they entered the waiting room. The child exploded into the room, shot from guns, and Mom trailed along behind, standing resignedly as the boy took the only remaining chair. I bit my tongue fighting the urge to suggest he let his mother sit down. He took in his surroundings and instantly bounded out of the chair and, in his attempts to amuse himself, bumped and jostled several people in the room.

He was sullen, surly and rude. Mom was apologetic and non-insistent. The one time she actually corrected his rudeness to her, there was no note of authority in her tone. Clearly, Mom does not know who she is, and equally as clearly, her son does! In the end, they left. Mom did not get her oil changed and the child got his way.

Moments later, a father and son pair came in. The child was quiet but busied himself in a very "6ish" way checking out the varying perspectives available to him by sitting frontward and then backward in the chair. He bothered no one and stayed contained in the chair, amusing himself quietly. At one point Dad leaned down and very quietly and privately said, "Know what? I love you very much." This was followed by some very quiet interchange I didn't quite catch. Then he said, "So, what do you want to be when you grow up?"

All this was very quiet and the exchange itself was not remarkable, but the tone was so tender, so oriented to fostering a quality relationship, I could not help but smile. As I was busy reading a counseling periodical, it was probably clear to everyone what I was smiling at. The tenderness of the exchange moved me nearly to the point of tears.

What does this have to do with us? Plenty! Ask yourself these questions concerning your closest relationships:

1. Do I accept the status quo as being too difficult to change or do I sow toward the desired end?
2. Do I routinely base my actions on what will provide me immediate but perhaps only semi-peace, or do I take the time and additional effort to do what works in the long run?
3. Am I concerned with appearances or am I concerned with substance and quality?
4. Do I walk in love at all times, even if that requires tough love and perhaps some inconvenience for me?
5. Do I allow fear to dictate my actions?

The father and son who drew my smiles had clearly been cultivating a relationship all along. As far as they were concerned their sojourn in that less than comfortable waiting room was an opportunity to spend time together. Instead of waiting for the perfect setting, they made use of what they had. For all they knew, these two might have been sitting at the end of a pier with fishing poles dangling in some crystal lake. They were together and that's what mattered.

Mom, on the other hand, was uncertain of the outcome from the moment she and her boy walked in. It was something to be endured (or not) until she could get junior home and gain temporary relief by plopping him in front of the TV or a video game. She is sowing to the future just as surely as Dad is with his boy.

Let's not make the mistake of seeking respite in the short run by forsaking the long run. Sowing is not always an easy chore but reaping a fine harvest is well worth the effort on the front end. And make no mistake, when it comes to relationships of any kind, the harvest will be great — either a field overgrown with briars and brambles, painful to walk through, or a field rich with golden grain. And it can all take place in a cold and grimy waiting room on a Saturday afternoon.

***

*Confession:*
Since seedtime and harvest is in effect (see Genesis 8:22), I will take responsibility for the seeds I sow, sowing them purposefully into every relationship from the most casual to the most intimate.

*Go Deeper:*
Proverbs 22:6
Genesis 8:22
1 Corinthians 13:4-8 (Amplified Translation)

*Minute by Minute:*
Begin by choosing your closest relationship and then rather than taking a purely academic interest, take the risk and ask yourself the suggested questions above. Be completely honest with your answers. You may be surprised. Consider sharing you answers with a trusted friend or accountability partner.

# Gabby's Way — Week 19

> *Train up a child in the way he should go,*
> *Even when he is old he will not depart from it.*
> Proverbs 22:6 NAS

With seven grown children, I generally see them in group settings, so it is rare and very special to have the opportunity to spend some time alone with any of them. In one such time with my eldest daughter and granddaughter, Nana was the one who learned something valuable.

In an effort to help my granddaughter live her increasingly complex then seven year old existence according to biblical principles, the two of them had devised a set of *remembrances*. Gabby shared them with me, with a bit of prompting from Mom. What they had designed was a means to help her navigate the uncertainties of the world of school and daycare with the many varied and often confusing expectations.

My daughter's hope was to impart to Gabby an understanding of the tools always at her disposal for navigating the rocks and shoals of being a child in today's world. From that need grew the following list which they called *5 Rules and Counting*. I think of it not so much as rules, but remembrances that can create valuable *aha moments* throughout the day. (Note: I have taken the liberty of breaking up number 5 to create a number 6.)

Since I am always on the lookout for practical applications of biblical principles, I was very taken by her presentation of these and I knew at once I could apply them to my own adult daily uncertainties. The principles are timeless, nothing new here, but simply and concisely stated, they are easy enough for a seven year old (and her sixty plus Nana) to understand, remember, and rely upon.

1. **Listen to the adult in charge.** How often do we forget that authority is a biblical principle, one Jesus understood and under which He operated. We do not ever outgrow the need to listen to the adult in charge. We would save ourselves a great deal of

*The Bible Minute*

---

heartache if we would first align ourselves with godly authority figures and then *listen* and *submit*. (Romans 13:1)
2. **Listen to the Holy Spirit.** How often do we remember that the Holy Spirit is speaking to us throughout the day, old and young alike? Do we think to stop and ask for guidance often enough throughout the day? We know that is a key role of the Holy Spirit, but so often we seem bent on muddling through on our own. (John 16:13-15)
3. **You will not always get your way.** Our own way is generally going to be self-centered. We teach our children this rule and then we turn around and demand it *ourselves*. God's way is perfect and will accomplish His will eternally, perfectly, for all involved. (Psalm 143:10; Romans 12:2; Psalm 40:8)
4. **Treat others the way you would like to be treated.** Easy to say, any child can repeat The Golden Rule but obviously not so easy to do or the world would be in far better shape than it is. (Matthew 7:12; Luke 6:31)
5. **Remember who you are.** This can be most simply accomplished by remembering *Whose* you are. Here's what my granddaughter says on the subject:
I am the apple of God's eye. (Psalm 17:8; Zechariah 2:8)
I am a princess, daughter of the King. (My granddaughter is learning the truth that this makes her a *real* princess, not just pretend.) (Romans 8:14)
I am the head and not the tail, above only and not beneath. (Deuteronomy 28:13)
I am the Righteousness of God. (2 Corinthians 5:20-21)
6. **Remember who you are not.** (Genesis 3:15)
I am not the devil's pawn, or as my little granddaughter says, *I am not the devil's queen!*

There is no denying it is a really tough world out there, whether you are seven, seventeen or seventy. In whatever form you choose to employ the Word of God and the guidance of the Holy Spirit in plotting your course, the important thing is that you *do* it, in His strength and wisdom, not your own.

Thank you Gabby (and Gabby's Mom) for the attitude adjustment!

*I will not leave you as orphans; I will come to you.*
John 14:18

\*\*\*

## *Confession:*
I am determined this day not to overcomplicate my Christian walk. I will remember that God is my Father and just as surely as I want those in my care to succeed, He wants me to succeed. I will keep it simple and focus on being pleasing to my Abba.

## *Go Deeper:*
Proverbs 22:6
Romans 13:1
John 16:13-1
Psalm 143:10; Romans 12:2; Psalm 40:8
Matthew 7:12; Luke 6:31
Psalm 17:8; Zechariah 2:8
Romans 8:14
Deuteronomy 28:13
2 Corinthians 5:20-21
Genesis 3:15
John 14:18

## *Minute by Minute:*
Gabby's confessions can be yours and mine as well. Consider adopting and adapting them yourself. Then, for a more comprehensive look at who you really are, in the eyes of your Father, try searching the New Testament letters for instances of *in Him*, *in Whom* and *in Christ*.

# Life in a Garden                                Week 20

*And the Lord God planted a garden toward the east, in Eden;
and there he placed the man whom He had formed.*
Genesis 2:8 NAS

Soon after God formed Adam, He placed His new creation in the garden He Himself had planted, the splendor of which we can only begin to imagine. Adam's Eve was brought forth from him in that garden and God Himself walked in Eden's splendor in the cool of the evening, in intimate fellowship with His newly created pair. Adam stepped out of God's will in that same garden and, as a result, was banned from that wondrous place of lush abundance. (Genesis 2:7, 8; 3:6, 8, 23, 24)

And it was in yet another garden that Jesus declared His surrender and obedience to God's will and plan, speaking it into the atmosphere for all of Heaven and earth to witness. The first Adam's transgression in the garden was cancelled by the second Adam's submission — in another garden. Adam was the accurate representative of all men by virtue of being first. And though it took 4000 years, God's carefully constructed plan came to pass in Jesus as the second Adam, the accurate Representative of all men by virtue of the carefully laid groundwork of lineage.

Even though Adam was removed from the garden, the garden was never removed from him. Like Adam before us, we are dust according to Genesis 2:7 and Psalm 103:14. The word used in both verses is *aphar*, meaning dust or loose earth. Any gardener knows that loose earth is the beginning of a great garden. Having been born of a garden, we maintain the properties of a garden and so we are highly "plantable." Jesus expands this concept in Mark 4 when He explains the sowing of the Word. The soil is our hearts, and, as in any garden, there are various kinds, some more conducive to abundant growth than others.

The process of sowing and reaping, planting and harvesting, was settled in its kingdom import from the very beginning, simply stated for us in Genesis 8:22, and confirmed as a New Testament principle in Mark 4:26-29. We cannot help but see the importance to God of the principles of the garden.

What is your garden experience? Are you in the garden of abundance right now? Or perhaps you are in the garden of decision, wrestling your flesh into submission to God's will. Or are you in the garden that feels like death? It is that very garden of death which can become your garden of victory (see John 12:24).

The most important factor is the state of the garden of your heart. It is this garden and how well you have tended it that will indeed create the *garden of your experience*. Remember Jesus' ultimate victory came in a tomb in a garden, (John 19:41), which many thought was surely the garden of death, but from which sprang not only His resurrection, but the resurrection of the whole world!

Now that spring has arrived, it is a perfect time to tend to the garden of your heart. The harvest will surely be found in the garden of your experience.

\*\*\*

*Confession:*
I will begin by insuring that the garden of my heart is guarded by watching over it, (Proverbs 4:23) in order to cultivate an environment in which no seeds of anxiety are sown. By diligently protecting it from known pests and invaders, I can be assured of nurturing an environment in which the resulting peace of God will protect my most precious garden. (Philippians 4:6)

*Go Deeper:*
Genesis 2:8
Genesis 2:7, 8; 3:6, 8, 23, 24
Genesis 2:7; Psalm 103:14
Genesis 8:22
Mark 4:26-29
John 12:24
John 19:41

***Minute by Minute:***
Most of us have allowed anxiety to creep into the garden of our heart unawares. It begins as the small garden pest of nagging worry. But worry always grows and multiplies and will soon begin to eat away at the peace of your garden. What small pests are you allowing, perhaps even entertaining? Choose one and, sharing it with your prayer/accountability partner, then begin, very specifically, to drive it out with the Word of God.

# *A Song of the Shepherd*              **Week 20**

*A Song of Ascents.*
*I will lift up mine eyes unto the hills, from whence cometh my help.*
*My help cometh from the Lord, which made heaven and earth.*
*He will not suffer thy foot to be moved:*
*he that keepeth thee will not slumber.*
*Behold, he that keepeth Israel shall neither slumber nor sleep.*
*The Lord is thy keeper: the Lord is thy shade upon thy right hand.*
*The sun shall not smite thee by day, nor the moon by night.*
*The Lord shall preserve thee from all evil:*
*he shall preserve thy soul.*
*The Lord shall preserve thy going out and*
*thy coming in from this time forth,*
*and even for evermore.*
Psalm 121 KJV

This beautiful and much loved Psalm is a song of the Shepherd, a song of *keeping*. In six different places in this psalm, the word *shamar* is used, translated as *keep*, but also *preserve* and *guard*.

The psalmist begins by establishing divine focus — His eyes are on the Lord, not on the circumstances. How often does our focus slip to the circumstances, to what is happening around us? When it does, we find we begin to look to ourselves, or to others to deal with circumstances, instead of to *the LORD, which made heaven and earth*.

The psalmist has his focus set on the Lord, the Keeper, and he knows this to be the source of his help. The Shepherd/Keeper is tireless in His provision for you. Not only does He keep you from natural danger, but He preserves your soul from all evil. The word *ra*, used for evil indicates an evil with a purpose, to keep you from being a benefit. The enemy is not anxious for you to fulfill your life's mission, and he knows you have one, even if you are uncertain. (Jeremiah 29:11)

If you have made the Lord the center of your life, you are among His sheep. He is guarding your goings and comings from now until forever. Walk in that knowledge. Speak it when you leave your house in the morning; speak it when you put your head on the pillow at night. Make it your last word and your last thought each night and your first word and your first thought each morning — *Lord I thank you that you keep me night and day, because I am yours. Not because I deserve it, but because* **I belong to you.**

*We are His people and the sheep of His pasture* (Psalm 100:3). Shepherds lead and sheep follow. This day, rest in the knowledge that you don't need to lead — all He expects of you is that you follow.

*For the Lord is good; His lovingkindness is everlasting, and His faithfulness to all generations*
Psalm 100:5 (NAS)

Hallelujah! That's good news!

\*\*\*

*Confession:*
Lord, I thank you that you keep me night and day, because You are my shepherd and I am your sheep. Not because I deserve it, but because I belong to you. I rest through the night and I am supported through the day in that awesome knowledge!

*Go Deeper:*
Psalm 121
Jeremiah 29:11
Psalm 100:3, 5

*Minute by Minute:*
Walk in the promise of the Shepherd. Take God at His word and follow the suggestions above. Speak the promises of Psalm 121 when you leave your house in the morning. Bring them to your remembrance when you put your head down for the night. Make it your last thought and your last word each night and your first thought and your first word in the morning. Make it your daily habit to refresh yourself in His love. *Lord, I thank you that you keep me night and day, because I am yours. Not because I deserve it, but because* **I belong to you.**

## *Common Opportunities*                           **Week 21**

*This is the day which the LORD hath made;*
*we will rejoice and be glad in it.*
Psalm 118:24 KJV

*The most common 'segment of opportunity'*
*we experience regularly is each new day.*
Dick Eastman[14]

Proverbs 3:5-6 exhorts us, *in all your ways acknowledge Him and He shall direct your paths.* In his article, Eastman teaches that the Hebrew for *ways* implies *regularly recurring segments of opportunity.*

As I mused on this, it became abundantly clear to me that life consists of a collection of segments, common opportunities, filling each of our days, and I began to think about how we approach these often fleeting moments of possibility.

- The 2-minute chance encounter in front of the Post Office — a common opportunity.
- A 3-minute chat with the checker at the grocery — a common opportunity.
- The regular 15 minute breakfast rush with the kids — a common opportunity.
- A 5-minute tersely polite phone call with your child's teacher — a common opportunity.
- Ten minutes with the police officer writing you a speeding ticket — a common opportunity.
- The 8 minutes between punching the snooze alarm and bounding out of bed — yet another common opportunity.

How do they relate to one another? Each presents us with a choice concerning a level of commitment to the abundant opportunities with which we are confronted each day, a choice to deepen and enrich relationships or to coast along in the shallows.

But first, we need to change our perspective on the events of our days, beginning to see every breathing moment as a segment of opportunity, a very real gift. Once we have accomplished this transition from the mundane perspective to which we are accustomed, we will begin to see the common as opportunity for the uncommon.

We have the power to turn each of these common segments of opportunity, and hundreds more like them each day, into uncommon kingdom interchanges.

Allowing for 8 hours of sleep a night, we are presented with 349,440 minutes per year which we can choose to see as slices of opportunity. We can choose to be ever at the ready to turn each of them into uncommon kingdom victories.

*I expect to pass through this world but once.*
*Any good thing, therefore, that I can do or any kindness*
*I can show to any fellow human being let me do it now.*
*Let me not defer nor neglect it, for I shall not pass this way again.*
William Penn, 1644-1718

Jesus exhorts us to *go therefore and make disciples* (Matthew 28:19). And we do that by first *being* disciples. Every time you open your mouth, you are displaying your discipleship; you are a witness of something. What will that be? Jesus made the choice — what about you?

*And I know that His commandment is life everlasting:*
*whatsoever I speak therefore,*
*even as the Father said unto me,*
*so I speak.*
John 12:50 KJV

\*\*\*

### Confession:
I commit to viewing each moment of each day as an opportunity — not one of them to be wasted on the common, mundane or

superficial, but each an *uncommon* opportunity. *For I shall not pass this way again!*

**Go Deeper:**
Psalm 118:24
Proverbs 3:5-6
Matthew 28:19
John 12:50

**Minute by Minute:**
 Rereading the list of opportunities listed above, how often have you viewed these in light of their annoyance factor, rather than seeing them as opportunities to advance the Kingdom. Rethink your every day interactions and purpose to change your perspective. After all, for most of us, it will be one person at a time we are called to impact. Very few of us will fill a stadium, but each of us can touch one person. Each of us can be salt and light (Matthew 5:13, 14). The ripples of influence will continue long after we are gone. The opportunities are common but the impact is eternal.

# Answering Questions — Week 21

*But a natural man does not accept the things of the Spirit of God;*
*for they are foolishness to him, and he cannot understand them,*
*because they are spiritually appraised.*
*But we have the mind of Christ.*
1 Corinthians 2:14, 16b NAS

In our enthusiasm to bring our friends and family into the kingdom, we risk becoming preoccupied with being able to supply answers to their every question. Questions arising from a position of challenge and a purely intellectual interpretation of biblical truths are extremely challenging to deal with. The field of Christian apologetics endeavors to provide rational justification to the Truth of God's Word. But unless we are well versed in the theology of apologetics, we risk doing more harm than good and ending up backed into a corner in a purely defensive stance regarding our faith.

We can be assured that all we need to know, not only to experience the New Birth but to live out our lives and callings, is already available to us within the pages of the Bible. If we believe we need more, it is a matter of the intellect, to satisfy curiosity or to counteract prevalent deceptions, and not of the spirit at all.

Occasionally I have been approached about answering the questions of doubting friends and relatives, especially in light of recent feature films causing many to question the Bible and its principles. Many have become curious about portions of the life of Jesus not included in the Gospel accounts. The Bible tells us everything we need to know, in order to satisfy our spirit man.

*And He went down with them (Mary and Joseph),*
*and came to Nazareth;*
*and He continued in subjection to them;*
*and His mother treasured all these things in her heart.*
*And Jesus kept increasing in wisdom and stature,*
*and in favor with God and men.*
Luke 2:51-52 NAS

*The Bible Minute*

We must never feel it is our responsibility to look anywhere other than the Bible to prove anything to questioners. It is simply not our job. It is the work of the Holy Spirit to draw people to Himself. It is He who stands at the doorway to our hearts and knocks. (Revelation 3:20) All we are required to do is help people change their focus and share what we know of the Good News. It is not our place to *make* them believe!

We don't "get people saved" as some people say. We just lead them to that place of decision, where the Holy Spirit will do His work. We never need to justify our beliefs to anyone. The Word is complete and, according to 2 Timothy 3:16, *inspired by God and profitable for teaching, for reproof, for correction, and for training in righteousness; that the man of God may be adequate, equipped for every good work.* (NAS) Presenting the Gospel to our friends is definitely part of *every good work*. It says nowhere that we need to add anything to the Word of God. In fact we are told that not one *jot* or *tittle* of the Word is to be changed (Matthew 5:18).

*For the word of God is living and active and sharper*
*than any two-edged sword,*
*and piercing as far as the division of soul and spirit,*
*of both joints and marrow,*
*and able to judge the thoughts and intentions of the heart.*
*And there is no creature hidden from His (the Word's) sight,*
*but all things are open and laid bare to the eyes*
*of Him with whom we have to do.*
Hebrews 4:12, 13 NAS

Peter put it very clearly, as was his habit, when he said that we have *a more sure word of prophecy* than even the audible voice of God which he heard on the Mount of Transfiguration. That is the Logos, the written Word of God. (See 2 Peter 1:19-21).

In our enthusiasm, we sometimes mistakenly believe we need to help God do His work and, in fact, when we do *more* than what we are called to do, we generally make a mess of it, utterly confusing the situation. We are called to live a life that is salt and light to the world, leading people to the perfect Word of God by our example as surely as by our words. We are then expected to intercede on their behalf, standing in the gap and believing that God *always* does His part.

***

*Confession:*
I will listen for the still small voice of the Holy Spirit, telling me what He has prepared me to be or do or say in every situation. I will not step out on my own, attempting to justify my beliefs. I will remember that my greatest value is as a model of the Christian life.

*Go Deeper:*
Revelation 22:18
John 10:35
1 Thessalonians 2:13
1 John 2:14
Matthew 5:14

*Minute by Minute:*
In Matthew 5:14, Jesus is speaking to His disciples. That includes us, for we are His disciples in these latter days just as surely as those who heard Him that day on the mountain. For me, one of the most encouraging statements He makes is that we are the light of world and the salt of the earth. Neither of these requires that I do or say anything to draw those around me. This addresses my character which most often speaks louder than all the right words.

Are you making a positive impact on those in your circle, your family and extended family, friends, coworkers and those you come in contact with along the way, without actively "preaching?" Does your character, who you are when no one is looking, testify to your integrity? Or would you need to check your attitude? Do your actions align with your words? In other words, do you talk the talk *and* walk the walk?

Ask the Holy Spirit to be your guide as you examine the value you are adding to your world. If you discover it is not what you thought, ask for guidance to bring your character and words back into alignment. It is never too late!

# *Summer*

*Now learn a parable of the fig tree;
When his branch is yet tender,
and putteth forth leaves,
ye know that summer is nigh:*
Matthew 24:32

# *Fruitful Perseverance*             **Week 22**

*Bear fruit with perseverance*
Luke 8:15 (NAS)

*By persevering produce a crop*
Luke 8:15 (NIV)

Jesus has just preached the parable of the sower, a pivotal teaching, an understanding of which is vital to operating according to the kingdom process. In Mark 4, He begins His explanation to the disciples by saying, *the sower sows the Word*, and He reminds them (Luke 8:10) that they are granted understanding of this mystery.

In this parable, only the good ground bears fruit thirty, sixty and a hundredfold. Why? The seed was the same in each instance, sown at the same time, out of the same bag, and we know that the seed was good...

The best seed, the uncompromised Word of God in this instance, must be sown in ground purposefully prepared to receive it. Then, and only then, will it yield the maximum harvest. You will never find the serious farmer sowing his precious seed on ground that has not been properly plowed and soil appropriately amended.

He understands the seed itself must be of the finest quality, but that is only the first step. Before he ever takes seed near the field, he has his work cut out for him. Only when this important step is performed, with perseverance, steadfastness and diligence (Proverbs 12:24), will he sow his seed.

Are our hearts properly prepared, the hardened ground broken up and yielded, to receive this precious seed of the Word of God? Or are we dashing off a psalm and a proverb before we toss off a cup of coffee and bolt for the train? Are we prepared to bear fruit *with perseverance*, not haphazardly sowing, but preparing our hearts with diligence to receive the Word — with an assured harvest?

Genesis 3:19 says, *for dust you are and to dust you will return*. We generally consider this to be humbling nearly to the point of humiliation. But, the word *dust* in this passage means *soft earth*, *loose soil, loam*, the perfect medium in which to plant seed and expect a harvest! It should not be a surprise that we were created to receive, nurture and bring to fruition the implanted Word of God.

Hallelujah! Our hearts are meant to be gardens for God's increase!

## *Confession:*
I will take time with the soil of my heart, softening it and preparing it to receive the seed of the Word. I will make time to sow properly and then, in faith and patience, I will await the assured harvest.

## *Go Deeper:*
Luke 8:15
Mark 4:3-20
Luke 8:10
Proverbs 12:24
Genesis 3:19
Genesis 8:22

## *Minute by Minute:*
Genesis 8:22 sets the stage for God's way of doing things — seedtime and harvest will never cease. Jesus confirmed this principle when He told His disciples that the kingdom of God was all about seed and how it is sown. Has your heart been diligently prepared to receive the precious seed of the Word? Or is the ground of your heart hardened, seared by life's pain, disappointments, disillusionments, unforgiveness and sin? We know that the seed is good and has within it the capacity to produce an abundant harvest. How can you better prepare the ground of your heart to receive and nurture the seed of the Word?

## The Diligent Hand — Ruling in Life         Week 22

*Diligent hands will rule,
but laziness ends in slave labor.*
Proverbs 12:24 NIV

In my quiet time one morning, the Holy Spirit prompted me to work on a hat I had been crocheting for my granddaughter. I had never felt prompted in such a direction before, but after a bit of initial wondering, I did what I felt I was being led to do. The Holy Spirit most often teaches me through the very simple things in my life, and since He dwells within each of us, that should be no surprise?

As I worked along in the early morning stillness, welcoming whatever fellowship or lesson He might have for me, the Holy Spirit showed me the following about my simple crochet project.

1. Make sure you have a vision. Keep a clear image before you at all times. It is critical to begin working from a good plan.
2. Assemble all the necessary tools at the outset. Check your gauge and skip none of the preliminaries.
3. Do not give up because the final outcome seems unclear. Trust the Plan.
4. Beginnings can be awkward. You may feel as though you are all thumbs. Don't be discouraged if your start is slow, or if you need to begin several times — press on. If you refer to the written plan frequently, the pattern will eventually emerge and become clear.
5. Once you have a well-established, easily recognized pattern, continue to refer to the plan. Never proceed totally from memory.
6. Stick with the plan until completion of the project. If you have not yet seen results, don't change the plan — consistency is the key! Complete each pattern as an integral part of the whole, leaving nothing out — no shortcuts.
7. By working with a known designer you will avoid errors in the plan, which will surely impact the outcome.

There's nothing new here, and those of us who crochet or sew or garden or perhaps do carpentry, whatever project we undertake, the rules are the same, if the outcome is to be assured. God is a god of process — not a single thing God has done and recorded has been done outside of process. How can we expect results in any area of our lives without operating in the same principle?

Consult the Plan early and often and make sure it is a Plan from the right Designer. Do what works, and *the diligent hand shall rule!*

\*\*\*

*Confession:*
I will consult the Plan early and often and know that my diligence will result in excellence in every area of my life.

*Go Deeper:*
Proverbs 12:24
Proverbs 10:4 NIV, KJV
Proverbs 21:5 NIV
Proverbs 22:29 KJV
Proverbs 13:4 KJV (Read *fat* as *satisfied*)

*Minute by Minute:*
Our Plan has been carefully laid out for us in Scripture. Are you one who carefully follows every step of a recipe or a sewing pattern but leaves the greater issues of your life to chance or intuition? If that is ever true of you, consider looking back over your decisions of the last month. Prayerfully determine if any of your decisions might have been different had you taken time to listen to the leading of the Holy Spirit and sought out Scriptural support for you decisions.

## *Dancing on Daddy's Feet*            **Week 23**

*I danced in the morning when the world was begun*
*I danced in the Moon & the Stars & the Sun*
*I came down from Heaven & I danced on Earth*
*At Bethlehem I had my birth:*

*Dance then, wherever you may be*
*I am the Lord of the Dance, said He!*
*And I'll lead you all, wherever you may be*
*And I'll lead you all in the Dance, said He!*
*(...lead you all in the Dance, said He!)*
Lord of the Dance
Traditional 19th Century Shaker Tune,
Lyrics by Sidney Carter

Before I knew how to dance, I danced on my father's feet. His bigger feet moving under my little ones, his skill and rhythm moved me easily around the room and all I needed to do was hold his hands. I have never danced as well, as unselfconsciously or with as little effort as I did in those days. Our heavenly Father offers us much the same experience, but on an eternal scale.

    When you are tired, your legs aching from trying to keep up with the complicated steps of this dance of life, take off your shoes and step up on Daddy's feet. You were never meant to do it all alone. After all, the dance is His and no one can do it any better.

*Even youths grow tired and weary, and young men stumble and fall;*
*but those who hope in the* L<small>ORD</small> *will renew their strength.*
*They will soar on wings like eagles;*
*They will run and not grow weary,*
*They will walk and not be faint.*
Isaiah 40:30-31 NIV

## The Bible Minute

As you grow and mature in strength through time in the Word and continual fellowship with your heavenly Father, occasionally you will step off His feet and, with your focus locked on Him, He will talk you through the complex steps. But you will never outgrow the need for that sweet time of rest that follows, when you step back onto His feet, into His space and flow with Him as He dances the dance He created before the world began.

Dancing on Daddy's feet means that you never lose the sense that you belong to Him, that you are cherished as His own precious child, that He is never too busy to whirl you around to the music he has composed just for your dance.

Why is it then that so many of us still struggle with the choreography? Why are we often too tired to continue, too discouraged, too spent? If that sounds familiar, perhaps you are trying to master the dance instead of dancing with the Master. When it comes time to step off Daddy's feet and dance on your own two feet, are you neglecting to keep your eyes on Him; have you lost your focus? Or have you made the all too common mistake of forgetting that the dance is not yours. It is His and He alone can orchestrate it.

It is true that we all must dance, but it is His pattern, His footsteps that we are meant to dance in. And when we forget and our smaller legs are tired and we feel very much like little children, overwhelmed with the complexities of the dance, all we need do is climb back on Daddy's feet, and looking into His eyes and, soaking up the love, hang on tight as He whirls us around to the music that is our own special song.

*Dance then, wherever you may be*
*I am the Lord of the Dance, said He!*
*And I'll lead you all, wherever you may be*
*And I'll lead you all in the Dance, said He!*

\*\*\*

**Confession:**

The dance is my Father's. I will not merely submit to His lead, but in my weariness, I will allow Him to carry me.

***Go Deeper:***
Isaiah 40:30-31

***Minute by Minute:***
If life weariness is all too familiar to you, begin by asking yourself if any of the above points apply to you. Are you trying to go it alone, desperately attempting to master the complex steps? Or is it perhaps a matter of focus? Have you forsaken your divine perspective, forgetting to keep your eyes on Him? Or have you gone off into a dance that is no longer His?

Prayerfully consider each of these and be open to the leading of the Holy Spirit as He guides you back to your Daddy's feet. Consider a period of rest, devoted to the simple, refreshing practice of delighting yourself in the Lord. (Psalm 37:4)

# *Thank You Daddy!*            *Week 23*

*Always giving thanks to God the Father
for everything, in the name of our Lord Jesus Christ.*
Ephesians 5:20 NIV

Every June we set aside a Sunday for honoring our earthly fathers and well we should honor them, not just in June but every day of every year! But while we are scanning the ads for that just right expression of our love and gratitude, perhaps it would be a good time to examine how well we are honoring our heavenly Father. And I know no better way to demonstrate honor than with a heart overflowing with expressions of gratitude.

Gratitude is merely the expression of thanksgiving – it is an attitude, a lifestyle. If you have ever had any trouble maintaining an attitude of thanksgiving, try this very simple but potentially life-changing exercise.

Not only will you become conscious of what you are thankful for in your daily walk, but it will very quickly lift your spirits higher than you may have thought possible, with no discernible change in your present circumstances. After all, it is not the circumstances that dictate our attitudes, whether we will walk in joy or not. It is our choices, plain and simple.

For just one day, though the exercise can become habit-forming, carry a small pocket sized notebook with you wherever you go and record everything (yes, everything) you are grateful for. For full impact, note each thing immediately, the moment it crosses your mind. Capture it quickly and simply, before your mind has a chance to process, assess and analyze. The idea is to capture simple child-like thanksgiving, the kind that registers delight at a patch of lily of the valley or running through the sprinkler. Recapture the simple joy of those moments and direct the thanks to your heavenly Father.

*Every good thing given and every perfect gift is from above,
coming down from the Father of lights,*
James 1:17a NAS

If you practice this exercise (and you can even do it in the midst of a meeting — just pull out your PDA and make a quick note), before long you will find you have recaptured the simple joy you have longed for and your attitude will be transformed from one of cynicism and discontent to simple joy and an understanding that the Father's love for you is a love which reaches even into the minutest details of your life. People will respond to the change in your demeanor; the attitude of a thankful person is and always has been gracious and attractive.

If you're driving down the tollway busying yourself with gratitude for your car, for the CD you are playing, for the breeze coming through the sunroof, for the encouraging message a friend sent you, it is practically impossible for you to react negatively to the driver who just cut you off. Instead, you will be immediately thankful for your deliverance from harm. In the midst of saying *thank you, Jesus*, you may even find you are able to hear and heed the prompting of the Holy Spirit to pray for the other driver.

Among all the great and important gifts with which God has blessed me, I am thankful also for much that is simple and often overlooked, those small treats that we love to give to our children; those things that say, *I notice you and I know just how you like things and it matters to me.* God gives me treats like that all the time. I just forget to stop and take note of them sometimes. I am thankful for hot coffee, for cinnamon, the scent of my crabapple tree in bloom, for warm socks and even for the lone bird that wakes me up at 5:00AM! And I know that those things matter to my Father, because He has promised that *He perfects those things which concern me* (Psalm 138:8).

Try the exercise for one day. It's worth the small effort involved to try something with the liklihood of such far-reaching results, isn't it? What better way to honor the Father than to tell Him you see his hand in every minute of every day.

And by the way, how about doing something similar for your earthly father — wouldn't he be thrilled to know you have noticed the concrete ways in which he has loved you over the years?

*Amen! Praise and glory and wisdom and thanks
and honor and power and strength
be to our God for ever and ever. Amen!*
Revelation 7:12 NIV

\*\*\*

### *Confession:*
I will make a purposeful effort this day to appreciate, with fresh and childlike thanks, all the good gifts my heavenly Father showers on me all day every day!

### *Go Deeper:*
Ephesians 5:20
James 1:17
Psalm 138:8
Revelation 7:12

### *Minute by Minute:*
Get out your notebook and begin first thing in the morning. Remember, nothing is too small or insignificant to record, as long as it matters to you. No one but you and God will know what you have listed. After only one day of focusing on what you are thankful for, you will be amazed at what a simple change of perspective it has accomplished! Try it.

## Study in Wisdom    Week 24

> *Study to show thyself approved unto God,*
> *a workman that needeth not to be ashamed,*
> *rightly dividing the word of truth.*
>     2 Timothy 2:15 KJV

The Bible is not always easy to understand. As a result, many of us begin our study by reading commentaries and articles by Bible scholars who we figure should know what they are talking about. These can be very valuable as supplementary studies, if we adhere to a few guidelines.

1. Beware of opinions. The opinions of men frequently lead to the teaching of men, which has often resulted in the traditions of men and the traditions of men render the Word of no effect. (Mark 7:13; Romans 4:14; Mark 7:8, 9)

> *'You have let go of the commands of God and*
> *are holding on to the traditions of men.'*
> *And he said to them: 'You have a fine way of setting aside*
> *the commands of God in order to observe your own traditions!'*
>     Mark 7:8-9 NIV

1. Begin with prayer — a good place to begin anything! Pray that the Holy Spirit will open your eyes to understand (Ephesians 1:18) and your heart to receive the incorruptible Word (1 Peter 1:23). Pray for the wisdom (James 1:5) to rightly divide the Scripture (2 Timothy 2:15).
2. Read everything the Bible says about the subject under study, making sure to follow any references to supporting Scriptures in both Old and New Testaments. You are filling your spirit with the Word. Don't be anxious about understanding all of it with your mind, at this point. It will become increasingly clear as you go and your spirit is thriving on it!

3. Be diligent about word studies, using a good comprehensive concordance to learn the nuances of the original languages.
4. Check often to make sure you are not putting your own "spin" on it.
5. *Then* read what others have to say. Stay with teachers who have proven they stand firmly and consistently on what the Word has to say and who do not veer off into the realm of opinion, those who have been shown to be careful in their study and trustworthy in their interpretations.
6. Immediately discount any commentaries based on negativity or criticism of others. Though there may be a germ of truth, sincerity or authenticity, those who resort to a negative approach pass along with it a spirit we must be especially cautious not to embrace. Their approach will ultimately tear down any truth and sincerity they may have begun with.
7. Be wary of absolute attitudes concerning areas of Scripture that remain in question among trusted Bible scholars. It is necessary for each of us to remain teachable, open to the Holy Spirit giving us interpretation beyond what may have become disputable denominational doctrine.
8. Make it a rule never to argue Scripture! The Word of God is not *debatable*; it is *revelatory*. God does not need your abilities as a disputer to bring about revelation in others. He says, *for I am watching over My Word to perform it.* (Jeremiah 1:12). He only needs you to speak the uncompromised Word, to say what He says; the Holy Spirit will be the Revealer (Ephesians 1:17) and God Himself will perform it.

*So shall My word be that goes forth from My mouth;*
*It shall not return to Me void,*
*But it shall accomplish what I please*
*And it shall prosper in the thing for*
*which I sent it.*
Isaiah 55:11 NKJV

\*\*\*

*The Bible Minute*

*Confession:*
I'll not be discouraged by my lack of understanding. I will spend time each day in the life-giving, saving, delivering, encouraging, empowering, comforting Word of God, knowing that He has promised it will accomplish His will and He Himself will bring it to pass.

*Go Deeper:*
2 Timothy 2:15
Mark 7:13; Romans 4:14; Mark 7:8-9
Ephesians 1:18
1 Peter 1:23
James 1:5
2 Timothy 2:15
Jeremiah 1:12
Ephesians 1:17
Isaiah 55:11

*Minute by Minute:*
Begin to employ the above suggestions in your own personal Bible study and consider sharing them with a study partner, Bible study or small group as well.

Choose an area of study you may have been avoiding, either because it seemed too difficult to grasp or because it is an area disputed among scholars. Approached systematically, you will find you are a more competent student of the Word than you supposed. You will have the additional option of commentaries available to you, but at the appropriate point in your study.

# Nuggets from the Proverbs
# Mining the Promise

Week 24

> *Choose my instruction rather than silver,*
> *And knowledge rather than pure gold.*
> *For wisdom is far more valuable than rubies.*
> *Nothing you desire can compare with it.*
> Proverbs 8:10, 11 NLT

When panning for gold, a prospector looks for nuggets, promising lumps of all sizes. His eye seeks morsels which, when assayed (examined and valued for use in the current world economy) and refined, will produce something outstanding, elegant, and of greater value than the original lump. In other words, he looks for *promise*.

Diamond mines yield gemstones which would be unrecognizable to the eye of the novice. But a trained gemologist deals in *potential value*. He is able to eye the compressed carbon rock and visualize it in its finished form and anticipate its class and value in the current world market.

However, the final value, when all is said and done, depends on the skill employed in the processes that follow. For gold, there is a rigorous refining process and for diamonds, often years of study and then the critical cutting. One wrong move and the raw materials are consigned to the waste heap.

In the coming days, we are going to begin to prospect the rich mother lode of the Book of Proverbs. And unlike the miners, we have already been told the true value of the gold and gems we are seeking, so we cannot possibly go wrong. The nuggets we will examine have *inherent value*, already there in all its fullness.

So we will work on determining the *personal value* of each nugget, its practical value in our own lives and situations, dependant only on our willingness and diligence to apply what we discover.

So please join me as we begin our expedition, mining our way through a couple of rich veins of Proverbs.

*There is gold, and a multitude of rubies:
But the lips of knowledge are a precious jewel.*
Proverbs 20:15 KJV

\*\*\*

### *Confession:*
This day I will faithfully seek the Word of God as choicest gold and, making it my own true treasure, I will apply it faithfully to my life and circumstances.

### *Go Deeper:*
Proverbs 8:10, 11
Proverbs 20:15

### *Minute by Minute:*
*Value* is a difficult concept to define and even more difficult to capture, being highly subjective, extremely transitory and, due to the fickle nature of humans beings, ever evolving! Essentially, value is a statement of worth to an individual or group of individuals at a given time and in a given set of circumstances. An item can be valued quite differently by a variety of people or groups, depending on the circumstances and those doing the appraisal! Value is determined by rarity, difficulty of procurement, current trends of popularity and current demand for the item or service.

Ultimately, it is about the most important element of all, the personal. Personal value is completely subjective. The most expensive opal in the world would have no personal value, other than resale, for someone who does not care for opals.

Over the next several days, think through how you have been assessing the value of your own life and experience as well as of the people around you. Consider the elements we have noted, *promise*, *potential*, *process* (the means of releasing inherent value) and *projected* or final value. By considering these elements are you better able to recognize and assign value through a wider lens? If so, how will this change your world view going forward?

# Nuggets from the Proverbs
## Fear of Fear

**Week 25**

*Do not be afraid of sudden fear,*
*Nor of the onslaught of the wicked when it comes.*
Proverbs 3:25 NAS

If we are honest with ourselves, this verse expresses what haunts us and it is most often not fear of a well-defined threat that harasses us. Ever since 9/11 we have been dealing with the threat of terrorism on some level continually. What exactly does that mean? It means we have been dealing with an enemy whose major weapon of mass control is terror, oppression by fear.

The Bible tells us clearly that we are not to be moved by fear of fear, particularly sudden fear, which is an apt description of the surprise element of terrorism. In the now famous words of his first inaugural address in 1933, *the only thing we have to fear is fear itself*, Franklin Roosevelt seems to have peered forward into the 21st century. We live in a time when our enemies have come to understand the most powerful weapon of control is within our own minds and hearts. If an enemy can move an entire people to days and nights of formless anxiety, he can eventually control the nation.

Proverbs goes on to tell us that the onslaught of the wicked does come, but we are not to fear that either,

*For the Lord shall be your confidence, firm and strong,*
*and shall keep your foot from being caught*
*[in a trap or some hidden danger].*
Proverbs 3:26 AMP

Our confidence is not in the level of national alert, nor is it ultimately in Homeland Security, nor does it rest with our extremely able military. The Lord is our confidence and He alone will keep us from the snare of fear. When we place our trust in Him and do what He says, regardless of how our minds might disagree, we can be assured of the promise of verse 24.

> *When you lie down, you will not be afraid;*
> *When you lie down, your sleep will be sweet*
> Proverbs 3:24 NAS

Declare this verse each night before you go to sleep, putting the Lord in remembrance of His promise that your sleep will be sweet. Does He need reminding? Of course not; but we do, and when we speak it, we hear just what we need to hear. As far as I am concerned, these are nuggets of *personal value*. We have no need to wonder if they are precious. They shine brightly up at us from the page!

***

### *Confession:*
The Lord is my confidence and so this day I actively choose faith over fear because, according to 1 John 4:4, *greater is He that is in* (me), *than he that is in the world.*

### *Go Deeper:*
Proverbs 3:25
Proverbs 3:26
Proverbs 3:24
1 John 4:4

### *Minute by Minute:*
First, how can you be personally assured that the Lord wants to be your confidence? Make sure your answer is not based on what you *believe* to be true, but solidly on Scripture.

Then, what does it feel like to actively choose faith over fear? In other words, how will you know that you have made that choice? Will it be something you feel?

Finally, how will you support the choice, making certain it has a firm foundation? If you will take the time to answer these questions and step out on your decision, no threat, real or implied, can stop you from fulfilling your God-given Mission on the earth.

## Nuggets from the Proverbs
## Choose Righteousness

Week 25

> *For the devious are an abomination to the LORD;*
> *But He is intimate with the upright.*
> Proverbs 3:32 NAS

This is exciting news! Read that verse again and let it sink in. Let's take a deeper look and see what Solomon was saying with this particular choice of words.

Whatever is labeled an *abomination* is morally disgusting, perverse. The root word means to turn aside from, to depart. Those who have chosen to turn aside, to depart from what they know to be pleasing to the Lord, generally end by becoming an abomination in His sight.

That's right, I said those who choose. Life is not about what happens to us, but about the choices we make in response. If we have become an abomination to the Lord, it is all about our choices. What do we do about them? Repent by turning in the opposite direction. You cannot reverse the choices already made, but you can obliterate them. Repentance and acceptance of the mercy and forgiveness available to all, separates you forever from your bad choices. (Psalm 103:10-12)

*Intimate* indicates a company of persons in close or secret talks. Intimacy with God means you are in His private counsel. Isn't this what everyone really wants, to feel a part of the inner circle? Here it is, the promise that the Lord includes those who are upright in His inner circle. But perhaps this is where you stumble. I am anything but upright you might say, so that's obviously not meant for me. But take a closer look.

*Upright* means to be right in the sight of the Lord and therefore to have His approval. If nothing else sinks in, take this truth and make it your own. If you have made Jesus Christ the Lord of your life, you have done so at the calling of the Holy Spirit and by the Blood of the Lamb. You did not do it on your own.

> *Here I am! I stand at the door and knock.*
> *If anyone hears my voice and opens the door,*
> *I will come in and eat with him, and he with me.*
> Revelation 3:20 NIV

With that choice, you have been made the righteousness of God in Christ. Read that again. You do not merely possess righteousness as an attribute; you *are* the righteousness of God. You can stand boldly, unashamedly, before the Throne of Grace. (Hebrews 4:16)

You can expect intimacy with your Abba Father. When you chose to belong to Christ, you became an heir according to the promise and you are now a beloved child. (Galatians 3:29) If you are not experiencing this intimacy, it is up to you to turn back and draw near to your Father. (James 4:8)

Just as Abraham believed and God counted it as justification, so belief in the Blood makes you righteous. (Romans 4:1)

> *But to the one who, not working [by the law],*
> *trusts (believes fully) in Him who justifies the ungodly,*
> *his faith is credited to him as righteousness (the standing acceptable to God).*
> Romans 4:5 AMP

How's that for good news?

\*\*\*

*Confession:*
I choose to make it my whole function to believe, according to John 6:29, and I accept that I am therefore pleasing in God's sight and I am forever in His inner circle.

*Go Deeper:*
Proverbs 3:32
Psalm 103:10-12
Revelation 3:20
Hebrews 4:16

Galatians 3:29
James 4:8
Romans 4:1
Romans 4:5

***Minute by Minute:***

Being pleasing to God is not an accident, but a choice. Life is not about what has happened to us, or the choices we made in the past. It is about what we choose *now*. And you are, at this very moment, no more than one choice away from being pleasing to God. It is literally that simple.

Choosing Jesus as Lord of your life is to acknowledge that His blood has already done what you could never hope to do, making you instantly pleasing to God, upright in His eyes. The intimacy that He has offered from the beginning is now available to you for the taking.

If you continue to feel like an unworthy outcast, always on the outside looking in, understand that it is by your own choice, a choice of which you may be sadly unaware. James 4:8 assures us that all we need to do is draw near to Him and He will draw near to us. What you have been unable to overlook in yourself, He has already washed away in His blood.

If accepting your position as righteous has been difficult for you, the simple solution is to ask to see yourself as He sees you and then accept what He shows you as the Truth. While this is simple, it is by no means easy and will require that you allow the Holy Spirit to change your heart. Submit to God's process, by your choice, and enjoy the intimacy of the inner circle!

# Nuggets from the Proverbs
## Walk in the Light

*The path of the righteous is like the first gleam of dawn, shining ever brighter till the full light of day.*
Proverbs 4:18 NIV

In the natural world, the process for finding the way is pretty clear. You determine your desired destination and then you consult maps, a GPS (*global positioning system*) and perhaps even your motor club to decide on the best, most direct route to your destination.

Once you have worked through the process of determining the route, you begin to travel along it, keeping watch at all times for signs to assure you that you have not lost the way. Your spiritual journey is no different. The natural realm is a reflection, albeit a distorted one, of the spiritual realm. So let us translate this into practical steps for determining divine direction.

First, *determine your destination*. You may already be clear about this. If not, don't waste another minute in aimless wandering. Discover your *Purpose* and your *Mission* and then begin to create vibrant *Visions* to support them. Now you are ready to travel!

Next, *decide where you are right now*. It is critical to determine exactly where you are in relation to your destination. Are you anywhere near it? There's an important clue in our foundation verse which assures that, *the path of the righteous is like the first gleam of dawn*.

Using this as an indicator, you can determine if you are on the right road, or at least somewhere near it. Is the path you are currently traveling growing ever brighter, even though it may be a new path and with only the "first gleam of dawn" right now? If you see it growing daily brighter, the Word assures that you are on the path of the righteous. The righteous are in right standing with God by virtue of the Blood of Christ. This is the best indicator of true and on-course direction.

Scripture is replete with references to the light of the Lord, likening it to the sun, making it very clear that the light for your path is the Son. If your path is brightening, it is almost surely His path for your life.

He is the first gleam of dawn, shining ever brighter, until the full light of day when the sun is at its zenith, the time at which His light shines the brightest. It is this ever-increasing light that tells you where you are and that you are on the right path and headed in the right direction. Begin today.

- Determine your destination
- Establish your current position
- Plot your course and head in the direction of the light!

\*\*\*

### Confession:
With the help of the Holy Spirit, I will purpose to lay aside my own plans, taking time to listen deeply for God to reveal His perfect plan for my life.

### Go Deeper:
Proverbs 4:18

### Minute by Minute:
The key is in understanding your place in the Kingdom Plan and working effectively through it for God's glory in the earth. True satisfaction and fulfillment follows. Personally identifying four fundamental elements is the starting point.

> *Purpose* is what you were created for — Discern it.
> *Mission* is what you are meant to do about it — Discover it.
> *Visions* are the evidence — Create them.
> *Goals* are the means of achievement — Design them

You must have a firm grasp of the first two elements before you can effectively carry out the last two. Time in the Word and prayer will reveal your Purpose and your Mission and it is only then that you can hope to go into the world and have the impact you are meant to with your vibrant Visions.[15] Life becomes exciting when you are walking in The Plan!

# Nuggets from the Proverbs
## A Light for Your Path

**Week 26**

*The way of the wicked is like deep darkness;*
*they do not know what makes them stumble.*
Proverbs 4:19 NIV

Are you right now trying to follow a path that does not seem to be daily growing brighter? Maybe you are even beginning to stumble and feel lost, and the way is becoming shrouded in deepening darkness. Perhaps you are so deep in darkness you can no longer recognize what is causing you to stumble.

The word *wicked* in Proverbs 4:19 is an interesting word. It does not begin as evil, but it implies a deviation, a winding, turning and twisting. Think of the twisted wick of a candle, and apply this to an individual whose confused and ultimately twisted thinking results in confused and twisted actions. If this continues, it results in complete departure from God's path.

The Bible tells us in Matthew 7:14, that *strait is the gate, and narrow is the way, which leadeth unto life, and few there be that find it*. So we want to be certain to stay on the path that is well illuminated, because the moment we move from it, we are stumbling about in darkness.

The Bible is clear that this deviation is a result of confused thinking leading to confused actions. If our path is in darkness and we are stumbling, we need to turn and see where we have deviated. We need enough light on the path to get us to the point of the first gleam of dawn ahead.

When ministering the Word in counseling, I tell people that my role is simply to hand out flashlights and show people how they work. I am not able to walk the path for them, and I cannot lead them by the hand. The path is narrow so we cannot both fit on it, but I can give them instructions for using their flashlight effectively.

If I hand you a flashlight, and I do not tell you where the on/off switch is, or where to put the batteries, or how to effectively wield it so it sheds light where you most need it, it would be of little use to you. But if I supply you with this valuable information, you will be able to travel your road in confidence and safety. We have that flashlight available to us. Psalm 119:105 tells us the *Word is a lamp to my feet and a light for my path*...

\*\*\*

***Confession:***
I set my intention this day to apply the Word of God to my path and as I do, it will become brighter until it is as bright as noonday.

***Go Deeper:***
Proverbs 4:19
Matthew 7:14
Psalm 119:105

***Minute by Minute:***
Try this simple exercise. Write out instructions for the use of a flashlight as though you will be teaching someone who has never seen one and has no idea what it is, its intended use, or how to operate it to best advantage. Be very detailed in your instructions, assuming nothing, and then teach your flashlight lesson to a friend or to your Bible study group. Have a flashlight with you in order to actually demonstrate to a member of your group.

Now take your flashlight instruction sheet and everywhere you have written *flashlight* or *light*, fill in *the Word* in its place. The Word of God truly is *a lamp unto my feet and a light unto my path* (Psalm 119:105).

# A New Song　　　　　　　　　　　　Week 27

*O sing unto the LORD a new song:*
*sing unto the LORD, all the earth.*
　　　　Psalm 96:1 KJV

I had an opportunity recently to minister to someone who shared with me that they had always cherished a dream of singing with a church praise and worship team, certainly a worthy ambition. But what is in this person's mouth most of the time is anything but praise. It definitely gave me pause.

I began thinking about how we define praise. Our word *praise* comes from the Latin for *value* or price. Praise then is a proclamation of God's value, His worthiness. The Hebrew word is *halal*, the root of which means to *shine* or to *celebrate*. Are we singing the prescribed songs or are we celebrating God's great worthiness, proclaiming the shining forth of His glory?

Is it something we do as a congregation at the beginning of a service? Is it a list of prescribed songs from a hymn book? Are we most comfortable with the familiar songs, hymns and modes of praise we know the best? Nine passages in the Bible from Psalms to Revelation exhort us to sing to the Lord a *new song*.

Or is our praise the (super)natural end result of the transforming power of the Word of God, of a heart and soul filled to overflowing with the revelation of the Love of God, the power of the Holy Spirit, the strength of His everlasting covenant, our redemption by the Blood, and on and on?

If these are the prompters of our praise, and if we take time to ponder them, to meditate on the character of God and His perennial lovingkindness toward us, then we will daily sing a new song as our hearts are freshly filled with wonder and awe at His Glory.

When we embrace the process of praise, we will continue growing supernaturally and we will be daily transformed by His Word and the awesome knowledge of Who He Is. We will truly move from glory to glory. (2 Corinthians 3:18) We will have little choice but to sing a new song from a transformed heart.

But what shall I sing, you ask. Sing to Him of where you were and where you are now and where you're headed. It will certainly be no surprise to Him. Sing to him of your concerns and your certainty that He knows them and is ever moving you from them to a large place of freedom (Psalm 118:5; Psalm 18:19) After all, that's what David did in so many of the psalms. He sang to Lord from his place of fear and anger, of hurt and shame. And as he sang of whatever was in his heart, it was *God* who filled it with a new song of praise.

In your devotional time, read through the Book of Psalms and you will see how often they begin as songs of lament born of deep distress and end as songs of praise. Try it for yourself — praise begins with taking your concerns to your heavenly Father and committing them to Him. He Himself will fill your mouth with praise. Then your every word will be a form of praise. Why even your countenance will become a form of praise, reflecting His glory upon your life!

> *And He has put a new song in my mouth,*
> *a song of praise to our God.*
> Psalm 40:3 (AMP)

\*\*\*

*Confession:* This day I will make time in the midst of whatever I am doing to *sing unto the LORD a new song, and his praise in the congregation of saints.* (Psalm 149:1 KJV)

**Go Deeper:**
Psalm 96:1
2 Corinthians 3:18
Psalm 118:5; Psalm 18:19
Psalm 149:1
Isaiah 54:2-3
Psalm 18:19
1 Samuel 13:44; Acts 13:22
Romans 2:11; Acts 10:34

***Minute by Minute:***

David sang to the Lord from the depths of his fear and anger, hurt and shame. He sang from peaks of joy and awe at God's greatness. He sang of whatever was in his heart, trusting *God* to fill His heart and then his mouth with new songs of praise. In all his humanity and imperfection, David was a man after God's own heart. (1 Samuel 13:44; Acts 13:22) By the blood of Jesus, you share that place in God's heart alongside David. (Romans 2:11; Acts 10:34)

Begin today!

Sing to the Lord a new song.
Sing to Him of where you were.
Sing to Him of where you are.
Sing to Him of where you are headed.
Sing to Him of your dreams.
Sing to Him of your sorrows.
Sing to Him of your joys.
Sing to Him of your certainty that He knows them all and is ever moving you closer and closer to a large place of freedom. (Psalm 18:19; Isaiah 54:2-3)

*The Bible Minute*

## *Magnify the Lord!*            *Week 27*

*O magnify the LORD with me, and let us exalt his name together.*
Psalm 34:3 KJV

*And Mary said, My soul doth magnify the Lord,*
Luke 1:46 KJV

*I will praise the name of God with a song, and will magnify him with thanksgiving.*
Psalm 69:30 KJV

*For they heard them speak with tongues, and magnify God.*
Acts 10:46 KJV

How often do we read these verses and give them a cursory look and think to ourselves, oh yes, let's definitely make God bigger; let's make Him bigger than everything else! After all, He is worthy.

Maybe I'm the only one, but that is how I used to see it. A closer look reveals something quite different. Webster defines *magnify* as, to extol or laud, to cause to be held in greater esteem or respect, to increase in significance, intensify or exaggerate, to enlarge in fact or in appearance. And finally, to have the power of causing objects to appear larger than they are. None of these quite fits the true essence of the word, seeming to far better describe the end result of magnification, rather than defining the act itself.

Think about a magnifying glass or a microscope. Its purpose is to focus in and completely fill the field of vision to enable closer, more detailed examination. In closely examining God in this way, the necessary end result will be holding Him in greater esteem, awe and respect and an increased awareness of His enormous significance in our lives. Psalm 34 perfectly illustrates this process.

There is no way we can make God any bigger than He is! But we can take the time to immerse ourselves in His Word and in fellowship with Him — our magnifying glass. We must focus on Him, filling our field of vision, shutting out anything that would intrude. And so, with the David, we will go forth exalting His Name!

\*\*\*

## *Confession:*
I will say along with Mary *my soul magnifies the Lord*. Looking beyond my situation, I will focus on Him only. I will praise the name of God with my song, and will magnify him, filling my field of vision with Him, in my thanksgiving.

## *Go Deeper:*
Galatians 5:22-23
Isaiah 6:3
1 Corinthians 3:6-9
Psalm 104
Psalm 102: 25-27;
Job 38, 40, 41
Hebrews 1:7-14
Isaiah 40
Psalm 34:3 KJV
Luke 1:46
Psalm 69:30
Acts 10:46

## *Minute by Minute:*
Has your divine focus slipped recently and you find yourself looking at the circumstances instead of God who is above the circumstances? Make a list of the life issues constantly nagging at you, ready to intrude at a moment's notice. Now find out what the Word has to say about your issues. Every time an issue threatens to fill your field of vision, begin to speak what God has to say about it. I do not promise that it will be easy, but it will change your outlook and that has the power to change your circumstances. Ask your pray/accountability partner to assist you in catching yourself. Magnify the Lord, not the problem!

# Take Heart — Week 28

*For whatsoever is born of God overcometh the world:
and this is the victory that overcometh the world, even our faith*
1 John 5:4 KJV

The key to living the victorious life is not in being free of problems, but in overcoming them by faith. There can be no victory where there is no battle. Someone needs to hear this today! In the midst of another project, the Holy Spirit stopped me one day and prompted me to send this message. If this is for you, be encouraged, your victory is already assured, take hold of it by faith and don't let go.

While Peter was the only one who had the faith to step out of the boat in Matthew 14, he still made the mistake of allowing himself to look at the circumstances and it was then that he shifted his eyes off the promise, and only then did he begin to sink. Even at that, Jesus was there to pull him up, to take hold of him and bring him safely into the boat. Matthew 14:31 tells us in fact, that *immediately Jesus stretched out His hand and took hold of him*. He did not say, *Peter because of your doubt, I'm not going to save you. I'm going to leave you floundering about in the waves to drown*. He did not forsake him, and He did not use near drowning to teach Peter a lesson!

He did rebuke Peter for his lack of attention to his faith. The scripture in the NAS translation reads, *O you of little faith, why did you doubt?* The *little* can denote value, but it can also indicate duration. We know that Peter's faith had value, or it never would have been enough to get him out of the boat in the first place. So, it is likely that Jesus was reproving Peter for not hanging onto his faith long enough. Had Peter kept his divine focus, and not begun to look around him at the circumstances, his faith would have been adequate.

Have you stepped out on a word from God, a promise, and are you becoming aware of the circumstances, and beginning to feel yourself sinking? Take heart, if your faith was enough to get you out of the boat, then your faith is enough to get you where you are going.

Hang onto the promise, *Take courage, it is I; do not be afraid... come.* (Matthew 14:27, 29) Jesus is speaking to you from across the waves and through the wind.

I don't know about you, but I needed to hear this, and I am blessed and encouraged!

***

*Confession:*
Once it has been activated by the Word of God, I will not allow my faith to be shipwrecked by looking at my circumstances. I will keep my focus on the Word calling me forth.

*Go Deeper:*
1 John 5:4
Matthew 14:22-33
Romans 10:17

*Minute by Minute:*
Has Jesus clearly called you across the water? Are you like the eleven who stayed cowering in the boat? Or perhaps, as is so true of many of us, you are like Peter, stepping out enthusiastically, only to be overwhelmed by the circumstances. If so, take time today to chronicle your call from Him.

Next, record the circumstances that seem to have overwhelmed you. Know that what God has called you to do can never be accomplished in your own strength, regardless of how favorable the circumstances. Just as Peter could no more walk on water on a calm day than in a stormy night, you cannot accomplish what only His power can bring about.

Step out of boat and, by faith, trust that same faith to take you the distance. Record every step in your prayer journal and stay attuned to the Word of God.

## *Lift Up Your Eyes*                       **Week 28**

> *Then the glory of the Lord will be revealed,*
> *and all flesh will see it together;*
> *for the mouth of the Lord has spoken.*
> Isaiah 40:5 NAS

Isaiah 40 is one of my favorite chapters in the Bible. It focuses on the greatness of God and the opening verse states the purpose, *Comfort, O comfort My people, says your God.*

We can be comforted, in whatever condition we find ourselves today, by focusing on the greatness of God. By consciously drawing our eyes away from the circumstances that beset us, from earthly hardships and human disappointments to the greatness of God, we will begin to see the situation the way our heavenly Father would have us see it.

> *So we don't look at the troubles we can see now;*
> *rather we fix our gaze on things that cannot be seen.*
> *For the things we see now will soon be gone,*
> *but the things we cannot see will last forever.*
> 2 Corinthians 4:18 NLT

Begin by consciously turning away from your problems and looking to God, not for answers, but for no other reason than to see His goodness, lovingkindness, and greatness and to bask in the radiance of His love. This will likely be the most challenging part of the process. Once you have begun magnifying God over your problems, recognizing and acknowledging His greatness and His glory, your eyes will begin to see with divine perspective.

When we are entangled in earthly chaos and confusion, when things look their bleakest, we must say with the psalmist,

> *I will lift up mine eyes unto the hills, from whence cometh my help.*
> *My help cometh from the LORD, which made heaven and earth.*
> *He will not suffer thy foot to be moved: he that*

> *keepeth thee will not slumber.*
> *Behold, he that keepeth Israel shall neither slumber nor sleep.*
> *The LORD is thy keeper: the LORD is thy*
> *shade upon thy right hand.*
> *The sun shall not smite thee by day, nor the moon by night.*
> *The LORD shall preserve thee from all evil:*
> *he shall preserve thy soul.*
> *The LORD shall preserve thy going out and thy coming in*
> *from this time forth, and even for evermore.*
> Psalm 121 KJV

\*\*\*

### *Confession:*
Heavenly Father, I am determined this day to look to You in the midst of the confusion, to focus on Your greatness, Your goodness and Your love, to magnify You, filling my field of vision with You. Then I will see this world as You would have me see it and act upon it as You would have me act. I will step out boldly on what You show me by Your Holy Spirit.

### *Go Deeper:*
Isaiah 40:5
2 Corinthians 4:18
Psalm 121
Hebrews 13:8

### *Minute by Minute:*
The first step is the most difficult. Turn away from your problems. Deliberately set them aside for the moment. In counseling, I occasionally give people *permission* to turn from what disturbs them for a predetermined period of time. We are then better able to begin gaining the perspective necessary to effectively address their issues. If you find this step too challenging for you, try giving yourself a specific timeframe to begin with and increase this as you become more comfortable with the process.

Next, turn your attention toward God, refreshing yourself in His Word. Remind yourself who He has been in the lives of His people and who He is still today (Hebrews 13:8). At this point, do not look for answers; simply see His goodness, His faithfulness, His lovingkindness, and His overcoming greatness and bask in the light of His love.

Your problems will be where you left them when you turn back, but your perspective will have changed and, with it, your ability to work through them.

# A Word of Encouragement                Week 29

> *Humble yourselves, therefore,*
> *Under the mighty hand of God,*
> *That He may exalt you at the proper time,*
> *Casting all your anxiety upon Him,*
> *Because He cares for you.*
> 1 Peter 5:6-7 NAS

While cleaning out some files, I came upon this Rhema Word that the Holy Spirit spoke to me a couple of years ago. It is certainly no surprise that it was exactly what I needed today, just as it was several years ago.

*All things are susceptible to the mighty hand of God!*

We can truly rest in that.

The Bible tells us that *the effectual fervent prayer of a righteous man avails much* (James 5:16). Our part is to pray, to the best of our ability in line with the word of God, and our constant Advocate and Intercessor (Romans 8:34; 1 John 2:1) makes sure it stays before the throne — in perfect form!

We can change the world this way, our own world (*oikos* in Greek) and the larger world as well. And we can because we take comfort in the mighty hand of God which is ever with us and for us. *Not by might, nor by power, but by My Spirit, saith the LORD of hosts* (Zechariah 4:6).

When I become discouraged, I remind myself that I am the apple of His eye, and He is the King of the universe Who commands the morning, and causes the dew to know its place (Job 38:12).

I read Psalm 104, Psalm 102:25-28, Isaiah 40, and God's powerful exhortation to Job in chapters 38-41. Then I am able to say, along with Job, *I know that Thou canst do all things, and no purpose of Thine can be thwarted* (Job 42:2).

That's good news!

\*\*\*

***Confession:***
All of my circumstances are susceptible to the mighty hand of God; so I commit them to Him anew this day.

***Go Deeper:***
Zechariah 4:6
Psalm 104
Psalm 102:25-28
Isaiah 40
Job 38-41
Job 42:2
1 Peter 5:7

***Minute by Minute:***
Read Psalm 104, Psalm 102:25-28, Isaiah 40 and Job 38-41. Magnify the Lord by filling your field of vision with His awesome splendor. We all need to be reminded that He is Elohim, Creator of heaven and earth and He is El-Elyon, the Most High God, the First Cause of Everything so that we can truly grasp the wonder that this same God has chosen to live in our hearts so that we can be united with Him for eternity. Nothing can drag you down once you have had that revelation!

# Daddy's Favorite — Week 29

*For I am convinced that neither death nor life,
Neither angels nor demons, neither the present nor the future,
Nor any powers, neither height nor depth,
Nor anything else in all creation,
Will be able to separate us from the love of God
That is in Christ Jesus our Lord.*
Romans 8:38-39 NIV

I became a grandmother today. Oh, it wasn't for the first time and God willing, it won't be the last. A beautiful baby girl, she is my fifth granddaughter. I have seven children and now six grandchildren.

But, in truth, she is my first grandchild. She is the most beautiful, most amazing, most miraculous baby I have ever seen. It is the most awesome birth I have ever been a part of.

Before you protest the unfairness of these statements, let me explain. Each of my children and grandchildren is extraordinary beyond words. Each is the most unique, most amazing, most beautiful creature I have ever seen.

Each birth was the most awesome experience I have ever had. One did not top the other and none stands out above the rest. And yet they are not by any means equal. Each is the epitome, the apex of my experience. My awe and enthusiasm have never lessened and each was thrilling beyond my capacity to express. Each of these thirteen people, my seed, is the most incredible human being ever born into the world!

These statements strike me just as curiously as they must you. They are simply impossible and yet they are absolutely true. I became a first time mother with each of my children and a first time nana with each of my grandchildren.

If you think perhaps you have experienced what I am attempting to express, then you are positioned to appreciate the love of God, your heavenly Father, toward you. We are unable to firmly grasp the intensity of this love with our finite minds, but our spirits know it and understand it well.

## The Bible Minute

*For God so loved the world*
*That he gave his one and only Son,*
*That whoever believes in him*
*Shall not perish but have eternal life.*
John 3:16 NIV

The love of God is well beyond our comprehension up until the moment when we look into the eyes of an infant who bears our name, whether by birth or adoption. We are immediately, completely, wildly in love. We would not hesitate to move mountains, take on enemies, stand in the way of bullets and give all that we have and all that we are in the face of what we perceive to be the child's needs and welfare.

Think about it a moment. That concept of love flies in the face of everything the self-centered world has taught us about affection. We are raised to love the lovely, the lovable and the deserving, and to withhold love from the unlovely and undeserving. And we often hold our love for ransom until an individual moves from a state of undeserving to deserving, by our definition. Yet we are in love with this infant with every fiber of our being, and the child has done nothing to deserve it, nothing to earn it. If you have ever experienced this, then you have touched the very tip of the infinite, the immeasurable love of the Father toward you.

You are His treasure, the apple of His eye, the pride of His heart, the heir of His creation. You are the reason He stepped from the throne and into the envelope of time; the reason He assumed the mantel of humanity and walked among us; the reason He absorbed every bit of sin, sickness, grief and despair into Himself and then, with all of that, offered Himself to be nailed to a cross. He stormed the gates of hell because eternity with you, His beloved, in His presence, is that important to Him. Each of us is His own most special creation.

With David, we can say with confidence,

*Keep me as the apple of your eye;*
Psalm 17:8a NIV

I cannot hope to understand it this side of Heaven and yet I can rest in the certainty that I am indeed my Daddy's favorite!

\*\*\*

*Confession:*
Nothing in creation, including me, will be able to separate me from the love of God my Father, which has been manifested toward me in Christ Jesus my Lord. I may not understand it, but I choose to believe it and walk confidently in it. (Romans 8:38-39)

*Go Deeper:*
Romans 8:38-39
John 3:16
Psalm 17:8a
Romans 8:38-39

*Minute by Minute:*
In working with people, in counseling as well as coaching, I find that an all too common underlying cause of many problems is an inability to understand who we are in Christ. When we are able to grasp the concept of our righteousness, our right standing with our heavenly Father, then truly nothing can separate us from his love.

Make a quality decision to accept about yourself whatever the Word has to say. Look through the letters written to the church, from Romans through Jude, and isolate each instance of *in Him, in Whom* and *in Christ* for a vivid picture of who you really are, through the eyes of your heavenly Father. You will come away knowing that you are indeed Daddy's favorite!

# Nearer God's Heart — Week 30

*Then the LORD God took the man and
put him into the garden of Eden to cultivate it and keep it.*
Genesis 2:15 NAS

While tending my annual garden, the Holy Spirit revealed to me a valuable lesson about unity in the Body of Christ.

The delicately flowered annual, impatiens, has always produced an abundantly satisfying display in midsummer as the reward of planting all those tiny seeds or seedlings in the spring. The initial sparse bedding gives way to a glorious mass of tiny blooms, so closely mounded, one plant sitting so near its brother they might be one huge plant, so closely positioned that weeds can only rarely break through. The display is quite breathtaking.

When the body of Christ grows and exists in unity, just as the mound of impatiens, each member remains a unique individual but the effect in and to the world is one of breathtaking colors in complete harmony, each taking his or her place in the total plan and picture. The overall effect is one of the seamless beauty of love and it is awesome to the beholder.

When one individual is missing, the result is glaringly obvious. Just try removing one plant in the middle of a display of impatiens and you will see what I mean. The hole it leaves becomes the focal point to any observer. (See Romans 12:4-5; 1 Corinthians, particularly verses 12 and 20). Truly, *every joint supplies*. Ephesians 4:16 The picture presented to the world is of one mind and one mouth glorifying God. (Romans 15:6) And that is without *doing* anything, just being who we are meant to be.

There are many godly principles displayed in the garden and is it any surprise? The principles of the garden appear throughout the Bible from the first reference in Genesis 1:11 to the final references in Revelation 22. You cannot go more than a few verses without appreciating that it is a gardening handbook.

There is an old poem that goes:

*The Bible Minute*

---

*The kiss of the sun for pardon,*
*the song of the birds for mirth,*
*one is nearer God's heart in a garden,*
*than anywhere else on earth.*
Dorothy Gurney 1858-1952

While you may dispute the sentiments, they are supported throughout the Bible. God is practical both in knowledge and application of His ways. Isaiah 55:8-11 clearly outlines the process by which He reveals himself. If you understand the principles of gardening, then God's principles will be clear and familiar to you and you will be open to His practical revelations.

Is someone you know missing, leaving an obvious empty space in the planting? Who better than you to reach out and tell them how sorely they are missed and how noticeable their absence?

*"I do not ask on behalf of these alone,*
*but for those also who believe in Me through their word;*
*that they may all be one; even as You, Father, are in Me and I in You,*
*that they also may be in Us, so that the world may believe that You sent Me.*
John 17:20, 21 NAS

\*\*\*

*Confession:*
I make a quality decision this day that I will not be among the missing, thinking that my presence is not valued or that my absence will go unnoticed. And I will dedicate myself to encouraging others who may be feeling unimportant within the Body as well.

*Go Deeper:*
Genesis 2:15
Study Isaiah 55:8-11
John 17:20-21

Using a Bible software or online Bible, search for gardening terms, such as garden, seed, reap, harvest, plant, water, farmer, husbandman, etc. Not only will you experience revelation through the Word, but your gardening skills will be sharpened as well.

Working with your Bible study or small group, trace the garden theme, with all its various implications, throughout the Old and New Testaments. Discuss its pertinence in this chiefly post agricultural society.

### *Minute by Minute:*

*As we are One.* In John 17:11, Jesus prays for unity, that His disciples (then and now) might all be one as He and the Father are One. Consider Jesus' words in light of your own life. How important is unity of the Body of Christ to you personally?

As evidenced by the above Scriptures, how important to God is unity of the Body of Christ?

Is it up to us, as members of the Body to call back those missing? If so, how can you, practically speaking, be a part of that movement?

# Heaven by Another Road        Week 30

*'And you know the way where I am going.'*
*Thomas said to Him, 'Lord, we do not know where You are going,*
*how do we know the way?' Jesus said to him,*
*'I am the way and the truth and the life;*
*no one comes to the Father but through Me.'*
John 14:4-6 NAS

We live in bizarre times. We legalize sin, killing infants at the moment of birth and calling it choice, fostering suicide for the elderly and those with grave illnesses, and calling it mercy, all the while legislating away the one Truth which provides all the answers to all the questions, all the pain and all the confusion of the world. How can we doubt the presence of the enemy in the earth when lies and death are legally acceptable, and Truth and Life are politically incorrect?

Religion, in this "brave new world," has become acceptable anywhere and everywhere, so long as it does not point the way to Jesus Christ. Buddha and his shrines are a regular sight in retail businesses. Wicca (the religion of witchcraft) has been recognized by many as the fastest emerging religion among young people of high school age. Freedom of religion is touted, but the spoken name of Jesus is not only unacceptable, it has even lead to the arrest of young children.

Ask the man on the street if he is going to heaven, and he will more than likely tell you that he believes he will because he has tried to be a good person. *Good* is such a relative concept that we have no choice but to conclude that he is attempting the impossible — to create his own road to heaven. Not knowing what it is, or where it is, he cannot possibly succeed!

There are many roads we might travel, and the road on which we now travel is of our own choosing. You might argue that often we did not choose our road; it is a matter of circumstances out of our control. It is true that many of us were set on the wrong road as children, but if we are presently on the wrong road, it is by our own choice. We can no longer blame the ignorance of our parents for our walk outside the Truth. It is time to come to personal maturity.

Jesus encouraged His disciples, telling them, *I go to prepare a place for you. And If I go and prepare a place for you, I will come again, and receive you to Myself; that where I am, you may be also.* (John 14:2-3)

When asked how they were to know the way, Jesus made what remains one of the clearest statements imaginable. He says,

*I am the way* (the path), *and the truth* (the essence of what is true), *and the life* (Zoë, the God-kind of life); *no one comes to the Father, but through Me.*
John 14:6 (The amplification is mine.)

In His conversation with Nicodemus (John 3:1-21), Jesus says, *Truly truly I say to you, unless one is born again, he cannot see the kingdom of God.* He goes on to explain that physical birth brings one into the earth, but rebirth of the human spirit, by the Holy Spirit, provides the open door into the kingdom. He tells Nicodemus, *you must be born from above.* (verse 7) Furthermore, *whoever* believes in Him will have eternal life (verse 16).

But how?

Romans 10:9 gives us the process, *if you confess with your mouth Jesus as Lord and believe in your heart that God raised Him from the dead, you shall be saved.* The word used here for saved is the Greek word *sozo,* which denotes both temporal (here and now in this life), as well as eternal deliverance.

Have you acknowledged Jesus as the Way, the only Way? Perhaps you have but you've allowed detours and side trips. If you have never acknowledged Him as the only Way, or if you desire to get back on track, do not allow any more time to pass without committing all to Him.

Tell Him, in your own words, that you have been on the wrong path until now, that you acknowledge His death and His resurrection on your behalf. Invite Him into your heart to be your personal Lord and Savior from this moment forward. Then go out and tell someone. Hallelujah! Mark it in your Bible as the day your eternal destination was established!

If you prayed such a prayer and really meant it from your heart, you are now born again and your feet are firmly planted on the only road to the Father. It is important to renew your mind daily in the Word of God. Your spirit is new and reborn, having moved from death in sin to life in Christ. But your flesh is stubborn and will only change as you daily give your spirit dominion through the Word.

***

*Confession:*

If you have never confessed Jesus as Lord, consider doing so today. You can use your own words, the words I suggest at the back of this book or you can simply read Romans 10:9, claiming it as your own personal confession. The only prerequisite is that the words come from your heart. If Jesus is already the Lord of your life, there can be no better confession than the renewal of that vow.

*Go Deeper:*
John 14:4-6
John 3:1-21
Romans 10:9

*Minute by Minute:*

This is an exercise each must personally design — on a daily basis. Specifically, how have you, whether consciously or unconsciously, attempted to make another way to gain the assurance of Heaven? Going forward, how will you catch yourself in attempts to take another road to Heaven?

## Prove Reliable — Week 31

> *So Samuel grew,*
> *and the LORD was with him*
> *and let none of his words fall to the ground.*
> 1 Samuel 3:19 NKJV

We're into the last month of summer already, that time when we wonder how it all flew by so quickly, when we begin to focus on resuming our forward movement. School begins once more and we find ourselves taking stock of where we stand.

How much have the kids grown over the summer? How have the summer's family adventures impacted everyone? Has there been any growing up, any maturing? It's not just for the classroom you know.

I was struck by this simple Scripture one morning in my quiet time. I saw a logical progression in these few words and began to realize that, even in my senior years, I need to continue growing up. I cannot afford to think I have reached maturity, not if I want to be all that God has for me to be.

If I want to continue growing and, in so doing, prove to be reliable, a person whose words do not fall to the ground, what must I do and what must I be aware of in all things?

1. *Grow up.* I like the NLT translation best for expressing the meaning behind this verse. The Hebrew for *grow up* expresses advancement, increase, becoming great, exceeding; in other words, *maturing*. No more babies crying for a bottle, whining for what they want, bickering, infighting and tattling. Sadly, this is not only indicative of the world's way, but is all too common in the Body of Christ as well. It is definitely time to grow up.

> *As Samuel grew up, the LORD was with him,*
> *and everything Samuel said proved to be reliable.*
> 1 Samuel 3:19 NLT

2. ***Discipline*** goes hand in hand with maturity. As much as we would like to avoid it, discipline is an integral part of the process of growing up and to reach true maturity is to come to value and appreciate discipline, to actively seek it in fact. Discipline is not bondage to harsh process, not at all what we dreaded as children. It is valuing and welcoming the serious process of learning and maturing. It involves dedication to instruction, but also to warning and reproof and yes, even correction. It is for the serious, not for the noncommittal.
3. The manifest ***presence of God*** is the result. *LORD*, in this verse translated from the Hebrew *Jehovah*, has from the beginning indicated relationship. As mature New Covenant people, we not only have the Holy Spirit ever present, but we are in *relationship*. God not only speaks, but now in the stillness born of maturity, we are capable of hearing Him. He is with us, omnipresent, and we can truly experience Him.
4. ***Wisdom*** follows. The mature individual is a reliable source of wisdom, which is the practical application of knowledge. Anyone can accumulate knowledge, but it takes maturity and awareness of what true wisdom is (see 1 Corinthians 1:30) to become a reliable source.
5. Finally, maturity is ***service oriented*** and understands that it's not all about *me*. It is a characteristic of childhood that, until about the age of twelve, children see the world as being *for* them, *about* them, and *because* of them. Approaching adolescence, in the normal flow of things, an awareness of other people and events as separate from themselves begins to emerge. If maturing continues unhindered, the young adult arrives at the place where reaching out, acting on behalf of others, becomes desirable. It is at this point, as Christians, that we become truly aware our gracious God has placed us here, not for ourselves but for one another.

*The Lord continued to appear at Shiloh*
*and gave messages to Samuel there at the Tabernacle.*
1 Samuel 3:22 NLT

Continue to grow, day in and day out, and you will be recognized and confirmed as a consistent, unfailing bearer of God's Words, a prophet for your times and in your circles. And God, knowing that you are trustworthy, will continue to speak to you and to use you, *there at the Tabernacle.* Stay connected.

> *The words of the godly save lives.*
> Proverbs 12:6b NLT

> *The words of the wise bring healing.*
> Proverbs 12:18b NLT

\*\*\*

*Confession:*
I determine this day to continue to grow and mature, to embrace discipline, to expect and welcome the very real presence of God and to walk in the wisdom that follows, in service to and on behalf of those God brings into my life.

*Go Deeper*
1 Samuel 3:19
1 Corinthians 1:30
1 Samuel 3:22
Proverbs 12:6b
Proverbs 12:18b

*Minute by Minute:*
Now that you have made this confession, how will you walk it out in the practical realm of your daily life? Ask yourself how you will grow and mature beyond where you are right now.

If you find it difficult to welcome discipline, perhaps your understanding of the true meaning of the word is the reason. Study discipline in light of discipleship and the fact that disciples of Jesus were those who seriously embraced His teaching and disciplined their lives accordingly.

How can you further foster an environment in which the constant presence of God becomes real in a very personal way? Do you need to turn down or tune out the voices of the world? List specifically those ways in which the world may be encroaching and drowning out the voice of the Spirit.

Finally, how can you begin to reach out, touching others in His name? Remember, you only need to touch one person at a time.

## Cafeteria Word? Make a Choice
### Week 31

> *Stop toiling and doing and producing for the food*
> *that perishes and decomposes [in the using],*
> *but strive and work and produce rather*
> *for the [lasting] food which endures [continually] unto life eternal;*
> *the Son of Man will give [furnish] you that,*
> John 6:27 AMP

Are you inadvertently treating the Word of God like a cafeteria line, picking and choosing only those dishes that are palatable to you? Mashed potatoes, but hold the gravy (too much fat), salad with just a little dressing on the side please, no lima beans — and absolutely *no* liver!

How often do we take the redemption without the healing (Deuteronomy 28:15-45; Galatians 3:13), forgiveness without the repentance (Luke 24:47), forgiveness without the forgiving, for that matter (Matthew 6:14, 15), resurrection, but none of the cross please (Matthew 26:42)?

We cannot embrace the resurrection without the cross (Matthew 26:54); we can have no harvest without seedtime (Genesis 8:22); and Zoé Life (the God kind of life) does not come without death (John 12:24, 25).

The Word is food to us (1 Peter 2:2, 3; John 6:27; Hebrews 5:12-14), but if we are to be truly nourished, we cannot stay with the milk only (the easy to receive and digest); we must grow and mature, graduating to the solid food of the Word, taking the *whole* Word, not just the *easy* Word.

> *For everyone who partakes only of milk*
> *is not accustomed to the word of righteousness, for he is a babe.*
> *But solid food is for the mature,*
> *who because of practice have their senses trained*
> *to discern good and evil.*
> Hebrews 5:13-14 KJV

That requires effort on our part. James exhorts us to act on the Word. His admonition is clear and straightforward. *But prove yourselves doers of the word, and not merely hearers who delude themselves.* (James 1:22 NAS) A tree is identified by its fruit. An apple tree is only an apple tree if it bears apples, regardless of any other evidence. We are doers of the word only if we prove it, if we provide concrete evidence.

But James does not stop there — he goes on to say that if we are hearing only, though we may well be hearing regularly and frequently, we are still deluding ourselves We need to take the Word *as it is*, digesting even those difficult bits that present a challenge to our spiritual stomachs, and then act on what we have heard — even if it seems like liver. The reward is a spiritually healthy system and a mature understanding of the importance of total nourishment!

Pass the lima beans please...

***

*Confession:*
Starting today. I will no longer be a picky eater. I will begin receiving the whole Word, including the liver and the lima beans. If God has put it on my plate, I will consume it!

*Go Deeper:*
John 6:27
Deuteronomy 28:15-45
Galatians 3:13
Luke 24:47
Matthew 6:14, 15
Matthew 26:42
Matthew 26:54
Genesis 8:22
John 12:24, 25
1 Peter 2:2,3
John 6:27
Hebrews 5:12-14
James 1:22
2 Timothy 3:16-17

***Minute by Minute:***
If you have been one who stays with those portions of Scripture that are fed to you, comfortable, easy to understand and digest, presenting little challenge to your current thinking or lifestyle, consider trying something new and different on your spiritual plate.

If, for instance, you have never focused on the healing power of God, why not commence your own study on the subject? Do not be satisfied with being fed, digesting only what others have to say about it. As a mature Christian, begin to feed yourself. Search the Word, gaining your own understanding. Approach it with an open mind and heart, asking the Holy Spirit to lead you and to reveal and interpret the heart of the Word to you.

*All Scripture is inspired by God and
profitable for teaching, for reproof, for correction,
for training in righteousness;
that the man of God may be adequate,
equipped for every good work.*
2 Timothy 3:16-17 NAS

# The Eye of the Storm  Week 32

> *Then the Lord answered Job out of the whirlwind...*
> Job 38:1 NAS

Near the end of the chronicle of Job's tribulations, we share in his revealing dialogue with God. Job experiences God's very presence and notice where He is speaking from! We are not going to address the age old controversy of Job's suffering, or who is responsible or even why. Instead let us take note that God comes to Job out of the whirlwind! I have always found that concept somewhat disturbing.

How could God, who tells me His very nature is love, come in a storm? It contradicts everything I have come to know personally of God's nature and certainly seems to contradict what the Bible says of Him. (1 John 4:8) So, I knew I must have missed it somewhere. And then I read Job 38:1 again — very carefully.

Does it say God is in the storm, really *in* the storm, at one with the tempest itself? That surely does not fit with what we know of Him. Nor does it fit with what we know of Jesus' own interaction with the storm on the Sea of Galilee. How could He be one with the storm and yet rebuke the wind and waves — ever, at any time? (See Matthew 8:26 and James 1:8)

Then I remembered 1 Kings 19:11 and Elijah on Mount Horeb. Multiple translations say the same thing, using exactly the same words,

> *But the LORD was not in the wind*
> 1 Kings 19:12

Yet clearly He speaks to Job from the whirlwind. And then I saw it, the whirlwind, the picture of the tumult, in all its destructive power, just as Job must have seen and experienced it, and at the very center of it all, the consummate and almost incomprehensible peace and stillness — the EYE OF THE STORM!

I realized that in the midst of the maelstrom is the Great I AM. I am convinced that this clear and present, transcendent, peace that God promises (Philippians 4:7; John 14:27) is what we call the *eye of the storm*. It is not part of the storm, not at all, but always present in the midst of the storm, the *I AM here* that we must focus on *in* the storm.

He is not intrinsic to the storm. Instead, He is the peace in the very midst of it! He is the blue sky that affords a glimpse of the heavens above the storm, the sweet air and quiet calm in the midst of the tempests of life.

He promised *I will never leave you nor forsake you* (Hebrews 13:5). He did not promise calm and trouble-free living. In fact, just the opposite; He warned us of life's tribulations, its crushing pressures. Have you ever noticed how heavy and oppressive the air is as a storm approaches? But at the eye, there is respite, space to breathe and gain strength.

God knows his people. Human beings still grapple with keeping their attention off the circumstances and focused on Him, but here God is showing us that He is present in the very *midst* of the circumstances. Just as they threaten to completely overpower us, there He is, His sweet presence strengthening, refreshing and reminding us that we are never without Him. His promise is true; He will never leave us nor forsake us.

If you are struggling to stand through the storm, be encouraged, He will speak to you from the midst of the storm. And, just as Elijah did and just as Job did, you too will hear the still small voice speaking from that place of complete peace — the very eye of the storm!

\*\*\*

*Confession:*

God has not promised me a trouble-free life, but He has promised He would never leave me nor forsake me. He is at the center of every whirlwind that threatens to overpower me. I expect to hear His voice.

***Go Deeper:***
Job 38:1
Matthew 8:26; James 1:8
1 Kings 19:11-12
Philippians 4:7; John 14:27
Hebrews 13:5

***Minute by Minute:***
    If you are experiencing storms in any area of your life, stop and take time to listen for the voice that would speak to you in the midst of the tempest. It will not happen by accident. If you are not already investing time at the beginning of each day in prayer and in the Word of God, I urge you to make it your practice. God has much to say to you from the storm, about the storm. Make the time to listen. Begin with 15 minutes and before long your will be ordering your day around that most precious time.

# A Great Calm Occurred[16]           Week 32

*And they came to Him and awoke Him, saying 'Save us, Lord; we are perishing!" And He said to them, "Why are you timid, you men of little faith?" Then He arose, and rebuked the winds and the sea; and it became perfectly calm.*
Matthew 8:24-26 NAS

We are all touched by the campus violence that has become an all too frequent news item. Worldwide terrorism continues as a threat, real and implied. Disturbed young people slaughter their own family members. Kids can no longer safely roam their neighborhoods exploring the world of childhood and too often are not safe in their own homes. Adults seek the relative safety of their homes as night falls to avoid the danger lurking in the streets of city and suburb alike.

In light of obvious threats and even not so obvious concerns, when was the last time we were calm, blissfully free from worry, fear, nagging concerns, emotional upheaval — stress? If we are really honest with ourselves, it has probably been some time. To be sure, we have moments of tranquility, perhaps during praise or prayer time. But these are islands in a sea of *surging waves*. (Luke 8:24)

We regularly move through life from incident to incident, reacting then recovering the best we can before facing the next crisis. Unfortunately, this cycle does not allow us full recovery before we must gear up for the next approaching wave. This stair-stepping is a familiar scenario to those who work in the field of Critical Incident Stress Management (CISM). Returning to the base state of complete calm rarely occurs in those who live with constant stress. What's to be done, aside from dealing with the existing cycle? And what exactly is the nature of calm? Do we even remember?

We do not often think of calm as being an active force. We generally define it in terms of the *absence* of a force such as anger, fear, worry, upheaval of any type, either internal to human beings, physical, or in reference to the forces of the natural world around us.

We might say, "The pain subsided and she was calm," or "his temper tantrum finally passed and the house was calm!"

In Matthew 8, we have the account, which occurs also in Luke 8 and Mark 4, of Jesus rebuking *the wind and the surging waves* (Luke 8:24 NAS). While these few words contain the material for countless lessons, let's remain focused on the calm. By definition, calm is a state of tranquil repose, with synonyms like still, serene, placid and peaceful. The verb is to *become* or *make calm*. This last is the only definition that even begins to describe what took place in our Gospel account.

Gale force winds with high waves can occur quite suddenly on the Sea of Galilee. Geographical placement of this clear water inland sea dictates the ferocity of these storms. Lake Kinneret, Hebrew for harp, so called for its shape, is in a basin shaped by the hills of the Golan Heights. Winds sweeping down from the hills are trapped in the basin and the normally placid beauty of the lake is rapidly transformed by often violent conditions. In 1992, one such extreme storm even sent waves 10 feet high pouring into the streets of the nearby town of Tiberias.[17] It is one such storm we read about in Matthew 8.

It is important to note what the disciples had been lately witnessing: *the blind receive sight, the lame walk, the lepers ...cleansed, and the deaf hear, the dead ... raised up... (and) the gospel preached.* (Luke 7:22) They had been with Jesus through it all, close at His side for every miracle, each healing. Every word spoken from His lips fell upon their ears.

Nonetheless, their reaction was immediate overwhelming fear, not faith as we might expect. Remember, however, they had not yet received the Holy Spirit (John 20:22), so their ability to process the divine was limited. They had Christ in their midst it is true, but they did not yet have Christ within. (1 Corinthians 2:16)

Though unexpected, they did understand what they witnessed that night. It is important we understand it as well. I feel sure the calm that Jesus invoked on the turbulent Sea of Galilee had a great impact on the disciples and was a factor in the boldness with which they approached their future ministries. How often they must have overcome fear with the *force of calm* as they spread the Gospel to the ends of the earth.

It is a principle that a force can only be overcome by a greater force. Calm is a greater force than violent upheaval of any kind. Calm is not the absence of upheaval, but a force that when purposefully applied to upheaval, internal or external, will completely obliterate it. It is a force stronger than the violent storms of life, a force capable of overpowering them, birthed as it is in that peace that passes understanding (Matthew 4:39; Philippians 4:7). Calm is anything but passive, as we see so well in Matthew 8. It is a dynamic force that must be actively applied to the circumstances.

Do you have a violent upheaval in your life right now, a roiling fear, a turbulent anger, waves of bitterness, worry about health or finances, fear for a loved one, doubt that threatens to drown you? Do as Jesus did — take action. (See John 14:12) Exercise your faith. Jesus did not reprimand the disciples for a lack of faith or even for not enough faith. He corrected them for the quality and endurance of their faith.

To each is given a measure of faith. (Romans 12:3) How we exercise it dictates the results we experience. The faith we have is enough to invoke calm in the midst of the storms of life. Begin right now to rebuke the wind and waves and replace them with calm. Speak peace into the situation and watch a great calm occur.

***

*Confession:*
I purpose this day to invoke the powerful force of calm and apply it diligently to the upheaval in me as well as around me.

*Go Deeper:*
Matthew 8:24-26
Luke 8:24 (See also Matthew 8 & Mark 4)
Luke 7:22
John 20:22
1 Corinthians 2:16
Matthew 4:39; Philippians 4:7
Romans 12:3

***Minute by Minute:***

Think of a specific personal stormy situation or relationship that has been troubling you, perhaps sometimes to the point of fear. If calm is a force and indeed an even greater force than violent upheaval, as illustrated in Matthew 8, how would actively invoking the force of calm as a purposeful action bring about change, in the situation and your attitude toward it? (See John 14:12)

# Wisdom Speaks
## The Power of Words

**Week 33**

> *For he who finds me finds life, and obtains favor from the LORD.*
> Proverbs 8:36 NAS

If we read multiple dictionaries and study carefully what the Word has to say concerning wisdom, we might arrive at the following definition describing wisdom as *the right, practical and prudent application of knowledge.* It is clear then that one can have a great deal of knowledge and possess little or no wisdom, but that one cannot possess wisdom without also having knowledge.

With this in mind, we begin to look at how and what wisdom speaks and then come to a clear recognition of what is truly wisdom and what is actually, as Shakespeare put it in Macbeth, *full of sound and fury signifying nothing,* or plain and simple *hot air.*

Most of us have some difficulty with our words and yet it is our words that are the surest indication of whether we possess wisdom or not. Even the world understands the power of words to. During WWII, movie houses across the country ran shorts between their feature films about the danger of careless tongues (*loose lips sink ships*).

The old adage, *sticks and stones may break my bones, but words can never hurt me* has been disproved by every child who ever endured the daily playground wars. Psychologists will attest to the long-range damage done by insensitive words spoken in ignorance or anger.

As Christians, however, we possess a deeper truth. We are made in the image of the Creator, (Genesis 1:27) whose entire creation is the result of His words (God *said* and then God *saw*, Genesis 1:3-31). The word *image* indicates an *exact likeness*, a reproduction in every way. Being truly made in God's image, our words must, like His, contain the same power. If not, we are nothing but a second-rate copy.

So, if we are to speak the words that wisdom speaks, the words of the Creator, and experience the full power therein, we need to know what they are, and we need to know how to get to a place where what we speak is in line with wisdom. And we need to fill our ears and eyes, and ultimately our hearts with those words. (Matthew 12:34)

Proverbs 8 is often referred to as the wisdom chapter. While Scripture as a whole has a great deal to say about wisdom, this chapter is a condensed treatment. So on the following pages, we will look at what wisdom speaks, according to Proverbs 8:6-14, and how we can experience the power of Wisdom's words in our own mouths — every time we speak.

\*\*\*

*Confession:*
*Set a guard, O Lord, over my mouth; keep watch over the door of my lips.* Psalm 141:3 NAS

*Go Deeper:*
Proverbs 8:36
Genesis 1:27
Genesis 1:3-31
Matthew 12:34
Proverbs 8:6-14

*Minute by Minute:*
Starting today, become aware of the powerful effect of your words on those around you. Begin by noting how often you speak without thinking. Pay close attention to the reactions of family, friends and co-workers. Ask the Holy Spirit to reveal to you what you need to see.

Do you frequently use words to encourage and comfort? How often are your words intentionally critical or demeaning? Are there times when your words are simply careless and might be construed as hurtful? At the end of the day, record your observations. Do you see a pattern?

Now think back through your own life and try to recall times when a word spoken to you in frustration or anger changed the course of a relationship or even your self-perception.

Finally, think about those times in your life when a word of encouragement or comfort at just the right moment was a key factor in freeing you from a difficult situation or was the catalyst that moved you forward toward a goal.

# Wisdom Speaks Excellence
## Week 33

*Finally, brethren, whatever is true, whatever is honorable, whatever is right, whatever is pure, whatever is lovely, whatever is of good repute, if there is any excellence and if anything worthy of praise, let your mind dwell on these things.*
Philippians 4:8 NAS

The kingdom of God is seedtime and harvest (Genesis 8:22), so today let's set our intention to sow words of wisdom into our surroundings, and we can expect the same kind of harvest that we see throughout Genesis 1 — God *said* and then God *saw*.

Today we will begin our look at exactly what Wisdom speaks, with our foundation Scriptures coming from Proverbs 8:6-14. As we dedicate ourselves to speaking the words that God has spoken, we are assured of a good harvest. (Isaiah 55:11)

*Listen, for I shall speak noble things; and the opening of my lips will produce right things.*
Proverbs 8:6 NAS

What changes would you see in your surroundings if the only words that came from your lips were excellent and each time you opened your mouth, the words which came out produced right things? The Hebrew word for *right things* is *miyshor,* meaning straightness, concord, honesty, equity, righteousness, a level land.

Thomas Jefferson said *Honesty is the first chapter in the book of wisdom.* So if excellence produces right things, then honesty, freely salted with love, would seem to be a good place to begin. Let's begin by checking to make sure our words are excellent and honest. Straight dealings with no twists or bends will be the result.

# The Bible Minute

*The quality of a person's life is in direct proportion
to their commitment to excellence,
regardless of their chosen field of endeavor.*
Vince Lombardi

\*\*\*

### Confession:
Jesus Christ has been made wisdom unto me. I have the Greater One in me, so I possess all wisdom and today I purpose to speak it into my world. (1 Corinthians 1:30 & 1 John 4:4)

### Go Deeper:
Philippians 4:8
Genesis 8:22
Isaiah 55:11
1 Corinthians 1:30
1 John 4:4
Psalm 19:14

### Minute by Minute:
Study Psalm 19:14 and then consider what right things would be produced in your relationships and the circumstances of your life if each time you opened your mouth, the words which came out were words of wisdom. Begin by monitoring your words closely, making a quality decision to speak from a heart filled with the Word of God. (Matthew 12:34)

# Wisdom Speaks Truth

*Week 34*

> *For my mouth shall speak truth;*
> *and wickedness is an abomination to my lips.*
> Proverbs 8:7 KJV

Wisdom speaks only truth and from this verse we know that anything but truth is wickedness and cannot be in the mouth at the same time as truth and still be called Wisdom. (See James 3:11) *Truth* and wickedness are not compatible on any level and nothing less than truth is acceptable to Wisdom.

Jesus said in John 14:6, *I am the way, the truth, and the life: no man cometh unto the Father, but by me.* And since we have learned that Jesus Christ has been made wisdom unto us (1 Corinthians 1:30), we can be assured that it all ties into one package. Jesus makes it abundantly clear to us that these all go hand in hand.

The Greek word for life in John 14 is Zoë and it denotes the God kind of life, the high life, if you will. If we take time to ponder it, we will admit that is the kind of life we are all looking for. Living in the Way will result in this high Life of God, and Truth and Wisdom are its characteristics!

Make a quality decision today to walk in the Way, speaking only the Truth and letting Wisdom have its way in your life. This will exercise your faith, but after all, we walk by faith and not by sight. (2 Corinthians 5:7)

\*\*\*

### Confession:

I set my intention this day to walk by faith and not by sight and to open up my life to the Wisdom of God by walking in Truth in all I do.

***Go Deeper:***
Proverbs 8:7
James 3:11
John 14:6
1 Corinthians 1:30
2 Corinthians 5:7

***Minute by Minute:***
    Do a word study of *truth* in both the Old and the New Testaments. Will you need to change your personal concept of truth in order to be in agreement with the biblical standard of truth?

# Wisdom Speaks
## The Treasure of the Heart

**Week 34**

> *All the words of my mouth*
> *are in righteousness;*
> *there is nothing froward*
> *or perverse in them.*
> Proverbs 8:8 KJV

Our Scripture today seems like a tall order doesn't it? If we are to check our talk alongside Wisdom, *all* our words must be morally and legally right. That means *nothing* can be distorted! How many of us can go an entire day without distorting or exaggerating? Often we aren't even aware that we are embellishing or amplifying, until we are caught in the act and it is brought to our attention.

And then verse 8 goes on to say that nothing we speak can be perverse. Sounds simple enough, since we all know what perversion is, right? But do we really know what Solomon meant when he used that particular word? The Hebrew word in this verse is *pathal* and it means to twine, to struggle (sound familiar?) or to be morally tortuous.

This can all be clarified by asking ourselves one question. Are our words our own or are we speaking the Word of God into the situations of our lives. Left to our own devices, we will err every time. Romans 3:23 says, *For all have sinned and come short of the glory of God.* That includes each one of us, exempting no one.

The Wisdom of our words is dependent upon the content of our heart. If we have filled out heart with God's words, then we will always speak in Wisdom.

> *A good man out of the good treasure of the heart*
> *bringeth forth good things:*
> *and an evil man out of the evil treasure bringeth forth evil things.*
> *But I say unto you, That every idle word that men shall speak,*
> *they shall give account thereof in the day of judgment.*

*For by thy words thou shalt be justified,
and by thy words thou shalt be condemned.*
Matthew 12:35-37 KJV

Ask your Heavenly Father to help you check your talk by confessing His Word.

\*\*\*

*Confession:*
Let the words of my mouth, and the meditation of my heart, be acceptable in thy sight, O LORD, my strength, and my redeemer. (Psalm 19:14 NAS)

*Go Deeper:*
Proverbs 8:8
Romans 3:23
Matthew 12:35-37
Psalm 19:14

*Minute by Minute:*
Keeping in mind that exaggeration and distortion are misleading and therefore conduct the listener away from the truth of the situation, try to go an entire day without distortion or exaggeration of any kind. If you find this difficult or impossible in your own ability, fill your heart with the Word of God, and you can be assured you will always speak in wisdom. Sound familiar? (Matthew 12:34)

## Wisdom Speaks
## The Straightforward Mouth

**Week 35**

> *All the utterances of my mouth...*
> *Are all straightforward*
> *To him who understands,*
> *And right to those who*
> *Find knowledge.*
> Proverbs 8:8a, 9 NAS

Words of wisdom are straightforward and right, very much like this statement. The Hebrew for straightforward is *nakoach*, correct and honest, straight on. And the word for right is *yashar*, upright, level, even and straight.

The shortest distance between two points is the straight one, often referred to *as the crow flies*, with no deviation from the course. Site the goal, focus on it, and set a straight path directly to it.

This doesn't mean we need to approach a matter harshly or with a sledgehammer. We are exhorted that by *speaking the truth in love*, thereby *we may grow up to Him in all things* (Ephesians 4:15). The Greek word for truth in this verse is *aletheuo* and it means to *be* true and to *speak* the truth. The implication is becoming a very familiar one to us — what we are within is what we will speak (Matthew 12:34-35)

How often do we try to circumvent, skirting the issues, dodging and avoiding without carefully chosen words, that which makes us uneasy? If we will but make the quality decision to fill ourselves with what God has to say, by daily taking in His Word, then when we speak, we can be assured it will be the shortest distance between any two points and Love will be the focus.

We no longer need to concern ourselves with the wisdom of what we say in a given situation if we say what the Father says about it and then expect His results.

Now that's good news!

\*\*\*

***Confession:***
I set my intention this day to fill my heart with the Word of God and to bring forth straightforward, good, and wise things from my mouth, in abundance, as a result. (Matthew 12:35)

***Go Deeper:***
Proverbs 8:8, 9
Ephesians 4:15
Matthew 12:34-35
1 Corinthians 13:4-8 (determine the connection between wisdom, love and straightforward words)

***Minute by Minute:***
How would you need to alter your words to be in line with what you have learned? Is it possible for you to be straightforward with your words, speaking in wisdom and love, in other words, speaking the truth in love? Would you need to change your approach? If so, how?

# Wisdom Speaks
# Discretion

Week 35

> *I, wisdom dwell with prudence,*
> Proverbs 8:12a NAS

Wisdom is permanently in close proximity to *prudence*, which is simply discretion and subtlety. Quite often dwelling together indicates a familial or very close relationship, which presents us with a tall order.

We learned in our last message that to check our talk against wisdom, we need to be straight on, truthful, not circumventing the issue. Can we be honest and straightforward, speaking only the truth and yet be discreet and subtle at the same time? We need to look to the earthly ministry of Jesus for our example. Jesus always took the shortest distance between two points, and being Love personified (1 John 4:8, 16), He always operated in *Agape* (the God kind of Love).

I am certain we can all agree that situations put to Jesus were dealt with straightforwardly, right to the heart of the matter, no padding, but always in Love. An excellent example of this approach is in Matthew 16:23. Following closely on Peter's striking recognition of Jesus the Messiah, Jesus was preparing His disciples for His death. We are told Peter *took Jesus aside and began to rebuke Him, saying God forbid it, Lord.* Jesus' response seems at first to be anything but gentle and encouraging.

*Get behind Me, Satan!* must have been quite a shock to Peter, especially following on the heels of *Blessed are you, Simon Barjona,* in verse 17 and *I will give you the keys of the kingdom of heaven* in verse 18 of the same chapter. (Please note that we cannot be certain of the actual time lapse between.) But Jesus was the Master of tough love and preparing people for what was to follow. Peter's role would require a great deal of spiritual and emotional maturing in a short time and out of His great love for Peter came the words he needed to hear. Note that Jesus did not speak in front of the others. The words were for Peter's ears only — that's discretion.

He spoke what Peter needed to hear, when he needed to hear it, and the motivation was based on a clear understanding of the entire situation and the role Peter was playing and would play in it — prudence and discretion.

But where's the subtlety you may ask. Jesus' declaration does not sound subtle at all! Two synonyms for the word subtle are *clever* and *ingenious*. Jesus definitely got Peter's attention in an ingenious and unexpected way and Peter surely understood what Jesus was saying! He wasn't identifying Peter as Satan himself. The Greek word means *adversary, anyone in opposition, standing between two points to keep them divided.*

Peter's passionate response was in opposition to the will of God, not only for Jesus, but for all of humanity. He inadvertently placed himself in the position of opposing God's plan of redemption. Jesus' response was indeed ingenious and undoubtedly had the desired effect!

***

*Confession:*

The Word is Wisdom. (Proverbs 2:6) The Word is Jesus. (John 1:1, 14) Jesus is Wisdom. (1 Corinthians 1:24, 30). When I speak what He spoke, Wisdom speaks through me in prudence, discretion, subtlety and Love.

*Go Deeper:*
Proverbs 8:12
1 John 4:8, 16
Matthew 16:23
Matthew 16:17, 18
Proverbs 2:6
John 1:1, 14
1 Corinthians 1:24, 30
1 Corinthians 13:4-8
1 Corinthians 2:16
James 1:5

***Minute by Minute:***

Time to take stock. True wisdom will be closely associated with prudence. Discretion (assessing the right opportunity at the right time) and subtlety (clever and ingenious means) are the earmarks of a prudent person. And the whole package is wrapped in agape love (1 Corinthians 13:4-8), covenant love that is not contingent on worthiness or changing emotions. This is a very tall order and yet if we would walk in wisdom, these qualities must be cultivated. Can you truly say you operate in prudence, and all it embodies? How do you know?

Working with a trusted friend or prayer/accountability partner, examine this portion of your wisdom walk. If you fall short, you are surely attempting it in your own strength. Look up each of the supporting Scriptures in the confession and make it your own. Jesus Christ has been made Wisdom on your behalf (1 Corinthians 1:30), available to you 24 hours a day. Know that you have the mind of Christ, Wisdom itself (1 Corinthians 2:16) and you have but to ask and it will be available to you (James 1:5).

# *Harvest*

*And another angel came out of the temple,
crying with a loud voice to him that sat on the cloud,
Thrust in thy sickle, and reap:
for the time is come for thee to reap;
for the harvest of the earth is ripe.*
Revelation 14:15 KJV

*The Bible Minute*

## Wisdom Speaks
## The Beginning of Wisdom

**Week 36**

> *The fear of the* L<small>ORD</small> *is the beginning of wisdom,*
> *And knowledge of the Holy One is understanding.*
> Proverbs 9:10 NAS

You may say, *I know I need to keep wisdom in my mouth, but how do I go about getting it there and keeping it there?* Scripture never leaves us with a command without the means to obey. Our key verse for today tells us where it starts. Wisdom begins with the reverential fear of the Lord. Let us be clear that this word does not imply terror, but rather the extreme reverence that results from extreme awe.

It is this awe at God's greatness, His overpowering love and mercy that weakens the legs and brings us to our knees. It is a personal revelation of Who He Is (remember that He introduced Himself to Moses as I AM).

Actively seek to be overpowered by this revelation. Ask for it. (Matthew 7:7) Do you believe for a minute that God will not grant you a revelation of His greatness in your life? After all, He has been trying to get the attention of His people for thousands of years. When one of His own is actively seeking it, be assured that it is on the way!

Proverbs 15:33 tells us that this same reverence is not only the beginning of wisdom, but is the instruction of wisdom. When you begin to have a revelation in the area of the fear of the Lord, you will be driven to the Word, passionately desiring to know more of this God whose love is so consuming, so transforming, so encompassing. As you bury yourself in His Word, you will learn that, according to Proverbs 2:6.

> *For the* L<small>ORD</small> *giveth wisdom:*
> *Out of His mouth cometh knowledge and understanding.*
> Proverbs 2:6 KJV

It is in His Word that we will find Wisdom. After all, He tells us that He IS His word (John 1:1), so everything we need is there!

\*\*\*

*Confession:*
I will seek the Lord in His Word, in reverential fear, and step into practical wisdom for my life and ministry.

*Go Deeper:*
The Word is Wisdom (Proverbs 2:6)
The Word is Jesus (John 1:1, 14)
Jesus is Wisdom (1 Corinthians 1:24, 30)
Proverbs 9:10
Matthew 7:7
Proverbs 15:33

*Minute by Minute:*
Set aside time to purposely concentrate on the awesome greatness of God, to flood your mind with it. Read and reread the greatness of God Scriptures we have discussed elsewhere in this devotional. (See Psalm 104, Isaiah 40, Job 38-41, Hebrews 1:7-14 and others you will find yourself). As you read and meditate, turning each over and over in your mind, revelation will come. That solid revelation of Who He is, is the very essence of wisdom. It grows in the good soil of a heart that is overwhelmed by the greatness and goodness of God. Do you want that as much as I do?

*The Bible Minute*

## *The Process*            Week 36

*For My thoughts are not your thoughts,
neither are your ways My ways,
declares the LORD. For as the heavens are higher than the earth,
so are My ways higher than your ways, and My thoughts than your
thoughts. For as the rain and the snow come down from heaven,
and do not return there, without watering the earth, and making it
bear and sprout, and furnishing seed to the sower,
and bread to the eater:
So shall my word be which goes forth from My mouth;
it shall not return to Me empty,
without accomplishing what I desire,
and without succeeding in the matter for which I sent it.
Isaiah 55:8-11 NAS*

Most people read verse 8 and 9 of this powerful passage and stop, grabbing hold and hanging on, quoting it as a reason to accept whatever comes their way. *Well, you just never know what God's going to do — His thoughts and ways are higher than ours, you know!* These are people who completely miss out on God's plan in the next verses and never exercise the dominion God intended. (See Genesis 1:26, 28)

A closer scrutiny of this passage actually reveals the process by which God has provided the remedy to the truth of verses 8 and 9! It is true that our natural, *unaltered* thoughts are not God's thoughts and our ways are surely not God's ways. A look at the morning paper will confirm that.

His ways are perfect and ours are sorely blemished, perverted by the selfishness, greed and sickness of spirit and soul that infects us from birth. Left to our own devices, we have surely attempted to pervert all that is good about God's creation.

The good news is that we have not been left to our own devices. In Isaiah 55:10, the thirsty earth receives exactly what it needs, life-giving water. As the earth soaks up the moisture sent from above, it cannot help but do what it is intended to do. It brings forth seed, with fruit and abundance following.

The earth does not need to take upon itself to do this. It must only soak up the precious moisture and the process goes into effect. Verse 11 assures us that the same principle applies to the Word of God. It *always* succeeds as the stated purpose of God.

Throughout Scripture, water and the word are linked and compared. It is well worth our time to do a study of the two as represented in the Bible. As we allow the water of the word to wash and renew our minds (Ephesians 5:26; Romans 12:2), we too are made to bring forth fruit in abundance. According to John 15, we have become branches on the vine that is Jesus Christ, grafted into Him, becoming part of Him, His life flowing through us.

A little further on, in John 15:15, He assures us that we are in Him and He in us. We are His *friends*, and *all things that I have heard from my Father I have made known to you*. His thoughts have become our thoughts, through the washing of the water of the word. Paul takes it a step further in 1 Corinthians 2:16, by reminding us that *we have the mind of Christ*. 1 John 4:4 wraps up the package with the truth that the greater One is *in* us, with us at all times and He is greater than the enemy.

The process in Isaiah 55 has come to fruition with our grafting into the Vine (John 15). As we abide (remain) and allow the water of the Word to do its work, as we are watered and flourish, we take our rightful place as branches of the True Vine, bearing good fruit for the kingdom.

> *These things I have spoken to you that*
> *My joy may be in you,*
> *and that your joy may be made full.*
> John 15:16 NAS

\*\*\*

## Confession:

I will submit to the processes God has placed in motion, not questioning what the Word says, but stepping out on it as a doer

(James 1:22). I do not have to understand it all to know that it works. Understanding will come to me as I act on it in faith.

*Go Deeper:*
Isaiah 55:8-11
Genesis 1:26, 28
Ephesians 5:26; Romans 12:2
John 15:15
1 Corinthians 2:16
1 John 4:4
James 1:22
John 15:16

*Minute by Minute:*
Isaiah 55 says you can trust God's Word as surely as you trust that rain will water the earth and seeds will sprout, grow and produce. The same God set both in motion.

In what practical ways would your life be measurably different if you ceased striving to make the process work and trusted the Creator who set it in motion?

List specific areas in your life that would benefit from trusting God's process. In what area(s) will you begin?

In what ways would your emotional and spiritual life benefit?

*Training Ground*  *Week 37*
*The Gift of Choice*

> Consider it wholly joyful, my brethren,
> whenever you are enveloped in or
> encounter trials of any sort or fall into various temptations.
> Be assured and understand that the trial and proving of your faith
> bring out endurance and steadfastness and patience.
> But let endurance and steadfastness and patience
> have full play and do a
> thorough work, so that you may be [people]
> perfectly and fully developed
> [with no defects], lacking in nothing.
> *James 1:2-4 AMP*

I love the epistle of James. With its beautiful prose, it is often referred to as the Proverbs of the New Testament. In its brief chapters are great truths, simply and concisely presented and expertly targeted. But I have always had difficulty getting past the point of exhortation in the second verse of chapter one. To exhort means to *push*, and this passage definitely pushes me!

Coming where it does, right after His very brief greeting, the words force us to stop for a moment before proceeding. Try as we might, we cannot comfortably move forward, until we have addressed the issue. I am sorry to say that for years I dealt with it by not dealing with it. I acknowledged it by mentally noting my inability to consider trials with joy, until finally, I felt compelled to dig deeper. If this is the first issue James addresses, then we ought also to tackle it, or we will probably not grasp the full substance of the rest of his letter.

I do not like trials! While I believe I can buck up with the best of them, I do not have a masochistic streak, and contemplating trials with joy seemed well beyond my ability. However, I do want to be *perfect and complete*, and I definitely want to *lack nothing*, so a deeper examination of this Scripture was in order.

As always, a closer look at the Greek concept of some key words will help us unravel James' meaning here. Joy, not surprisingly, means what we might think, mirth, gladness of heart, calm delight and cause for bliss.

The word *trials,* however, leads us to an unexpected, though very logical, implication. The same Greek word is also translated as *temptation.* Oh my, we don't like those! But what exactly is a temptation? Temptation is actually nothing but an option, an opportunity to choose. It is a point of decision, a moment when the rubber meets the road and we have the choice to align actions with words. We all know it is one thing to talk the talk and definitely another to walk the walk. This is an opportunity to prove that we are not just spouting hot air. Now that is cause for joy!

No one said it would be easy. When an athlete begins training for an event, he knows he must face intense challenges, first in the process, and then in the performance. It will take knowledge, wisdom, wits, plenty of practice and pushing every single trained muscle to its utmost and beyond. But the athlete welcomes the challenge, the opportunity to prove readiness. Paul said in Philippians 3:14, *I press toward the mark for the prize of the high calling of God in Christ Jesus.*

James goes on to assure us in verse 12 that endurance during the testing will bring victory, and with it the laurel wreath, the symbol of triumph, in this instance the crown of Zoë life, the abundant life of God! There is no *maybe* implied here but a full-fledged promise, *they will receive the crown of life that God has promised to those who love Him.* (NLT)

***

*Confession:*
I will daily learn to welcome points of decision, those challenges that offer me opportunities to prove my readiness. I am grateful for the gift of choice. As I am diligent to be prepared in season and out, I know I will experience the promised victory.

***Go Deeper:***
James 1:2-4, 12
Philippians 3:14

***Minute by Minute:***
  Set aside some time to reflect on a personal victory, an incident which required that you face a trial squarely, a point of decision becoming unavoidable. Think about your course of action, how you approached the decision. Now reflect on how you felt once your decision was made and you were successfully carrying out your plan of action. In this instance, how was the trial a gift of choice?

# Training Ground
## Persevering to Victory

*Week 37*

> *Blessed is a man who perseveres under trial;*
> *for once he has been approved he will receive the crown of life,*
> *which the Lord has promised to those who love Him.*
> James 1:12 NAS

As encouraging as this Scripture is, we need to dig deeply into verses 3 and 4, and get as much nourishment from the Word as possible, so we know exactly what is expected of us in gaining the victory in verse 12. Sometimes what God feeds us in Scripture is steak and sometimes it is liver but it will always nourish us supernaturally, growing and developing our spiritual musculature enough to take on whatever comes our way.

> *Knowing that the testing of your faith produces endurance.*
> *And let endurance have its perfect result,*
> *that you may be perfect and complete, lacking nothing.*
> James 1:3-4 NAS

*Knowing* in this Scripture is the same kind we see in Psalm 46:10, *Be still and know that I am God.* It is an intimate experiential knowing. James assumes that we not only have practice in this area but knowledge based upon it as well.

*Testing* is the application of a criterion, a measure or standard. It is the determination of whether someone or something makes the grade, hits or misses the mark, whether they have prepared physically and mentally to succeed, to go over the top in a given area.

*Faith* in the Greek is more than the English word *believing* implies, which is often rather weak by translation. The Greek demands knowledge, assent, and confidence in divine truths. This is a kind of believing on which you can hang everything. It demands action and ultimately becomes an entire system, a way of life.

*Endurance* is a combination of two traits, a firm stance, which is steadfastness, and the addition of patience, the ability to postpone your expectations until the time is ripe, *stick-to-itiveness*. The two together are unbeatable! You will always win, as long as you outlast the competition!

*Perfect* is an often misleading translation of the Greek, which occurs throughout the New Testament. It can be discouraging to those who do not dig deeper into the meaning. It need not be interpreted as flawlessness, but rather maturity, completeness, reaching the goal. We can be mature, though we may not be perfect — we just need to grow up!

James is telling us something about developing *character*, and what we must do to reach a point of maturity of temperament that can take on whatever challenge comes and will emerge victorious. Let's put it all together. The following is my suggested paraphrase.

> *Consider it to be the cause of full and complete gladness of heart and exaltation, when you are given the opportunity to test yourself. Just as an athlete or a student trains and prepares, testing allows you to put your choices into action, knowing from experience that doing so, where it comes to your belief structure (faith as a way of life), develops muscles in the area of standing fast. And standing fast, hanging on, never letting go, will always see what it is standing for. The result will be maturity, completeness and victory, without fail.*

I am greatly encouraged and will continue to ready myself to meet the challenges for which I have been so long preparing. A look at the next several verses of James chapter 1 will reveal a resource with a different origin, wisdom from God, a crucial resource if we are to be truly victorious. Character is our responsibility; but wisdom must come from God to be truly effective. Put them together and they are virtually unbeatable!

*Hallelujah*! We have the resources; we are trained and ready for what comes our way. Don't avoid the tests. Instead, be prepared to show yourself approved (2 Timothy 2:15)

\*\*\*

*Confession:*
I will consider it to be the cause of complete gladness of heart and exaltation, when I am given the opportunity to test myself. Testing allows me to put my choices into action, knowing from experience that doing so where it concerns my faith as a way of life develops my muscles. The result will be maturity, completeness and victory, without fail.

*Go Deeper:*
James 1:12
James 1:3-4
Psalm 46:10
2 Timothy 2:15
Philippians 3:14

*Minute by Minute:*
Are there areas that keep reappearing, areas that continually present a point of decision you may have been avoiding? Begin to record these as you think of them and then make a quality decision not to avoid the trials, but to prepare for them. While trials are not easy, they can be approached with increased confidence as you diligently dedicate yourself to training for them. Daily time in the Word of God, prayer, fellowship and hearing from the Holy Spirit will build your spiritual musculature. According to Philippians 3:14, victory awaits.

# Pass It On — Week 38

> *Verily I say unto you, Inasmuch as ye*
> *have done it unto one of the*
> *least of these my brethren,*
> *ye have done it unto me.*
> Matthew 5:40 KJV

Today I ran out early to do a few errands before my "real" day began. It's heavy and humid today; the air is oppressive. We are faced with the prospect of an unseasonably hot holiday weekend with highs in the 90s. I have more on my schedule to do today than there are hours for, or energy enough to carry me through.

Due to the early hour, I was forced to run into a store I avoid as often as possible and I wasn't very happy about it. Prices are high and service often impersonal.

My mood might have soured very quickly.

As I stepped into the checkout line, the lady in front of me signaled me to go ahead of her. Now I have done this same thing countless times, but I cannot remember the last time anyone did the same for me.

Transaction completed, I turned to thank her once more and tell her she had set the tone for the rest of my day. Responding that she was glad to do it, her expression backed up her words. The checker remarked, *oh, she's a sweetie*, and we all walked into our day with a smile.

When we say with Isaiah *Here am I; send me*, (Isaiah 6:8) or when we say, *God, please use me*, often we have in mind some great kingdom mission, some revelatory, life-changing word or some great evangelistic undertaking. We forget Jesus' words from today's text exhorting us, *Inasmuch as ye have done it unto one of the least of these my brethren, ye have done it unto me.*

The greatness to which we are called begins with who we determine to *be*, more than what we determine to *do*. Jesus reminds us in Matthew 5:13-14 that we *are* the salt of the earth and the light of the world. If we give attention to who we are first, all that we do will follow in kind.

I firmly believe there is no way to calculate the radiating effect of these random acts of kindness. I was personally so moved this morning that I came right home and set down this Bible Minute.

If even one of you applies this principle just one time today as a result, the effects will reverberate indefinitely — and all this will be credited to the account of the lady in the check-out line! And it will be credited to my account and to yours, if you join in. Now, that's a chain we don't want to break. Pass it on.

*** 

### *Confession:*
I set my intention this day to be increasingly aware of the impact of my actions, large and small, on those around me. I will be salt and light in all I do.

### *Go Deeper:*
Matthew 5:40
Isaiah 6:8
Matthew 5:13-14

### *Minute by Minute:*
Jesus exhorts His disciples to be the light of the world and the salt of the earth. This is something we are, not something we do. It addresses our character, who we are when no one is looking. Random acts of kindness follow as naturally as breathing when we are who God intends and equips us to be.

What is the impression you leave as you pass through? Do you know? Do those you regularly encounter expect kindness and consideration from you?

If you are serious about Jesus' exhortation, begin by writing a paragraph describing yourself as you believe others perceive you. Then consider sharing your observation with a trusted friend, family member or accountability partner to help you determine the accuracy of your self-perception.

If you are less than satisfied with what you learn, do not be discouraged. Renew your mind daily in the Word and ask the Holy Spirit to guide you minute by minute in each situation you encounter. As you make progress, repeat the exercise and again share it with your accountability partner until you feel confident you are well on the road to spreading joy, one encounter at a time.

## Questions, Questions, Questions    Week 38

*All Scripture is inspired by God and profitable for teaching, for reproof, for correction, and for training in righteousness; that the man of God may be adequate, equipped for every good work.*
2 Timothy 3:16, 17 NAS

Everything we need to know, not only to experience the New Birth but to live out our lives and callings, is waiting for us on the pages of the Bible. If we think we need more, it is a matter of the mind, not of the spirit, to satisfy curiosity or to build a case for or against prevailing deceptions.

We must continually guard against the lure of resources (both real and contrived) outside the Word of God for purposes other than historical or cultural background. Certainly any such sources are not anointed to prove anything to the lost. Faith does not come as a result of increased knowledge, but by hearing the Word of God (Romans 10:17).

It is the responsibility of the Holy Spirit to draw people to Himself. The Holy Spirit stands at the doorway to our hearts and knocks (Revelation 3:20). As believers, we are charged with interceding for the lost, helping to position them in a place and an attitude disposed to hear, supporting those within our sphere in changing their focus, and boldly proclaiming the Good News we know. But it is *not* our job to make anyone understand or believe.

We do not "get people saved" as I sometimes hear Christians say. However, by being trustworthy witnesses to the goodness of God and the truth of His Word, we can lead them to that place where the Holy Spirit can and will do His work. We need never justify anything to anyone. The Word is complete in itself.

Presenting the Gospel to our friends is part of "every good work." (See Colossians 1:10 NAS) We are never told to add anything to the Word of God. In fact Jesus Himself tells us not one jot or tittle, the smallest of Hebrew markings, will be changed. (Matthew 5:18)

## The Bible Minute

> *For the Word of God is living and active and*
> *sharper than any two-edged sword,*
> *and piercing as far as the division of soul and spirit,*
> *of both joints and marrow,*
> *and able to judge the thoughts and intentions of the heart.*
> *And there is no creature hidden from His (the Word's) sight,*
> *but all things are open and laid bare*
> *to the eyes of Him (the Word) with whom we have to do.*
> Hebrews 4:12, 13 NAS

Peter made it clear beyond a shadow of a doubt when he said we have *a more sure word of prophecy* than even the audible voice of God. He was referring to the Logos, the Word of God to which we have unlimited access. (See 2 Peter 1:19-21).

In our zealousness, our passionate love for God and for the lost, we sometimes think we need to help God do what only He can do. In fact, when we do more than what we are called to do, which is to live life as salt and light to the world (Matthew 5:13) and lead the lost and suffering to the perfect Word of God, we only confuse the situation.

***

*Confession:*
I have faith that God knows how to draw His children to Himself. After all, He drew me!

*Go Deeper:*
2 Timothy 3:16, 17
Romans 10:17
Revelation 3:20
Colossians 1:10
Matthew 5:18
Hebrews 4:12, 13
2 Peter 1:19-21
Matthew 5:13
Matthew 11:30

***Minute by Minute:***
Make a list of those for whom you have been praying and to whom you have been witnessing the Word. Now think about how often you have felt frustrated in each of these situations, not having seen them move any closer to that saving relationship you so desire for them?

Now, one by one, commit each of these people to God. Purpose to speak the Word, as you are led by the Holy Spirit, but keep your focus on how you present yourself. Do people seem to clear the area when you draw near? Are you light and salt or are you perhaps a *Scripture spewer*, peppering your every conversation with verse after verse? If this is true of you, unload your burden. (Matthew 11:30) It is not your job to save them. Just be attractive as light and salt are attractive and let the Holy Spirit do the rest.

# *Change*                    *Week 39*
## *Four Keys to Smooth Transitions*

> *For I am the Lord, I do not change;*
> *that is why you, O sons of Jacob, are not consumed.*
> Malachi 3:6 AMP

The only constant in change is that it is always with us. The changes I am observing lately seem to be increasing in intensity! Join me and learn 4 simple keys to handling what is arguably the most unsettling kind of change we experience.

Change, which we so cleverly avoid, has three faces, *alteration*, modification which is often imperceptible or limited, *swapping*, exchanging one distinct entity for another and *transformation*, movement from one distinct state or condition to another, often as a passage experience. Transformation is the most unnerving face of change and often throws us completely.

In Lewis Carroll's *Alice's Adventures in Wonderland*, Alice, in her curious experiences, becomes familiar with transformation. Her size changes alone are so pronounced they have their own designation, *transmogrification*, or gross transformation.

Raised in the Victorian era, ever the polite child, Alice misses her opportunities to take control of the topsy-turvy world of Wonderland. As her size moves back and forth between tiny and huge, surely we can imagine her bewilderment and anxiety at these unsettling and highly disruptive changes. What might Alice have done differently, or for that matter, any of us experiencing bewildering, unsettling experiences with transformation? Try these commonsense suggestions.

### *1. Stop and Take Stock*

Alice missed her opportunity for this and consequently seesawed from one alarming size to another. Once she chose to react in desperation, the possibility of mastering the unsettling circumstances of change flew out the window.

To avoid Alice's mistake, do what it takes to land on solid ground, however briefly. Stop the cycle of knee-jerk reaction and begin thinking in terms of *planned response*. Your final outcome will benefit from a brief rationality break. But how do you gain that moment of clear thought when you are in the throes of life altering circumstances?

If the transformation is *external*, such as a move, the loss of a home or job, a divorce or separation from a loved one, a change in your designation, try to step away briefly, temporarily removing yourself from the scene of the mayhem. It will still be there when you return, but you will be better able to deal with it.

If the change is *internal*, one you cannot walk away from, a physical transformation such as comes with age or maturing, or which might come with diagnosis of an abnormality or a perhaps a distinct change in your understanding which would affect your philosophy going forward, try to withdraw your *mind* from the circumstances. I do not suggest that this will be easy, but with practice and perseverance, it is possible.

## *2. Move Slowly*

Now that you have taken stock and you have moved some distance from *emotional reaction* and toward *mental response*, deliberate action is crucial. Did you ever try to walk on a moving train? It is very similar to the sensation of navigating transformation. Move slowly until you get the hang of it.

Do not be afraid to take time to consider each move carefully before executing it and then build on it, assessing the results before moving on. If the transformation you are facing is of a fast-paced or emergency nature, it does not disallow this action. Talk with any skilled first responder, a fire fighter, paramedic or police officer who has learned to operate effectively in just this manner. Countless lives and futures repeatedly hinge on their ability to function in just this way. Speed of response does not disqualify wisdom and careful consideration, but it does require practice.

Practice weighing options and making carefully considered decisions under normal conditions, before transforming change overtakes you. Train your brain exactly how you want it to perform under the challenging conditions of change.

### 3. Maintain A Spot Of Familiarity

However brief, *visits* to a spot that remains untouched by the transformation process will go a long way toward keeping you steady when the newness of the circumstances threatens to overwhelm you. Prayer and time in the Word create the most valuable spot of familiarity there is and neither requires a geographical location. Both are readily available in all situations. Remember that the secret place of the Most High God is ours at anytime. (Psalm 91:1)

If have the luxury of planning the transformation is planned, incorporate this step into the plan at the outset. It may not seem necessary to you when you are in the distant perspective of the blueprint stage, but you will be glad you made provision for a comfort station once your journey of transformation begins!

Do not skip this step. It may well be the difference between victory and failure in coming through transformation relatively unscathed.

> *He who dwells in the secret place of the Most High*
> *shall remain stable and fixed*
> *under the shadow of the Almighty*
> *[Whose power no foe can withstand].*
> Psalm 91:1 AMP

Finally,

### 4. Expect the Unexpected

When Alice decided to enter the mirror image world in Carroll's *Alice Through The Looking Glass*, she would have done well to apply this principle. As soon as she noted that things were getting *curiouser and curiouser*, it was a sure sign that the unexpected was to be expected!

In his 1886 classic, *The Strange Case of Dr. Jekyll and Mr. Hyde*, Robert Louis Stevenson's main character not only invites, but himself engineers the appearances of his malevolent alter ego, all in the name of science. However, he misses this all-important step when designing the truly grotesque transformation to his evil counterpart, Mr. Hyde. He mistakenly expects to retain control of the separation between the two sides of his nature, but of course he cannot and the results are horrific.

Alice loses her ability to discern dream state from reality and her reactions reflect this critical error. Both characters fail to expect the unexpected. But if you have made use of periods of normalcy as practice ground for *responding* rather than *reacting*; if you have formulated a Vision of how you will handle yourself in times of change and upheaval, if you are prepared to move deliberately, then you will have prepared yourself to shine in your own personal moments of passage.

You will maintain a clear-headed ability, discernment and control of yourself in the process, and may even find yourself standing at the helm and plotting the course for others as well as!

To summarize:

When you are planning transformative change, or as soon as you sense its approach, begin to look for a *spot of familiarity* or enduring normalcy. Begin *taking stock*, recording your observations to better enable you to process them as the transformation progresses. Make *no sudden moves*; consider your responses carefully. Then *expect to be surprised*, knowing that the unexpected can be around any corner and is definitely the order of the day.

*\*\*\**

*Confession:* In periods of transition and transformation, when I feel most pressured, I will remember that the Lord never changes and therefore I will not be consumed. (Malachi 3:6)

***Go Deeper:***
Malachi 3:6
Psalm 91:1

***Minute by Minute:***
None of us can avoid transforming change. It is a fact of life. So before transformational change appears on your horizon, practice the suggestions above, weighing your options and making carefully considered decisions. Train your brain by practicing the steps outlined.

Choose a transformation you are currently facing, considering or actively planning. Sit down with an accountability partner, and move through the steps above.

Identify your *spot of familiarity* and make provision for it, before you do anything else. *Take stock.* As much as you are certain you will remember all, you won't. Record everything. It will go a long way toward helping you maintain a true perspective. Make no radical or *sudden moves.* Your accountability partner will be invaluable in this. And then, plan for and *expect the unexpected.* Look at consequences you might not ordinarily and consider how you would handle them.

While no one is ever totally prepared for the transformations of life, it is possible to have your emergency kit at the ready.

# *Change*
## *Standing in the Storm*

*Week 39*

> *...and having done all [the crisis demands],*
> *to stand [firmly in your place].*
> *Stand therefore [hold your ground]*
> Ephesians 6:13b-14a AMP

It is an understatement to say that change is not well-tolerated by we human beings! And of the three faces of change, *alteration*, *swapping*, and *transformation*, the last is the most radical and decidedly the most challenging to weather.

The definition of transformation conveys the gritty truth that life, as we have known it, has changed and will never be the same again. A caterpillar, once transformed into a butterfly, will never squeeze back into the cocoon and emerge in its former state. An elemental change has occurred and the former reality no longer exists.

Transformation is often the straw that breaks the camel's back, catapulting us right over the edge of our endurance. But the good news is that there are some steps we can take and some characteristics we can cultivate that will find us still standing in the wake of the storm.

In planning transformative change, or as soon as you sense it is imminent, begin to look for a spot of familiarity or residual normalcy. Begin to take stock, recording your observations to help you manage them as the process unfolds. Make no sudden moves, considering your responses carefully, and finally, expect to be surprised, knowing that the unexpected can be around any corner and is surely the order of the day.

Here then are a few characteristics which can help you emerge victorious from transforming change. Cultivating these characteristics will increase your change hardiness. When all is said and done, you want to be standing when the dust clears. It has always been "change or be changed." So let us begin.

## Flexibility

One of the connotations of flexibility is elasticity. But better still and more valuable is suppleness. What a wonderful image.

A teammate on my son's high school wrestling team was the picture of suppleness. He was a risk taker whose positions were, more often than not, precarious. But he was so lithe, he would slither out of every hold, repeatedly, a pleasure to watch. This same characteristic is useful when change seems to have you pinned. The key is in accepting or rejecting appearance. Our wrestler never settled for what *appeared* to be his defeat.

The ability to completely relax, go loose in the face of the tidal wave of change, instead of tensing, will insure the suppleness to slither through the toughest elements of transformation. I am not advocating unnecessary risks, but a sense of adventure and fearlessness is helpful.

## Willingness

Are you motivated? Whether the transformation is your idea or is being imposed on you, willingness will lessen the discomfort of the process.

Be prepared to view the situation through other eyes, purposely taking on a new point of view. It may not alter your thinking about the change and its necessity, but it will adjust your perspective and that is healthy. You will develop valuable insight into the origin of the change you are dealing with and your future insights, pro and con, will be more valuable.

## Vision

Those who have worked with me, in my classes, workshops or in my private practice, know where I stand on Vision. It is stimulus and influence, the key to success in all areas of life.

> *Then the LORD answered me and said,*
> *Record the vision*
> *And inscribe it on tablets,*
> *That the one who reads it may run.*
> Habakkuk 2:2 NAS

The first step to everything, however, is knowing what you are doing here in the first place, your Mission. Once clear on that, Visions are what shape futures and are the evidence to the world of your life's Mission. Without Vision, you meander aimlessly though life, dissatisfied at every turn. And without Vision, change of any kind will plow you under.

With Vision comes clarity, the understanding of your role in a given situation and the ability to focus your efforts and energies on the area that is specifically yours. From clarity of Vision comes carefully designed Goals, which will bring the Vision to fruition.

When you are clear, focused and motivated, change is not so daunting. Strong clear Vision births passion and ideates Goals. What more could you ask in the midst of the changes we are so frequently faced with in life?

*Confidence*

True self-confidence, not cockiness or brashness, is a valuable commodity whatever the challenge. A true understanding of your core value, your worth, will see you through the most traumatic types of change. It begins with self-esteem, that rare commodity in a society obsessed with self-improvement. I am definitely not against reasonable self-improvement, not as an end in itself, but as a tool in furthering a Vision, a focus and a plan.

We are constantly beset by allegations that we cannot be worthy without whatever is currently for sale. Pick up any magazine and you are reminded on every page that your hair, clothes, skin, body shape, etc., do not measure up to some shifting standard set forth by those expects we call "they."

*And the disciples were amazed and bewildered and perplexed at His words. But Jesus said to them again, Children, how hard it is for those who trust (place their confidence, their sense of safety) in riches to enter the kingdom of God!*
Mark 10:24 AMP

Self-esteem cannot be applied from the outside and then migrate from the outside in, but must come from the life within. It is knowing you are intrinsically valuable, worthwhile, whether your home is upgraded, whether your wardrobe, body and hair are currently in style, whether you drink designer coffee or corner donut shop. It is certainty at your core that you have a Purpose, a relationship with your Creator, a job to do, your Mission, and you are the best one to do it.

Assurance arises from that, security in your mind, freedom from self-doubt, and that brings you to the point of confidence. Know that you have something to offer that only you can offer and the world is waiting for you.

## *Resiliency*

Resiliency might easily be confused with flexibility, but it has another dimension we need when facing radical transformation - durability, hardiness, the ability to come back strong, no matter what.

The perennial comes to mind. In my garden I have a number of annuals which grow quickly, bloom profusely and spread actively, providing that burst of instant garden we love. But they have no staying power, no durability. At the end of the hot summer, they are spent, ready to be yanked out of the garden. They are lovely while they last, but they are short-lived.

Ah, but the perennials, slower to grow, slower to bloom, often not profuse until several summers down the road, continue on year after year, putting down strong root systems and withstanding the toughest winters.

Showiness has its place, but the hardiness and ability to come back after the deep freeze and the driving snowstorm, now that's something to possess.

## *Sense of Adventure*

A true sense of adventure involves a willingness to step out of your comfort zone, taking calculated risks and experiencing a certain enjoyment at the prospect of exploring the unknown. Children possess this characteristic and know how to bring it to almost every game. Somewhere along the way from childhood to adulthood, it is misplaced. If you don't accept the risk, you will never successfully ride the change wave and may not even begin the process. Run it by your accountability partner, someone with a proven track record, someone you can trust.

### *Fearlessness*

> *And do not [for a moment] be frightened or intimidated in anything by your opponents and adversaries, for such [constancy and fearlessness] will be a clear sign (proof and seal) to them of [their impending] destruction, but [a sure token and evidence] of your deliverance and salvation, and that from God.*
> Philippians 1:28 AMP

If you haven't faltered yet, this may be the characteristic that gives you pause. But take a closer look and you will see fearlessness of itself is not cultivated. It is the *end result of cultivating the rest*. Flexibility, willingness, self-confidence, hardy resiliency and a childlike sense of adventure bundled together wear the tag of fearlessness. Fearlessness develops as the end result of courage, which is simply acting in the face of fear. Cultivate these characteristics. You are not born with them, so you have as good a chance as anyone to develop them.

In planning transformative change, or as soon as you sense it is imminent, remember to start looking for a spot of familiarity or of residual normalcy. Begin to take stock, recording your observations to help you manage them as the process unfolds. Make no sudden moves but consider your responses carefully, and finally, expect to be surprised, knowing that the unexpected can be around any corner and is surely the order of the day.

***

**Confession:**
I am ready to go forth into the raging wind of change, knowing that not only can I withstand the experience but I am well-equipped to add value in the process.

***Go Deeper:***
Ephesians 6:13b-14a
Habakkuk 2:2
Mark 10:24
Philippians 1:28

***Minute by Minute:***
    Change is unavoidable, so change hardiness must be cultivated. The list of traits above, though perhaps not all-encompassing, includes some of the characteristics that will foster your ability to withstand transformation.

    Working with a trusted friend, do a personal inventory in each of these areas to determine your change hardiness so you will be well prepared for changes that may be just over your horizon.

# The Changeless God — Week 40

*Every good thing bestowed and every perfect gift is from above,
coming down from the Father of lights,
with whom there is no variation or shifting shadow.*
James 1:17 NAS

Every good gift and every perfect gift is from above,
and cometh down from the Father of lights,
with whom is no variableness, neither shadow of turning.
James 1:17 KJV

How often in our reading of James have we glossed over this awesome promise? Have we stopped to ponder (*selah*) on the implications of this promise? I like the King James translation of shifting shadow, *shadow of turning*, because it paints a picture of the results of the changing of position. There are always outcomes and consequences of changing position and they are observable. We will never see a shifting shadow with God. His position is changeless!

In the Old Testament, we are promised, *For I am the Lord, I change not* (Malachi 3:6), and in Hebrews we are told that in His physical manifestation as Jesus Christ the Man, He *is the same yesterday and today and forever* (Hebrews 13:8). But what does this mean to us?

It means that we can commit everything to His promises in the word. In John 14:6, He tells us He is *the way, the truth and the life*. In Exodus 15:26, He says he is the Lord that heals. Then he steps into the earth and the entire New Testament relates how He upholds His word. In Deuteronomy 8:18, He tells us that He is the God that gives us the power to create wealth to spread His covenant; and on and on. Depending on who you ask, there are anywhere from 3,000 to 30,000 promises. That covers any subject of concern to us. Will we take Him at His word?

Which of His promises are you standing on right now? Do you need healing? Do you desire to walk in a greater manifestation of the power of the Holy Spirit? Do you have a heart to give into

His work in the world, but your checkbook is flat? Whatever you are believing, find the promise in His word. I assure you it is covered. Then hold that promise before Him and know that He has not changed. Step out on His word for your life today and, according to Isaiah 55:11, you can know with certainty that He will back you up with an unchangeable stance!

*\*\*\**

*Confession:*
I refresh myself this day in the sure and certain knowledge that you are the God of good and perfect gifts because, according to 1 John 4, You are love and it is the nature of love to give.

*Go Deeper:*
James 1:17
Malachi 3:6
Hebrews 13:8
John 14:6
Exodus 15:26
Deuteronomy 8:18
Isaiah 55:11
1 John 4:8, 16
1 Corinthians 13:4-8

*Minute by Minute:*
Study the referenced Scriptures, using several different Bible translations. Then determine how the knowledge you have gained might change the practicalities of your daily life, your confidence, your approach to difficult relationships, your response to disappointments, etc. Be specific, and if possible, share your thoughts with a close friend or a prayer/accountability partner.

# Lord, Lord...              Week 40

One morning during my customary quiet time, I heard the following in my spirit. I cannot remember if I was reading Isaiah 22 specifically at the time, but verse 11 of that chapter certainly confirms and personalizes what I heard in my spirit:

> *All the good plans are God's (of long ago).*
> *There's nothing new here;*
> *it was all God's plan long ago.*
> *Consider Him and depend on Him*
> *in executing all your plans.*

Do you ever feel stuck? You love the Lord and you desire to move forward in the plans He has for you, but it can be a bit like trying to run in chest deep water, slow going with heavy resistance. Here are a couple of suggestions that the Lord ministered to me. Perhaps they will help you to lift your feet off the bottom and allow the water to carry you.

Start by doing what you already know to do. (James 1:22) We all know a great deal more about the next steps than we realize. God has already communicated much to us on the subject.

***Take communion regularly***, whether with your congregation, in your own home as a family or alone with the Lord. Be reminded of the covenant promises He has made to you as you receive His body broken for that purpose and the cup of blessing. (Luke 22:19; 1 Corinthians 11:25)

***Feed yourself three times a day*** with three well rounded meals of the Word of God. Consider tithing your time for a season. Fill yourself with His promises concerning your situation, and stand on them rather than looking at your "stuck" circumstances.

***Practice intercession***. Get your mind off yourself and your circumstances and pray for those around you. Give yourself over to mediating on someone else's behalf. Pray for the salvation of a loved one or even for someone who has wronged you. (Matthew 5:44)

Or step out and pray fervently for someone you will likely never meet. Be led by the Spirit. As you back away from concentrating on yourself and your own situation, you give God room to work on your behalf, as well as setting wheels in motion for change in the lives of others. Pretty economical isn't it?

**Make prayer and fellowship with the Holy Spirit your priority.** We all know we are meant to pray. 1 Thessalonians 5:17 tells us to *pray without ceasing.* Sounds like a pretty tall order doesn't it? It probably seems if you do that you will never have time for anything else.

But I don't believe this scripture means we are to be on our face before the Lord 24 hours a day (although some drastic situations require drastic measures). I think it means more what evangelist Smith Wigglesworth was getting at when he said he never prayed longer than half an hour and he never went longer than half an hour without praying. He was talking about fellowship. He was alluding to the kind of fellowship you have with a friend of many years. You can spend a great deal of time with such a friend and never say a word, but remain in close company. As you walk along together, the companionable silence may be only occasionally broken with a comment, an observation or perhaps a remembrance.

That's fellowship. Fellowship is not conversation speckled with *thee's* and *thou's*, high and fancy verbiage, but closeness that is never broken; camaraderie that is continuous. Such intimacy often has a sort of spoken shorthand birthed by years of understanding, or sometimes, as in the case of twins, words that no one but the two of them understands.

**Commit all things.** (Psalm 37:5; 1 Peter 5:6, 7) Be faithful in this, committing *all* things. That means no moving out on your own. Maintain constant divine focus and divine connection. (Ephesians 1:18) If you had a friend who you understood to have all the answers you needed to get through your day, wouldn't you be on the phone to that friend many times in a day? Would you risk a move without a consultation? Well?

**Stand on scripture**, establishing your foundation on the Rock. (Luke 6:46-49) The Word, the logos of God, was made flesh and gave us the way, the example by which to walk out this life. Take the Word and apply it to your life.

**Love Him** in the way He has shown us to love Him. That's obedience according to John 14:16-31. According to Isaiah 1:19, *If ye be willing and obedient, ye shall eat the good of the land*: We have a tendency to skip the willing part, and grit our teeth at the excruciating obedience. That is not at all what God is trying to tell us. If we are willing, we will be obedient, and it won't hurt a bit. Obedience will be the fruit of love.

In Luke 6:46, Jesus says, *And why do your call Me, 'Lord, Lord,' and do not do what I say?* Why would we continue to call out to Him and not do as He says when He answers us? His answers to our cries are enclosed within the covers of our Bibles (the *Logos* Word), as well as in the still small voice of the prompting of the Holy Spirit (the *Rhema* Word). Let's begin by doing what we already know to do, and listen for further instruction. Lift your feet off the bottom and swim with the current!

\*\*\*

*Confession:*
The next time I feel stuck, I will go back to the simple steps, to what I already know to do and begin there.

**Go Deeper:**
Isaiah 22:11
James 1:22
Luke 22:19; 1 Corinthians 11:25
Matthew 5:44
1 Thessalonians 5:17
Psalm 37:5; 1 Peter 5:6, 7
Ephesians 1:18
Luke 6:46-49
John 14:16-31
Isaiah 1:19
Luke 6:46

***Minute by Minute:***
Consider following the plan outlined by the points above. It need not take place all at once. You surely did not become "stuck" all at once — it was a process. Patiently follow the process to release yourself. Begin by feeding yourself a healthy spiritual diet, spending daily time in the Word of God and in communication with Him. Begin with fifteen minutes in the morning and you will soon want more. When you are no longer fitting your time with God into your lifestyle, but building your lifestyle around it, you will no longer be able to remember what "stuck" felt like.

# The Lord is My Keeper                    Week 41

> *The LORD shall preserve you from all evil;*
> *He shall preserve your soul.*
> *The LORD shall preserve your going out and your coming in*
> *from this time forth, and even forevermore.*
> Psalm 121:7, 8 NKJV

We are all familiar with Psalm 23, many of us having committed it to memory. It is routinely brought out and dusted off for funerals. But a deeper reading will assure us it is anything but funereal. It is the song of the Shepherd.

Psalm 121, beloved by many as well, is another example of a song of the Shepherd. It is a song of *keeping*. In six different places in this psalm, the word *shamar* is used. It is translated as *keep*, but also as *protect*, and *guard*.

The psalmist begins establishing divine focus right away in verse one. This *song of ascents* was employed on mounting the steps to the Temple in Jerusalem, a pilgrimage during which focus must shift from the current circumstances to God as the central point of all. When we begin to focus on circumstances around us, we also begin to look to ourselves, and to other human beings to deal with what we see and feel.

But the psalmist has his focus set on the Lord, the Keeper, the Shepherd, knowing that He is the source of all true and lasting help. The Keeper is tireless in His provision for us His sheep. Not only does He keep us from the natural, but He preserves our souls, keeping us from eternal evil. The word *ra*, translated as *evil* in verse 7, indicates an evil that is imposed to keep one from being a benefit. The enemy is definitely not anxious for us to fulfill our God-given purpose (Jeremiah 29:11).

If you have made the Lord the center of your life, you are one of His sheep. Know that He is keeping your goings and comings from now until forever. Walk in that knowledge. Speak it when you leave your house in the morning; speak it when you put your head on the pillow at night. Make it your first word and your first thought each day and your last each night.

*We are His people and the sheep of His pasture* (Psalm 100:3). Shepherds lead and sheep follow. This day you can rest in the knowledge that you do not need to lead. All He expects of you is that you follow. *For the Lord is good; His lovingkindness is everlasting, and His faithfulness to all generations* (Psalm 100:5). That's for us, Hallelujah!

\*\*\*

*Confession:*
Lord, I thank you that you keep me night and day, because I am yours, not because I deserve it, but because I belong to you.

*Go Deeper:*
Psalm 121
Psalm 23
Jeremiah 29:1
Psalm 100

*Minute by Minute:*
As you purposely shift your focus from the natural to the divine, how will a revelation of being continually protected, guarded and kept, by the Creator of the universe, the ultimate Good Shepherd, change your confidence as you walk through life? Isolate specific examples of areas in your own life which will be impacted by this new understanding.

## Mingled Tears — Week 41

> *Jesus Wept.*
> John 11:35

Many sermons have been preached and many theories put forth about this shortest verse in the Bible, but what really interests me is that these words are even there. Tears sprang to Jesus' eyes even as they spring to ours. What a wondrously comforting thought!

We weep for many reasons, all of which are very much a part of the human condition. Whatever you believe is the reason, Jesus wept very human tears in this situation, and we can take heart that He is intimately and personally familiar with tears.

What deep comfort there is in knowing that our Savior, in His humanity, understood weeping, giving place to the importance of tears and even shedding them Himself on several occasions. Hebrews 5:7 tells us that *in the days of His flesh, He offered prayer with strong crying and tears unto Him that was able to save him from death.*

> *And God shall wipe away all tears from their eyes;*
> *and there shall be no more death,*
> *neither sorrow, nor crying,*
> *neither shall there be any more pain:*
> *for the former things are passed away.*
> Revelation 21:4 KJV

Revelation tells us that tears are not in our eternal future. But while this verse assures us that this time is coming, for the present tears are a part of being in the days of our flesh. Tears of gladness, tears of sorrow and tears of pain are part of living and if we are to give the fullest meaning to them, we must be prepared to share them.

Recently this word from the Holy Spirit came to my sister, a hospital chaplain who sees tears of all kinds on a daily basis. What the Holy Spirit spoke to her on a day when she had shared tears with others was a precious word for all of us.

*When you spend your day with other people's tears on your face, you know you have done something precious for the Lord.*
By the Holy Spirit

It is not enough to simply witness the tears of others, or even to acknowledge them, but God honors our mingled tears, our cheeks wet with the tears of others, our shoulders damp with weeping. How dear are the tears that are shared. When we offer our own cheeks to wear the tears of others, we are truly demonstrating the heart of the Savior toward those who sorrow.

It is often our instinct to run from sorrow, to turn the other way at tears, not quite knowing what to say to staunch their flow. But it is not always necessary that we do. Until we stand before our heavenly Father with His own gracious hand wiping every tear from our eyes, sometimes we can be the strongest witness of God's love to those we meet by simply sharing their tears and wearing them on our own cheeks.

*Weeping may endure for a night, but joy comes in the morning*
Psalm 30:5 NKJV

*They that sow in tears shall reap in joy. He that goeth forth and weepeth, bearing precious seed, shall doubtless come again with rejoicing, bringing his sheaves with him.*
Psalm 126:5-6 KJV

**Confession:**
Until I am in the presence of eternal joy, I will seek out those who weep alone, sharing my cheek, and the precious powerful seed of the Word, in their sorrow.

**Go Deeper:**
John 11:35
Hebrews 5:7
Psalm 30:5

## The Bible Minute

Psalm 126:5-6
Using your concordance, make your own study of tears and weeping in your Bible.

**Minute by Minute:**

> *I know there are brook-gladdened meadows ahead,*
> *And mountains of wearisome height;*
> *That the road passes on through the long afternoon*
> *And stretches away to the night,*
> *And still I rejoice when the travelers rejoice*
> *And weep with the strangers that moan,*
> *Nor live in my house by the side of the road*
> *Like a man who dwells alone.*
> From *The House by the Side of the Road* by Sam Walter Foss

When was the last time you simply shared tears with another? Are you one who shies away from this most human emotional display? If so, ask the Holy Spirit to strengthen you not only to lend your shoulder but to share your tears with others. Often the greatest comfort is the companionship of mingled tears.

# *Mirror, Mirror*                                     **Week 42**

> *For He hath made Him to be sin for us,*
> *Who knew no sin; that we might be made*
> *the righteousness of God in Him.*
> 2 Corinthians 5:21 KJV

What do you see when you look in the mirror? If you are anything like me, at some point in your walk of faith, perhaps right now, you have had difficulty seeing yourself the way this Scripture describes you. *I'm anything but righteous,* you say, *and what's more, I have no hope of measuring up to God's standard of righteousness! I see a person who has failed repeatedly and I don't see how a sinless God can accept me the way I am!* The world defines righteousness as *being* free from guilt or sin, having a nature recognizable by perfection. Which of us can begin to live up to that?

We know that Righteousness means being in right standing with God, like being *teacher's* pet, perennially within God's good graces, sinless in His sight. We may be able to accept this explanation, but are we able to receive it as our own? Are we personally worthy?

In Christian coaching and biblical counseling, I deal with this subject with alarming frequency. A majority of the issues that surface in the Christians I work with lead back to a lack of understanding of what it really means to be the Righteousness of God in Christ. We confess it but we often have absolutely no idea how to live it.

Righteousness is God's standard and it is nothing less than absolute perfection, flawless judgment according to Him Who established the measure. Righteousness must address perfection because it issues forth from Perfection.

The Law, given by God as the standard of measure, while absolutely impossible for man to satisfy, acted as the open door to divine mercy and the Gift of Jesus Christ. It is in acknowledging our inability to meet the standard that we make the way for the Savior. By entering into the deep and unbreakable Blood Covenant with Him, our sin natures are exchanged for His perfection. This is the great mystery revealed! In our covenant relationship with God who is Perfection, we enter into that very perfection. Covered, clothed in the Blood, we *become* acceptable, righteous.

In the parable of the wedding feast in Matthew 22, we see the king looking over the last minute guests his servants have recruited from the streets after the invited guests declined. He approaches one guest questioning, *Friend, how did you come in here without wedding clothes?* The guest, who has dropped everything to attend the feast, is without explanation, and so he is bound *hand and foot and cast into the outer darkness* into a place where there is *weeping and gnashing of teeth.* (Matthew 22:12-13 KJV)

As unfair as this may seem to the modern reader, Jesus' contemporaries would have understood that the appropriate wedding clothing was provided at the time of the invitation. This guest *chose* to come before the king in his street clothes, assuming they would be good enough, and consequently fell far short of the requirement, dishonoring the king in the process. This parable was meant to make it clear that our wedding clothes, the clothes of Righteousness, have been provided for us, but only if we are willing to accept the exchange made for us at the Cross.

It should be no surprise that this is an area on which the enemy concentrates heavily. Guilt, shame, condemnation and the resulting sin cycle run rampant in the lives of millions of people, chiefly because they have never realized who they are in Christ.

Don't waste another minute questioning your worthiness. Cast off your own utterly worthless attempts at righteousness. Accept the wedding finery the Savior has provided and enter into joy unspeakable. (1 Peter 1:8)

\*\*\*

## *Confession:*

I will don my wedding clothes and walk boldly into the presence of the King (Hebrews 4:16), knowing that I am accepted as family through my relationship to the Firstborn of many brethren. (Romans 8:29).

***Go Deeper:***
2 Corinthians 5:21
Matthew 22:12-13
1 Peter 1:8
Hebrews 4:16
Romans 8:29

***Minute by Minute:***
Look up every instance of *in Him, in Whom, in Christ, by Him,* and *through Him,* in the New Testament, particularly in the Epistles (Romans through Jude) and you will see the amazing picture God paints of who you really are when you enter into that deep and abiding relationship with Him through Jesus Christ.

Now, using your journal or prayer notebook, list the ways in which this knowledge of how God sees you could change, not only the way you see yourself, but your perception of others as well. In what ways will this new understanding change your daily life and relationships?

## Divine Focus                                    Week 42

> *And he said, Listen, all Judah,*
> *and you people of Jerusalem, and King Jehoshaphat!*
> *So says Jehovah to you,*
> *'Do not be afraid nor dismayed because of this great multitude.*
> *For the battle is not yours, but God's.'*
> 2 Chronicles 20:15

What others do to you is simply not your concern — *none of your business!*

That is a pretty strong statement to make in a world where all we have to do is get into our cars and drive to the store to see how many people actually appear to be out to get us. If we are sons and daughters of God, it is not what others do to us but rather our own response that must concern us. What others do or do not do to us is dealt with in their *own* relationship with God. Our response is dealt with in *our* relationship with God.

*Divine focus*, our eyes on the Father and not on the circumstances, breaks the bonds of fear, offense, resentment, anger, envy, and jealousy, ultimately anxiety and eventually discouragement and depression as well. If we are to be truly free of suffering at the hands of others, we must focus first, last and always on the Father, through the Word, prayer and fellowship. In committing to divine focus, we are giving our vision over to God, causing us to see everything through His perfect eyes, the eyes of Love, not our own flawed, warped, hypersensitive, self-centered vision.

Some years ago, at a particularly stressful time in my life, the Holy Spirit arrested me one day with an exhortation. He spoke to me firmly but tenderly, as one might to a child and said, *just keep your eyes on Me*. At the time, I was quite surprised, thinking that I was being asked to surrender my responsibility of "tending to business." After all, isn't it conscientious to carry the concerns of our lives, to tend to the people and problems that present themselves? I was sure I was *including* God in my situation. Yet day after day, for weeks, I heard the same words, *just keep your eyes on Me*.

In Psalm 34:3, David appeals to us to magnify the LORD with him. What exactly is he asking us to do? Surely he is not expecting us to make the Lord any bigger. What then, does it mean to magnify the Lord? Very simply, it means to fill your field of vision with Him and nothing else. A drop of water under a microscope does not change in size, but the microscope enables our eye to view the drop in detail, shutting out all else.

Several months later, after many promptings, it had become my habit to look to Him in all things. Why? Because He told me to. When I realized I was not going to be given further explanation, I set about obeying. So when the Holy Spirit asked one day if I wanted to know why, I was surprised. I found that I didn't feel I needed to know why, but clearly it was now important that I be told.

He showed me that I was not meant to become irresponsible, going through life inattentive to the circumstances of my life or lacking in diligence. But when I observe the world around me, whether it be people or circumstances, through my own eyes, my perspective is warped, rather like looking through the bottom of a thick old-fashioned bottle. But when I look to Him first, I will see the scene reflected in His perfect eyes, the eyes of love. (1 Corinthians 13:4-8.)

Fill your field of vision with Him, consciously putting His Word first, placing His Name above all else, above all other needs and desires, above the wishes and weaknesses of the flesh, above the attacks of the world or the enemy. (Philippians 2:9, 10)

Let God be God and He will clarify for you what He will do *for* you and what is your part to do. Fellowship constantly with Him, not only in petitioning, which we are commanded to do in Philippians 4:6, but in listening. Take time to be still and really *know* Him (Psalm 46:10). Asking the Father for your part in His plan, how you might serve Him each day, will be the natural result. Delight yourself in Him only, bending your will to His in all things (Psalm 37:4, 5). Then rest in the knowledge that He is God and you are not!

\*\*\*

*Confession:*
My responsibility is to maintain divine focus and walk in love, according to 1 Corinthians 13:4-8. What others do to me is not my business; how I respond is my only concern.

*Go Deeper:*
2 Chronicles 20:15
Psalm 34:3
1 Corinthians 13:4-8
Philippians 2:9, 10
Psalm 46:10
Psalm 37:4, 5

*Minute by Minute:*
We have learned that divine focus is the practice of magnifying our heavenly Father above all else, exchanging our warped vision for His perfect perspective. What can you do daily to further magnify the Lord? How can you more effectively fill your field of vision with Him and bring your world into healthy focus? The keys are in *Word*, *Prayer* and *Fellowship*.

*Word*
Begin by consciously putting His Word first. Make a quality decision to begin each day in the Word. Whether it is 15 minutes or 2 hours, take the step and set that time aside. If it means going to bed earlier to get up earlier, you will receive benefits far beyond your investment

*Prayer*
If you have allowed your prayer time to slip, there is no time like the present to begin again. Prayer is portable! Any time is the perfect time for prayer. Keep in mind that prayer is a conversation and a conversation is two-sided. Allow as much time for quiet attentiveness as you do for talking and petitioning. Your Father has much to tell you!

*Fellowship*

Aside from the serious interchange of prayer, have you ever simply enjoyed the presence of our heavenly Father, basking in the knowledge of His love? The Bible tells us that in His presence is fullness of joy, where He promises us pleasures forever. (Psalm 16:11) Jesus made it a practice to regularly go off alone and spend intimate time with the Father. Share your heart with Him as you would with any intimate friend and He will share His heart with you.

## *For I Will Contend*                    *Week 43*

*And Moses said to the people, 'Do not fear, stand by, and see the salvation of the LORD, which He will accomplish for you today: for the Egyptians whom you have seen today, you will never see them again forever. The LORD will fight for you, while you keep silent.'*
Exodus 14:13-14 NAS

*For I will contend with the one who contends with you, and I will save your sons. And I will feed your oppressors with their own flesh, and they will become drunk with their own blood as with sweet wine; and all flesh will know that I, the Lord, am your Savior, and your Redeemer, the Mighty One of Jacob.*
Isaiah 49:25-26 NAS

*And he said, Hearken ye, all Judah, and ye inhabitants of Jerusalem, and thou king Jehoshaphat, Thus saith the LORD unto you, Be not afraid nor dismayed by reason of this great multitude; for the battle is not yours, but God's.*
*Ye shall not need to fight in this battle: set yourselves, stand ye still, and see the salvation of the LORD with you, O Judah and Jerusalem: fear not, nor be dismayed; tomorrow go out against them: for the LORD will be with you.*
2 Chronicles 20:15, 17 KJV

Read these verses over several times and let them sink down deep inside your heart. They make an overwhelmingly powerful statement. Take the time to study each passage in depth and see what God is saying to your personally.

    Focus first on God's promises made to the Israelites in Exodus 14. There are a number of powerful promises packed into these two short verses, which we are liable to overlook, if we neglect to examine them closely.

## *Do not fear*

This oft-repeated admonition throughout the Old and New Testaments never comes as a suggestion; always as a directive. As we are so frequently charged with conquering fear, this must be a key element to receiving what it is God has for us.

What is it about fear that God so consistently warns us? There are those who would tell us that fear is healthy, that it keeps us from standing dumbly unaware as danger overtakes us. It stimulates flight. It also provokes rash actions and reactions, impeding clear thought and strategy. It alters our focus. Fear rarely causes wise action — fear only knows to run or freeze, paralyzed.

## *Stand by*

God would have us stand. Standing does not describe the kind of paralysis that fright can bring on. The term *stand by* actually means to take your stand, and then not waiver. James tells us in chapter 1, verses 6 and 7, that wavering and shifting is double-minded, doubting, and that nothing can be received from God in such a changing position.

This should be no surprise to us. I cannot give you a gift if you refuse to stand still and let me put it into your hands. What are you believing God for? Have you taken a stand on His Word, His promises, and purposed not to move from it?

## *See the salvation of the Lord — today*

Salvation is always for today. The freedom that God has for us (see Luke 4:18, 19) is never for another time; it has *already* been proclaimed; so it is for today. The word for salvation in this passage is *Jeshua*, the Hebrew for Jesus. He is the fulfillment of this promise in our lives for each of our todays. Confess this promise over your circumstances each day, *I will see the salvation, the deliverance of the Lord this day.*

## *You will never see them again forever*

This does not promise there will never be other enemies, other Egyptians, or other circumstances, but it does promise that the enemy of the day is defeated, *never* to resurface. The only way the Israelites could have been harassed by the Egyptians ever again would have been if they continued to relive the fear, continuing to resurrect it. Let the defeated enemy die!

### *Keep silent*
How good are we at keeping silent and allowing God to be God in our lives, allowing Him to fight for us. How often are we all about telling God how to do what He has promised? How often are we clogging communication with our continual begging? The Lord said to me one day *Stop flooding heaven with your words and start flooding the earth with Mine.* Confess His words into the situation and then be silent — there is nothing more that needs to be said.

Take heart, in whatever you are facing this day. God is neither surprised nor bewildered by it. He knew from before time and prepared a way out for you in advance. Take your stand on His word concerning your circumstance, witness the salvation, the deliverance of God, made manifest in Jesus Christ!

\*\*\*

### *Confession:*
I will keep silent except to speak His promises and I will let God be God in my situation. I confess that His defeat of my enemies has been complete and I will never see these enemies again! (Nahum 1:9)

### *Go Deeper:*
Exodus 14:13-14
Isaiah 49:25, 26
2 Chronicles 20:15, 17
Luke 4:18, 19
Nahum 1:9
Hebrews 4:12

### *Minute by Minute:*
Take the time to study each passage in depth and see what God is saying to you personally. All three of our Scriptures have essentially

the same message, which is no surprise because our God never changes and His Word is ever fresh and alive. (See Hebrews 4:12.)

Each of the commands that Moses passed along from God in Exodus 14 was critical to the Israelites experiencing the full deliverance God had for them.

Are you looking to the Lord for deliverance in some area today? The exhortations of Moses in Exodus 14:13-14 are just as real and pertinent as they were when God used him to speak them. Follow the steps outlined above to know your own deliverance. Work with a trusted friend who will encourage you in the Word and pray with you, holding you accountable to your decision to set yourself, stand still, and see His salvation on your behalf. (2 Chronicles 20:17)

## *Death of the Devil*                        *Week 43*

> *And the devil that deceived them was cast into the lake of fire and brimstone, where the beast and the false prophet are, and shall be tormented day and night for ever and ever.*
> Revelation 20:10 KJV

Why does God allow the enemy to continue? Why doesn't He just destroy the devil? Be honest now, how many times has that thought crossed your mind? If He is truly a loving God, and we are His beloved children, why doesn't He just make it easy on us and destroy the devil once and for all?

The reason God does not step in and dole out total destruction to the devil is a simple one — He already has! He has already totally stripped the enemy of his power, once and for all. Satan is right now nothing but a naked and vanquished foe. (Colossians 2:15) The devil is merely a shadow, clinging desperately to the brief time he has remaining before being cast into the lake of fire. (Revelation 20:10) But, if you do not have this valuable knowledge, you are left open to his deception. Make no mistake, he can and will, if given the opportunity, still cause you damage, vanquished foe or not.

Think of a thief breaking into your home. You might say, *but why don't the authorities pass a law against breaking and entering*, as though this alone would be enough to insure your safety. If you are unaware that breaking and entering is already covered under the law, you will simply submit to this lawless act. You will be rendered helpless and seemingly without resource in your hour of need. You will be forced to listen to and acquiesce to the lies of a criminal.

On the other hand, if you know the truth (John 8:32), you will inevitably take action on it (James 1:22). You will defend your home and family with whatever is at hand, knowing that you have the right, by law. You will call the authorities, in the certain knowledge that they are obliged to respond.

The next time the devil tries to muscle his way into your home, your family, your health, your dreams, or your finances, be sure you have knowledge of your rights. You can be certain Satan does. Then be a doer of what the Word tells you (James 2:14), and exercise your God-given authority over him. Do not buy his lies or let him convince you he has any rights in your life because of something you said or did (or didn't say or do), or whatever deception he is employing that day.

Call on the Name above all Names (Philippians 2:9, 10), and when the devil tries to remind you of your past in order to gain entrance into your present, you just remind him of his future!

Hallelujah! What are you waiting for? The work is done; the enemy is cast down! Don't wait another minute. Hasn't he stolen enough from you? Know your rights and exercise them boldly today.

*\*\**

### *Confession:*
The devil is a defeated foe, whose only weapon is lies. I will know the Word, know my rights and boldly act on them in the face of his every deception.

### *Go Deeper:*
Revelation 20:10
Colossians 2:15
John 8:32
James 1:22
James 2:14
Philippians 2:9, 10
Ephesians 6:13-14
Genesis 3:1
John 8:44

### *Minute by Minute:*
Do you know your rights? Or are you at the mercy of the enemy and his fabrications? Worse yet perhaps, do you know just enough of the Word of God that the devil can twist it as he did with Eve in the Garden in Genesis 3:1? Once Satan had planted doubt in Eve's

mind where confidence should have been, she became muddled in her attempts to explain God's instructions. The rest is history.

Are there situations in your life right now in which you are uncertain of God's will? Was it God who brought sickness on you or a family member? Is it His will for you to be healed? Are you experiencing financial challenges so God can teach you something? If you have not taken the time to search His Word, you will have no way of knowing when the enemy comes to you with his lies. (John 8:44)

Start by listing your areas of concern and then find the Scriptures in the Word of God that express God's will for you in each area. Now make a quality decision, by an act of your will, to shut out the lies of the devil and the confusion of the world by being a doer of the Word. (James 1:22) Stand firmly on Scripture, regardless of appearances. (Ephesians 6:13-14)

## *Practicing Christianity*  *Week 44*

> *Come unto me, all ye that labour*
> *and are heavy laden,*
> *and I will give you rest.*
> Matthew 11:28 KJV

Are you a devout, practicing Christian? Perhaps you are not really sure what that means and you need a little time to think it through. In the meantime there is one thing you can know with absolute certainty. Every one of us is called to make a difference!

If your answer to the question is a resounding "yes," then read on. If you agreed without hesitation, then I suspect you are also experiencing more exhaustion, and perhaps even frustration, than the rest Jesus promises in our foundation Scripture.

If you are experiencing fatigue and occasionally feel as though it is too much to keep the whole thing together any longer, then I submit to you that you may be *practicing Christianity*, much like an attorney practices law. He puts into daily practical application everything he has spent years learning. Does that sound familiar?

> *For my yoke is easy,*
> *and my burden is light.*
> Matthew 11:30 KJV

Stop struggling to *perform* and instead begin to *yield* to the resources already within you. Yes, it is absolutely true! When you made Jesus the Lord of your life, at that very moment, you were equipped with all that you need to do all that He asks of you.

As soon as you gave your heart to Him, He went to work filling your re-born Spirit with all the attributes necessary to live a victorious life. He planted His own supernatural nature in you in the form of the Fruit of the Spirit.

*But the fruit of the Spirit is love, joy, peace,
patience, kindness, goodness, faithfulness,
gentleness and self-control.
Against such things there is no law.*
Galatians 5:22 NIV

Do your own study of each of these attributes, following each throughout Scripture, particularly the New Testament and see the tremendous resource you have within you. Instead of *practicing* Christianity, keeping tabs on yourself, your behavior and your progress, and fighting discouragement at every turn, yield to the supernatural qualities in you, much as you would when settling into a large, comfortable easy chair.

You have already been given all that you need to carry out the superhuman call the Lord has placed on His body here in the earth. He never meant you to do it in your own power — give that up; it simply cannot be done. Just get your natural self out of the way and relax into His power to perform!

\*\*\*

### *Confession:*
I will yield to the very nature of God residing in my human spirit, knowing that only then will the world look at me and truly see Jesus.

### *Go Deeper:*
Matthew 11:28, 30
Galatians 5:22
Mark 16:15-18
Zechariah 4:6

### *Minute by Minute:*
In your enthusiasm to be the disciple Jesus commissioned in Mark 16:15-18, have you perhaps lost sight of the difference between performing and yielding? If you are tired, overwhelmed and frustrated, chances are that there is some confusion.

*The Bible Minute*

In getting on track for the long run, it is essential that you understand what it means to you to have been equipped with all that you need to do all that He asks of you?

Do an in-depth study of each of the characteristics known as the Fruit of the Spirit, following each throughout Scripture, particularly the New Testament, in order to gain an understanding of the power available to you from within. As you do, consciously begin yielding to these supernatural qualities in your reborn spirit, much as you would to the ease and comfort of your favorite chair.

Remember that you have been provided all that you need to carry out your part in God's plan. Refresh yourself in the Word.

*Not by might nor by power, but by my Spirit,*
*says the LORD Almighty.*
Zechariah 4:6 NIV

# Winning Combination  Week 44

*For our gospel did not come to you in word only,
but also in power and in the Holy Spirit and with full conviction;
just as you know what kind of men we proved
to be among you for your sake.
You also became imitators of us and of the Lord,
having received the word in much tribulation
with the joy of the Holy Spirit.*
1Thessalonians 1:5, 6 NAS

If you are anything like me, you sometimes feel completely inadequate in the face of the Great Commission as recorded in Mark 16. But the encouraging news is that we were never intended to undertake the tall order of spreading the Gospel under our own power. So why do we continue to try?

In this Scripture, Paul gives us a concise picture of the manner in which the Gospel is effectively spread. He gives us three elements. While it is possible to deliver the Good News without all three in place, the burden becomes heavy, the labor is ours alone, and we neglect to recognize with Whom we are yoked.

*Come to Me, all who are weary and heavy-laden,
and I will give you rest.
Take My yoke upon you and learn from Me,
for I am gentle and humble in heart;
and you shall find rest for your souls.
For My yoke is easy and My load is light.*
Matthew 11:28-30 NAS

Paul is responsible for setting down two-thirds of the New Testament and for effectively spreading Christianity beyond the confines of Palestine in his three epic missionary trips. It is Paul who was called to reach us, the gentiles (John 17:20-21). And it is Paul who effectively took an assortment of people and formed them into the Church. Paul is the consummate expert on spreading the Gospel and his credentials are impeccable. Let us examine the elements as he reveals them to us.

He begins in verse 5 by identifying the Gospel as good news (the Amplified Bible calls it glad tidings), using the Greek word *euaggelion*. The original meaning is a *reward* for good news. According to the Greek definition, good news brings reward for the bearer as well as the recipient. It is not good enough to hear alone, you must hear and receive. The reward follows the hearing *and* receiving. Only then will what you hear lead to action.

> *But prove yourselves doers of the word,*
> *and not merely hearers who delude themselves.*
> James 1:22 NAS

Hearing does not take a great deal of effort but receiving necessarily requires faith, and faith always steps out (James 2:14-26). How then can we effectively present these glad tidings in such a way that both the bearer and the recipient experience full reward? Paul goes on to identify the three elements necessary for the Gospel to be fulfilled in the lives of both.

### *The Word (Logos)*

This is the same word John uses when he tells us *in the beginning was the Word and the Word was with God and the Word was God.* (John 1:1) The Greek indicates first the intelligence and then the expression of that intelligence.

For our purposes, it is the mind of God expressed in written form, as well as in Jesus, both the preincarnate Christ (John 1:1), and the incarnate man, Jesus Christ. (John 1:14) In 1 Thessalonians, Paul is referring to the written and spoken word of God as a tool of the Good News. We are people of language, and whatever other means we use to express ourselves, language is the primary one. It is no mistake that Paul gives the Word first place.

### *Power (Dunamis)*

*Dunamis* is a wonderful word, and like so many in the Greek, it is difficult to express with one English word. Power is an accurate translation, but it does not tell the whole story. If we think about what we know of dynamite, we will better understand. Dynamite may bring to mind explosion, but that's only one element of the character of dynamite.

The actual explosion isn't even necessary to an understanding of dynamite. Dynamite can exist indefinitely without ever exploding, and it is still dynamite, losing nothing of its essential nature. The true character of dynamite is expressed in its *inherent power*, constantly available ability, its capability. The explosion is not built in (that's simply a onetime display of the *result* of the power). It is the *ability* that is built into its character. On hand power, in constant readiness — that's dunamis.

### Holy Spirit (Pneuma)

The literal translation for pneuma is breath, but the implication is of the wind, unseen and powerful, the breath of God. It is the breath of God that brought Adam to life, a living being, a speaking spirit (Genesis 2:7). It is the breath of God breathed into a young Hebrew maiden that brought Jesus into the world as Emmanuel, God with us (Luke 1:35). And it is the breath of God that brings new life to our sin-deadened spirits (John 3:5) when we accept Jesus as our personal Savior.

Finally, each of the three is accompanied with *plerophoria*. It is translated in the New American Standard as full conviction, but the word implies even more. It is confirmation, fullness, completion, and the final steps to perfect certitude. During Jesus' earthly ministry, He performed many miracles, the translation of which is actually *attesting miracles*. The purpose of these signs and wonders was to confirm the word, to insure perfect certitude! They were meant to lead people back to the Word, to the promises, and to *attest* to them.

Paul then adds a critical ingredient we all too often leave out. He says *you know what kind of men we proved [ourselves] to be among you for your good*. (1 Thessalonians 1:5 AMP) What kind of men and women do we prove ourselves to be among those we witness to? Do we give them the Word but prove to be something less than godly in character? Just as it was Paul's character which drew the

Thessalonians, it is our own characters that will draw people to the Word, the power and the Spirit.

The result of the Word, in power and the Holy Spirit, and Paul's character, was that the Thessalonians became imitators of who they saw — Paul. In so doing, they became imitators of Who they did not see, the Lord Jesus Christ. Isn't that our goal as well? We are here for one reason only, to draw people to the person of Jesus Christ.

We have been given the necessary tools to accomplish that with which we have been charged, the spread of the Gospel. We have the Word and we have the power of the Holy Spirit, in revelation and in attesting miracles (see John 14:12). Let's tend diligently to our characters, making sure we prove ourselves godly witnesses before we open our mouths, and then let's get on with the work at hand. There's a troubled world out there and we have what they are looking for!

\*\*\*

## *Confession:*

I will step out in confidence that I have been equipped with what I need to do what He asks of me, the Word, the power and the Holy Spirit. I will attend to that key ingredient, my own character, that I may truly and honestly reflect Him Who has sent me.

## *Go Deeper:*
1Thessalonians 1:5-6
Mark 16:15-18
Matthew 11:28-30
John 17:20-21
James 1:22
James 2:14-26
John 1:1, 14
Genesis 2:7
Luke 1:35
John 3:5
1 Thessalonians 1:5 AMP

John 14:7-9, 12
1 Corinthians 13:4-8
Matthew 5-7

***Minute by Minute:***
As was Paul, we are equipped with *Logos*, the mind of God in written form and in the Man Jesus, *dunamis*, on-hand power in constant readiness, and *pneuma*, the breath of God. Each is essential to the spread of the Gospel, today as in Paul's day. Set in place by God Himself, each will operate as He directs.

The personal component, the one that has the potential to draw people or push them away, is *character*, our character, not the character of God, which is represented in Jesus Christ. (See John 14:7-9) As was true of Paul, people will be drawn by our authenticity or deflected by our duplicity. Which do you convey?

## *Praise Sets the Stage*                             Week 45

*And at midnight Paul and Silas prayed,*
*and sang praises unto God: and the prisoners heard them.*
Acts 16:22-25

*Behold, God is my salvation; I will trust, and not be afraid:*
*for the LORD JEHOVAH is my strength and my song;*
*He also is become my salvation.*
Isaiah 12:2

Praise sets the stage for a move of God. Praise brings about the loosening of bonds; opens doors, and shakes off fetters. Praise ushers in freedom in the circumstances. Praise, a sacrifice of praise, is the sacrifice He desires of us today. (Hosea 6:6) And He Himself will enable us to offer it.

Paul and Silas had been beaten with rods and then thrown into this dank, dark, sewage and rodent infested Roman prison, into what probably amounted to solitary confinement, *the inner prison* (verse 24). It is in the midst of these unthinkable conditions that we see Paul and Silas bursting into prayer and songs of praise at the midnight hour!

They didn't wait until they were free. Instead, they praised Him unashamedly and loudly (v25), in the midst of the circumstances. The result was what might have seemed like a localized earthquake, affecting only the prison, loosening the fetters, and opening the doors, impacting everyone near these two prisoners.

They were not removed from the situation; they were set free *in* it. In the natural they had the ability to flee, but unlike Peter in Acts 12, they were not instructed to leave. The result of this incredible act of obedience was the salvation of the jailer and his entire household. (Note that this was more than his entire family, but included any servants and slaves as well). It is difficult to assess the far reaching implications of Paul's actions that night.

Their legal release came later (v.35) but they acknowledged and received their freedom while still *in* the circumstances. Take care not to confuse *release* with *freedom*. The release was a natural, physical phenomenon, but true freedom was within Paul and Silas. Freedom begins in the inner man, and cannot help but eventually impact the physical circumstances.

Do you have a midnight hour in your life right now; a place in which you are confined and even bound hand and foot? God will turn your situation around as surely as He did Paul's and, what's more, God Himself *is* our song. I do not believe for a minute that Paul and Silas were able to sing praises in their own strength. They were undoubtedly miserable, but they were obedient and lent their souls and their mouths to prayer and praise, and the Lord filled them. Freedom from the circumstances followed.

Anyone can be freed from the circumstances and then praise God as a result, but to be free in the circumstances is real freedom, true freedom, and only those for whom He has become their Song can know that salvation.

Isaiah 11:10 says, *And His rest shall be glorious*. The New American Standard says, *and His resting-place shall be glorious*. That place of His glorious rest can be right in the midst of the circumstances! It was for Paul and Silas, and it can be for you. Now that is good news!

*** 

### Confession:
I set my intention this day to praise the Lord, regardless of the appearance of my circumstances, knowing that, according to John 8:36, if the Lord has made me free, I am free indeed. I will no longer allow the facts of circumstance to rob me of the truth of inner freedom.

### Go Deeper:
Acts 16:22-25
Isaiah 12:2
Hosea 6:6
Acts 12
Isaiah 11:10

Consider a study of the range of emotions expressed in the book of Psalms. The Hebrew word for Psalms is *tehillim*, meaning praises. But the book encompasses a great deal more than what we generally associate with praise. Every human emotion is expressed within this section of the Old Testament. David, most prolific and best known of the authors of the psalms, did not pen them only in his moments of triumph and joy. He was often distressed and mournful, angry and repentant, as well as joyful and victorious. But each of the psalms eventually turns to praising God *in the circumstances*.

### *Minute by Minute:*

*Freedom begins in the inner man, and cannot help but eventually impact the physical circumstances.*

What circumstances are you even now allowing to create a prison for you? Is it a difficult relationship, financial concerns, sickness and disease? Or is your prison an emotional or even a spiritual one? Are you perhaps, like Paul and Silas, literally imprisoned and prison has bound your soul as well? Take careful stock and record each area which is keeping you bound hand and foot, keeping your soul locked away in darkness.

Now, take a step of faith in the Word you have heard and begin to praise Him, actively and decisively, *in the midst* of each of these circumstances. Praise Him for no other reason than that He is worthy. Do not praise Him in order to *change* your circumstances, but *in spite* of them, and you will be amazed at what follows!

# Finding No Way  Week 45

> *But finding no way because of (the crowd),*
> *they went up on the roof and lowered him,*
> *with his stretcher through the tiles into the midst,*
> *in front of Jesus.*
> Luke 5:19 AMP

If you are anything like me, you have more than once come up against a brick wall, with no way through, over, around or under it. Giving up on a dream, a friendship, a marriage, even a child is never what we would willingly choose, but often seems to be the choice the situation has made *for* us. Finding no way, convinced it's the end of the road, how many of us have simply given up and turned back? Sound familiar? But our Scripture says otherwise of this man's friends.

*Finding* no way, they *made* a way! They refused to accept, to be hampered, hindered, held back or stopped by the circumstances. They had a vision of placing their friend *right in the center, in front of Jesus* (Luke 5:19 NAS). Their focus was on Jesus and healing for their friend, not on the circumstances, which provided no way. Instead, being unwilling to accept the existing conditions and finding that traditionally accepted means were unavailable to them, they looked to the radical and employed the unusual (as Jesus so often did) and kept their focus on their vision for their friend.

And how did Jesus respond to this abrupt invasion, this intrusive demand placed on His healing anointing? Verse 20 says *and when He saw their faith...* It appears that He didn't see disrespect or even take notice of the interruption. He didn't see the damage to the roof. He saw their faith and *when* He saw it, He spoke! And that's when healing manifested for this man, spirit, soul and body. No rebuke, just reward. The man walked away, body healed and sins forgiven, more than his friends had envisioned — and theirs was a dynamic vision!

Hebrews 11:6 (AMP) tells us that *without faith it is impossible to please and be satisfactory to Him,* and in the same verse, that *He is the rewarder of those who earnestly and diligently seek Him.* The paralytic's friends did not yet have this Scripture to stand on, and they surely didn't stand on ceremony, but they did stand on their vision of Jesus the Healer and their friend the healed, and they earnestly and diligently took action. Dire circumstances require drastic measures and mountain moving faith!

Let's contrast this with another "no way" account in Scripture. In John 5, we are introduced to another invalid, a man who had suffered *a deep-seated and lingering disorder for thirty-eight years.* (v.5) Unlike the man in Luke 5 whose focused friends sought Jesus on his behalf, Jesus Himself took notice of this man and approached him, finding him full of excuses as to why in all that time he had been unable to get into the water when the angel stirred up the healing. So he lived his entire life embracing a "finding no way" attitude.

Jesus touched Him, but not until He questioned how earnestly he desired restoration. In verse 14, Jesus exhorted the man to sin no more. Confusing? After all, he was sick, not sinful, right? But a look at the Greek word for sin, *harmartano,* used in this account clears it up for us. It describes one who keeps missing the mark, specifically in relationship with God.

Let's put it together. If it is impossible to please God without faith, and the Bible calls it *sin* to miss the mark in relationship with Him, then it is not much of a leap to see that lacking in faith misses the mark. Our friend at the pool had never reached out and grabbed what was available by *making a way* into the presence of his miracle. Instead, he lived in and even made a doctrine of *finding no way.*

If you find no way, if the bridge is washed out, the road closed, the door slammed, or too many others are in line ahead of you, or if you *have nobody* (John 5:7), do you settle into *finding no way* or do you activate divine focus? Keeping your sight on the inner vision, the dream God has given you, do you plow through, around, under or right over the circumstances to divine manifestation? (See Revelation 2:7.) The choice is yours — all yours!

\*\*\*

## The Bible Minute

***Confession:***
Having stimulated and strengthened my faith in the Word, I will step out. Finding no way in the natural realm, I will be unmoved. I will look to the radical and employ the unusual, understanding that dire circumstances require drastic measures and mountain moving faith!

***Go Deeper:***
Luke 5:19
Hebrews 11:6
John 5:5
John 5:7
Revelation 2:7

***Minute by Minute:***
Desperate situations require drastic measures. What is your personal barrier? What obstacle is standing between you and the realization of your Vision? What desperate situation in your life would require you to look to the radical and employ the unusual?

Finding no way, do as the paralytic's friends did and *make* a way! You too can refuse to accept, to be hampered, hindered, held back or stopped by the circumstances. The paralytic's friends were ordinary people just like you and me but with an extraordinary need and a willingness to employ drastic measures.

It all begins with Godly Vision. Set aside time to build a vibrant Vision. You must be able to see your need fulfilled and unwilling to accept the circumstances as they currently exist.

At all times, be attuned to the voice of the Holy Spirit and, as the great evangelist Oral Roberts once said, expect insights, concepts and ideas. The only thing that remains is to step out and take action!

# Word Power — Sword of the Spirit    Week 46

*Take the helmet of salvation and the sword of the Spirit,
which is the word of God.
And pray in the Spirit on all occasions with
all kinds of prayers and requests.
With this in mind, be alert and always keep on praying
for all the saints.*
Ephesians 6:17, 18 NIV

The Holy Spirit arrested me one day with this: *The Word is as much a manifestation of God as is Jesus, with the same power, two forms of the same Thing.*

I am sure everyone is in agreement, until we come to the words *with the same power*. We acknowledge that Jesus is Lord and accept the triune God, Father, Son and Holy Spirit. But the Word as a manifestation of God, the *same* as Jesus, might take some *consideration*. And the Word having the same power as Jesus; now that may be a *real* stretch for many.

Let's dig into the Word together. Follow along with me for a few minutes and see how this comes alive for you.

We must not stand on the interpretation of one Word. Every word is confirmed by two or three witnesses (2 Corinthians 13:1, Deuteronomy 17:6 & 19:15 and Matthew 18:16) and we know that the Holy Spirit will never give a personal Word that is not confirmed in the written Word. If the interpretation is correct, it will stand the test and the personal Word from God will be born out in Scripture. The Word of God is eternally consistent and the testimony of any Word is confirmed by the totality of the Word.

John 1:1-3 states, *In the beginning was the Word, and the Word was **with God**, and the Word **was God**. The same was in the beginning with God. **All things were made by Him**; and without Him was not any thing made that was made.* (The emphasis throughout is the mine.) We know from a careful reading of Genesis 1 that all things were created by God's spoken Word. Throughout chapter one, God *said* and then God *saw*.

The Word was not only with God at the beginning, but we are told they are One and the same, and verse 3 tells us that *All things were made by **Him***. The Word is referred to as *Him*, which is further confirmation of the oneness of the Word and God. Verse 14 goes on to tell us *And the **Word** was made flesh, and dwelt among us, and we beheld **His** glory, the glory as of the only begotten of the Father, full of grace and truth*. We know the reference is to Jesus Christ, but clearly as a manifestation of the Word. Verse 16 confirms it, *grace and truth came by Jesus Christ*. The Word, the Father and Jesus Christ, all are of a common character, *grace and truth*.

Jesus assures us that when we have seen Him, we have seen the Father (John 14:9). We can be sure that Jesus is not a watered down version of the Father, and if we had any doubt at all, this scripture dispels it. So we can also be certain that the Word of God is not a watered down version. After all, the Word created everything that is seen. (Hebrews 11:3)

The Word spoken into the womb of a young Hebrew maiden became the very manifestation of God as Man. The Word spoken to Lazarus gave us a foreshadowing of the ultimate power of the Word over death. And the Word of God spoken by sinners brings a new birth of the spirit and transformation into sons and daughters of God.

The Word of God has lost no power over the ages. When the Lord Jesus splits the eastern sky and returns to claim the earth in power and glory, there will be no lessening of the power of the Word; they are still One and the Same (see Acts 1:9-11 & Revelation 19:11-16).

Do you long for the power of God in your situation? Then speak the Word He has given you. The Word has inherent power whether as the Creator of all things, as the Son of Man, as the Glorious Lord, or spoken in your mouth — the power is in the Word.

Hallelujah!

\*\*\*

*Confession:*
Death and life are in the power of *my* tongue. The words I speak will bring dynamic power into my circumstances, and into the cir-

cumstances of those around me. I will experience the fruit of this power in my life and ministry. (Proverbs 18:21)

*Go Deeper:*
Ephesians 6:17, 18
2 Corinthians 13:1
Deuteronomy 17:6; 19:15
Matthew 18:16
John 1:1-3
Genesis 1 (God said and God saw)
John 14:9
Hebrews 11:3
Acts 1:9-11
Revelation 19:11-16
Proverbs 18:21
Jeremiah 1:12

*Minute by Minute:*
Has the Holy Spirit spoken a very personal Rhema Word to you? If you are in the Word daily and remain in prayer and fellowship, you may be sure He has spoken to you. Perhaps you are uncertain what to do about it. Begin by recording and dating each personal Word you believe He has spoken to you, either in your prayer journal or on separate note cards.

Then get out your Bible and find confirmation in Scripture. A Rhema Word spoken to you by the Holy Spirit will never contradict the Logos Word as recorded in the Bible. Record the confirmation Scriptures. Then watch for and expect the Word to come to pass. (Jeremiah 1:12)

# Step In!                        Week 46

*The Lord is my shepherd [to feed, guide, and shield me],*
*I shall not lack.*
Psalm 23:1 AMP

Are you weary of striving to fulfill your needs, exhausted just trying to keep up with the necessities for yourself and your family? Be encouraged today and know that it is not your job!

It is not the place of the sheep, not their job to provide for themselves; it is the shepherd's responsibility to provide. Everything you need has already been made available in the spirit realm by the Blood of the New Covenant into which He freely offers you entrance. (See Philippians 4:19)

Once you have established that it is according to His will, speak your desire, (Psalm 37:4), believing that He is Who He says He is (John 14:14; Hebrews 11:6) and He will do what He says He will do (Mark 11:24).

At a buffet, you step up and say *I would like of some of this and some of that on my plate, please*, and it will be transferred from what is AVAILABLE and becomes what is YOURS, on your plate, for your exclusive use.

If you cannot see it or hold it in your hand (whatever your God-given desire is), you have not been availing yourself — *you do not have because you do not ask* (James 4:2).

Step in, step up and step out on the Word of God today. Whatever you need is available. Now that's good news!

***

### Confession:

I do not come as a beggar. God Himself has prepared a table for me and I will not dishonor the gift or the Giver by not receiving what His Blood has paid for.

***Go Deeper:***
Psalm 23
Psalm 37:4
John 14:14
Hebrews 11:6
Mark 11:24
James 4:2

***Minute by Minute:***
First, commit this day to ***step into*** the Word in greater measure. How will you do this?

Then, how can you ***step up*** to God's expectation and call on your life? What will you need to do differently?

Finally, in what specific ways will you need to ***step out*** of your comfort zone and out onto the water to walk in His power?

## *Living in the Harvest*                          *Week 47*

> *But the fruit of the Spirit is*
> *love, joy, peace, patience, kindness,*
> *goodness, faithfulness, gentleness and self-control.*
> *Against such things there is no law.*
> Galatians 5:22-23 NIV

This is the time of year when we see the evidence of harvest everywhere we look. We celebrate the time of gathering into the storehouses culminating in the day set aside as our national day of Thanksgiving. It is the beginning of a new season representing the end result of the year's sowing, watering and nurturing of what we have planted.

It is a perfect time to look at Galatians 5:22 which records the nine characteristics we know as the *Fruit of the Spirit*. Note they are not called "fruits." This is an awkward form of speech for us, but we know that not one word in the Bible is an accident or an oversight. It seems to me that what this phrasing indicates is that these *fruit*, while they may bear different names, are really so completely connected to one another as to be collective. It might be helpful for us to think of it as a basket of fruit that must be received as a whole or not at all.

When we make the decision to welcome Jesus Christ as the center of our lives, we receive the *Fruit of the Spirit* as part of the package. The Holy Spirit takes up residence within us and with Him comes the supernatural nature, the very character of God. We need neither ask nor beg nor even deserve it. It is part of the binding agreement we know as the New Covenant. When we hear the admonition to walk in the Spirit, it is this basket of fruit that not only evidences the walk but largely enables us to walk it as well.

A study of the Greek for each of the fruit would be a great Thanksgiving undertaking. There is no greater proof of the harvest of the Son of Man than for us to walk in the *Fruit of the Spirit*. And there is no greater chance for success than to begin with all the necessary materials already in place!

## The Bible Minute

We have within us *right now* Love (that particular Love that is described in 1 Corinthians 13), Joy (the joy of the Lord), Peace (the New Covenant shalom), Patience (expectant endurance), Kindness (excellence in character and demeanor), Goodness (virtue), Faithfulness (the same Greek word as faith, constancy), Gentleness (a particularly powerful force, humility), and Self-Control (temperance, the supernatural ability to hold steady the walk of faith, to maintain until Jesus comes).

We cannot hope to walk in this harvest, the *Fruit of the Spirit*, in our own power, and the natural human versions of the fruit are fleeting, puny, underdeveloped fruit at best. But if we will yield to God's character within us (yes, simply yield, much like sitting back in a comfortable chair and yielding the body to the rest it offers), we can graciously and victoriously walk out *any* situation facing us.

We will need to be more and more dependent on the *Fruit of the Spirit* in these last days if we are to accomplish all that God has for us. These are exciting and dangerous days, but we have been fully equipped to deal with them in the power of the Spirit. As we move out in confidence in this equipping, without fear, we will surely see His Glory fill the earth, even as He has promised. (Isaiah 6:3)

May this be a powerful season of harvest for each of us!

*I planted the seed, Apollos watered it, but God made it grow.*
*So neither he who plants nor he who waters is anything,*
*but only God, who makes things grow.*
*The man who plants and the man who waters have one purpose,*
*and each will be rewarded according to his own labor.*
*For we are God's fellow workers; you are God's field,*
*God's building.*
1 Corinthians 3:6-9 NIV

### *Confession:*

Hallelujah! Encouraged by the good news that I have all that I need to do all that the Father asks of me, I will step out in new confidence that when the world sees me, they see the Fruit of the Spirit. They see the heart of Jesus!

***Go Deeper:***
Galatians 5:22-23
Isaiah 6:3
1 Corinthians 3:6-9

***Minute by Minute:***
Gaining access to the power of the Fruit of the Spirit when your fleshly versions of each are falling short can seem overwhelming. Try this simple exercise the next time you are physically exhausted and heading toward your favorite chair. As you relax into it, allowing the chair to surround you and, giving in to its support, imagine yourself similarly yielding to the Fruit.

When your patience is running short or your self-control is gone, sit back into the Fruit of the Spirit and *allow* them to take over. Practice the physical sensation and then make the spiritual connection the next time your situation calls for more than your natural attributes. Yield to God's supernatural nature which has been born in you for just such a time.

# The Wicked Prowl — Week 47

*The wicked prowl on every side,
when vileness is exalted among the sons of men.*
Psalm 12:8 NKJV

*H*elp, Lord! For principled and godly people are here no more (Psalm 12:1). How often have you, along with David, cried out to God in a similar way? It is November and we are all beginning to gear up to go into shops and malls to take on the challenge of Christmas shopping. The challenge is not in choosing gifts for loved ones, but in moving out into a world growing daily angrier and more degenerate.

Psalm 12 gives us insight into both the root of the problem and the remedy. We share David's frustration in verse 1. Principled, godly people seem to be fading further and further into the background. And vileness is exalted more and more every day, in every arena.

The dictionary tells us that vileness is not only despicable and abhorrent, but its tendency is to degrade. Vileness describes the basest and most disgusting forms of conversation, entertainment and activity — and we are surrounded by it. Vileness is exalted.

Vileness is fast becoming the norm, the benchmark for all forms of recreation, those which we observe, as well as those in which we participate. Enjoyment and pleasure, which God intended for His people, have become so perverted and abused that we are beginning to perceive of pleasure as a dirty word. Vileness is exalted.

We are witnessing an alarming increase in hate crimes, organizations based on the core principle of hatred, are rising up publicly. Sadly, such groups are not new in the world, or even in this country, but today we see them emerging in the daylight, no longer cloaked in darkness and secrecy. Vileness is exalted.

Books on witchcraft and its evil arts have become teaching tools in many schools and sad to say, even in some churches, having been clothed in a mantle of harmlessness, normalcy and popularity. The old cry of *but everybody's doing it*, still seems to work. Aimed toward children and teens, these tools are being employed to raise up our own children and grandchildren as the unsuspecting army of the enemy. Vileness is exalted.

Sex crimes have skyrocketed and become inextricably linked with violence of the most heinous kind. Our society ventures further into the realm of darkness by staunchly protecting the right to spread such poison under the pretext of freedom of expression. Vileness is exalted.

We have unwittingly become part of the problem by standing for the principles upon which this country was founded, without first making sure we truly understand them. We have allowed the unspeakable to be spoken in the name of free speech. We have allowed the vultures to gather in the name of free assembly. We have legislated murder in the name of a woman's right of sovereignty over her body. Our very naïve hearts have been in the right place, but vileness is exalted nonetheless.

When spiritually immature people have brains and talent, they have the potential to become very dangerous. We are witnessing the truth of that right now. Where does that leave us? Are we to be relegated to hiding, a cowering band of believers fearing persecution? That is, after all, how it appears. And while we are often persecuted, we surely cannot claim surprise at that. Jesus warned us that tribulation was coming, but He also promised us that He had already overcome the world and we would find our peace in Him. (John 16:33)

Here is the good news.

> *'Now will I arise,' says the Lord;*
> *'I will set him in the safety for which he yearns.'*
> Psalm 12:5 NKJV

And how will we see that for which we long?

> *The words of the Lord are pure words,*
> *Like silver tried in a furnace of earth,*
> *Purified seven times.*
> *You shall keep them, O Lord;*
> *You shall preserve them from*
> *this generation forever.*
> Psalm 12:6-7 NKJV

We return to the preciousness and power of the Word of God — always. Our covenant with God provides us with all-powerful resources, if we will but avail ourselves. We have the Word, the Name and the Blood, and with the Holy Spirit to direct us, it is all that we need to do all that He asks of us.

The Word planted in our hearts cannot help but be spoken and God's Word will not return to Him void, according to Isaiah 55:11, but will accomplish His purpose and prosper in His will. Speak it into the circumstances and watch the living, active, powerful Word go to work. (Hebrews 4:12)

We have been given the Name, not only as our new family name, but to invoke as well. All the demons in hell must fall back at the Name and at you when you speak it and they know you are of the Name.

And we have been given the Blood, the precious, life-giving, life-sustaining, world-overcoming, sin-eradicating, blessing-providing, Blood of the Lamb. Come under the Blood, truly knowing its power and operate from that vantage point.

*The Word, the Name and the Blood.* Jesus promised He would not leave us as orphans, that He would come to us, and He has left us well equipped, not only to maintain but to advance the kingdom until He comes.

Vileness is exalted it is true. But we have His promise that every knee will bow to Him and *every tongue should confess that Jesus Christ is Lord, to the glory of God the Father.* (Philippians 2:11 NKJV)

Let us go into the world then, not discouraged, dejected and afraid, but encouraged that although time is short, we can have a significant impact in every minute of every day that remains, even in a vile, unbelieving and perverse generation.

***

*Confession:*
Though the wicked may prowl, I will continue to plant the Word in my heart. Out of the abundance of my heart I will speak into the circumstances, knowing that the Word cannot return to God void,

## The Bible Minute

according to Isaiah 55:11, but will accomplish His purposes, in His power and prosper in His will.

*Go Deeper:*
Psalm 12
Isaiah 55:11
Philippians 2:11
John 16:33
John 14:27
John 16:33
Philippians 4:7
Matthew 12:34
Luke 6:45
Hebrews 4:12 AMP
Romans 14:11 AMP
Philippians 2:10
Revelation 12:11
John 14:18
Philippians 2:10-11
Matthew 17:17
Mark 16:15-18
John 14:12

*Minute by Minute:*

While our society is at best becoming sensitized to vileness and at worst exalts it, we need not be discouraged. We have available to us, at all times, all that we need to do what God has called us to do. Study the Scriptures above.

Then determine how the Holy Spirit, the Word, the Name and the Blood are not only your protection but your equipping to go out into the midst of it, to accomplish what Jesus charged you with (Mark 16:15-18), under the same anointing as Jesus Himself in His earthly ministry (John 14:12).

# Reflections on Joseph
# Man in the Shadows

**Week 48**

> *Then Joseph her husband, being a just man,*
> *and not willing to make her a publick example,*
> *was minded to put her away privily.*
>     Matthew 1:19 KJV

For the next several messages we are going to look at Mary's husband, Joseph. It is easy to forget that he was chosen of God as surely as Mary or the magi or the shepherds or even the heavenly host, for that matter. He is often all but forgotten in our portrait of that first Christmas. So, for every one of us who may have felt forgotten at one time or another in God's plan, let us look and learn.

What do we really know of him, this man chosen to be the adoptive father of our Lord, chosen to raise the boy Jesus? We are told very little of this man in the shadows, attending the main players in the eternal drama. But if we piece together what Scripture does reveal of him, a portrait emerges.

We know Joseph was of the House of David (Luke 1:27), the prophesied line of the Messiah. (2 Samuel 7:12-17) That is well documented for us, the Jews being well known for their meticulous record keeping. If the detailed lineage is not enough, we have confirmation in Luke 2:4 that he went to Bethlehem, the town seat of the House of David, to be taxed, and there to be recorded in the Roman census.

This is no small matter. Joseph's lineage establishes beyond a doubt Jesus' claim to rightful inheritance of the throne of the long awaited Messiah King. And it is the one place in which we see Joseph stepping to the forefront in the telling.

The lineage having been established, what then of the character of this man? We know he was a carpenter (Matthew 13:55), a difficult trade for the area in which he chose to settle his family, I'm told, wood not being in abundant supply. Perhaps this is an indication that he was a man of *patient perseverance*.

Can it be said of each of us that we are willing to patiently persevere in those times when we feel that no one is taking note of our diligence, our struggles or our triumphs, knowing that our heavenly Father is always aware?

\*\*\*

*Confession:*
*If you call me in the nighttime, I'll get on my knees and pray. If I am never seen of men, and if I always work behind the scenes, still I will be faithful.* (From daily prayer of Kenneth E. Hagin[18])

*Go Deeper:*
Matthew 1:19
Luke 1:27
2 Samuel 7:12-17
Luke 2:4
Matthew 13:55

*Minute by Minute:*
God positioned Joseph in such a way that his role was a quiet fulfillment of Messianic prophecy. We see him in the shadows and often seemingly forgotten and forgettable. But examination has shown that his role is anything but!

Has God positioned you strategically, as He did Joseph, to make a difference for the kingdom? Have you been overlooking your importance in God's scheme because you may not be on front stage, in a highly visible role? Take a deeper look at what you have perceived to be your unique contribution and ask the Holy Spirit to give you revelation concerning your part in God's greater plan. There are no unimportant players in this eternal drama!

## Reflections on Joseph
## As the Lord Had Bidden

**Week 48**

*Then Joseph being raised from sleep
did as the angel of the Lord had bidden him,
and took unto him his wife:*
Matthew 1:24, 25 KJV

What else can we learn of this man Joseph who appears on the scene as the protector of the child Jesus and His mother, a man obedient to the word of the Lord in dreams and the link to messianic prophecy? Who was this man who was willing to turn his life upside down, and even to face ridicule for a child that was not of his own blood, but Who would claim his bloodline nonetheless?

We know, of course, that he was not Jesus' biological father (Luke 1:35), but Matthew has spent the first 17 verses of his account establishing the legality of Jesus' claim to the throne — *through his adoptive father.* We begin to see that this is no small role he played. Matthew 1:16 says, *And Jacob begat Joseph the husband of Mary, of whom was born Jesus, who is called Christ.*

This established, without a doubt, the importance of Joseph's bloodline in the claim of Jesus to the throne of the Messiah King. (Matthew 1:1) Adoption in that day and culture was a tie as strong as birth. This established line of inheritance was in God's plan all along, and His prophets set it down for all generations to see. In this, we see Joseph's role as earthly father firmly established.

And perhaps most revealing of all, we know Joseph was given the all important right to announce the child's name as Jesus, even though the name had been established before the beginning of the world. (Matthew 1:21)

\*\*\*

### Confession:

If I you call me to lay aside my own plans and dreams and, in silence, support those you have decreed for another, still I will be faithful, knowing that Your plan is the only perfect plan (Jeremiah 29:11), and in my obedience is my love for you revealed. (John 14:1)

*Go Deeper:*
Matthew 1:24, 25
Luke 1:35
Matthew 1:16
Matthew 1:1
Matthew 1:21
Jeremiah 29:11
John 14:1

*Minute by Minute:*
We have seen that Joseph set his own plans and perceptions aside in order to submit to God's plans for him. A child not of his body was to claim his lineage and Joseph would be the earthly father of a child whose birth brought with it the risk of shame. But he was obedient. Joseph did not have the whole picture, but he understood obedience to God.

Think of a time when God clearly communicated His will to you and you had difficulty understanding your role or you were certain that obedience would negatively impact your life and future. How did you respond and what was the outcome?

## Reflections on Joseph
## For Such a Time

**Week 49**

> *And knew her not till she had brought
> forth her firstborn son: and he called his name JESUS.*
> Matthew 1:25 KJV

We are continuing to get to know Joseph, chosen of God to shelter the infant Jesus and His mother. Examining what we know of him will help us to better understand how God's plan for each of us fits into His great plan for all mankind and how each of us plays a key role, even if God is the only one to see it!

Joseph and Mary were espoused (legally bound by pledge to one another) but they had not yet *come together*. Betrothal in the Jewish tradition was a legal union, a binding covenant, bringing with it many of the benefits we associate with marriage, so binding in fact, that breaking it involved a bill of divorcement.

It can therefore be no mistake, rather a fulfillment of prophecy (Isaiah 7:14) that Mary remained a virgin, with the marriage yet in the betrothal stage (Matthew 1:18; Luke 1:34). We know that Joseph was *obedient*, one who heard from God and heeded what he heard, regardless of his legal rights in the situation. In this, as in everything else, he was guided to play his role in obedience, in the fulfillment of prophecy.

Though we know from Matthew 1:19 that he was a *just* man, Joseph often appears to us to be a mere pawn in this drama which has altered all of life on earth. But that being the case, his character would not have entered into the account. Not only did his integrity keep him from divorcing Mary and publicly disgracing her, but looking beyond, we may conclude that he had an impact on the child Jesus for which we have no written account.

He must have been an influence during Jesus' early years, of which we are only told, *And the Child grew and became strong in spirit, filled with wisdom. And the grace of God was on Him.* (Luke 2:40; Luke 2:52) We know he was a man obedient to the will of

God, which was surely essential to God's choice of Joseph to assign his bloodline *and himself* to the boy Who is the Messiah.

I believe we all have a similar *for such a time as this* in our lives, as did so many we see in the pages of Scripture. (See Esther 4:14). Joseph embraced his time, embraced obedience to the will of God and, along with it, embraced the Messiah as his own. May the same be said of each of us.

*\*\*\**

### *Confession:*
Father, like Joseph, I will quietly embrace your will for my life and place it above my own plans and ambitions. May I be one who seeks and hears your voice and one who trusts Your plan and follows.

### *Go Deeper:*
Matthew 1:25
Isaiah 7:14
Matthew 1:18; Luke 1:34
Matthew 1:19
Luke 2:40; Luke 2:52
Esther 4:14
2 Timothy 3:16-17

### *Minute by Minute:*
*Joseph embraced his time, embraced obedience to the will of God and, along with it, embraced the Messiah as his own. May the same be said of each of us.*

Joseph's integrity and character were the pivotal factors in his ability to embrace his time, embrace obedience and embrace the child Jesus. He was obedient and faithful and just, not merely on the outside. Integrity and character are words we would certainly freely apply to Joseph and the way he lived his life.

*Integrity* refers to core strength. When a hurricane hits a major coastal city, we may hear reports of cosmetic or peripheral damage that did not compromise the integrity of structures. The same is true of human integrity. It is the strength at the core of an individual.

Joseph's integrity, his core strength, remained intact throughout the challenging times and events surrounding the birth of Jesus. Joseph's integrity was solid and was not broken down by the circumstances. His faith kept him sound.

*Character* is the real person, who we are when no one is looking. Joseph's character in private was reflected in who he was publicly. It was the same in the personal moments when he must have wrestled with his emotions, in the silent times with God and in the face he presented to the world around him.

Have you done a self-assessment recently? If not, consider taking a meaningful and prayerful look inside. Has your integrity remained intact through the storms of life or has it been weakened by repeated buffetings? And what of your character? Are you the same person in public as you are in private or have you begun to put on a different face to the world? Ask the Holy Spirit to reveal to you any areas of weakness and begin to purposefully strengthen those areas with the Word of God. (2 Timothy 3:16-17)

## *Reflections on Miriam*[19]
## *Be It Done to Me*

*Week 49*

> *My soul exalts the Lord,*
> *And my spirit has rejoiced in God my Savior,*
> *For He has regard for the humble state of His bondslave;*
> Luke 1:47, 48 (NAS)

Who was she really, this maiden chosen to bear the infant Jesus? What do we really know about her from the pages of Scripture?

> *...She was found to be with child by the Holy Spirit.*
> Matthew 1:18, 20, 21 (NAS)

We know her part in the story represents prophecy fulfilled.

> *Therefore the Lord Himself will give you a sign:*
> *Behold, a virgin will be with child and bear a son,*
> *and she will call His name Immanuel.*
> Isaiah 7:14 (NAS)

Luke, universally recognized as a careful investigator (see Luke 1:3,4), as well as one of the most literarily gifted of the Gospel writers gives us the most detail, beginning with Gabriel's visitation.

> *The Holy Spirit will come upon you,*
> *and the power of the Most High will overshadow you;*
> *and for that reason the holy offspring shall be called*
> *the Son of God.*
> *For nothing will be impossible with God.*
> Luke 1:35b, 37 (NAS)

She didn't question her worthiness; she didn't ask for time to prepare herself; she didn't question the decision. Her only question was *how*, not *if*, or even *why*. She didn't say *I'm not ready to receive Him yet*. Her response was immediate, *be it done to me according to your word* (Luke 1:38). She offered herself to the process, to being filled with God, set apart for His use — for the rest of her life.

Her greatness was in her humility, another one of those paradoxes we find so well illustrated in the Beatitudes. (see Matthew 5) In the upside down world of the Word, the last shall be first (Matthew 20:16), and the humble shall be exalted. (Matthew 19:30) Her greatness was in her willingness to be used, to be a receiver, a vessel, the container for greatness. But first, she had to set *herself* aside.

Are we meant to be any different than Mary? Are we not also intended to be vessels of greatness? Too much for you? Consider this — Father, Son and Holy Spirit are One God. (Matthew 8:20:19) And yet we lose sight of what we carry within us. Mary was the vessel, the vehicle for the manifestation of the Son in the earth, so that we could be the vessels, the vehicles for the manifestation of the Spirit in the earth.

\*\*\*

## *Confession:*

Along with Mary, I say with all my heart, *be it done to me according to your word*. I too offer myself to God's process in my life, to being filled with His Spirit, set apart for His use for the rest of my life. I am intended to be a container for greatness, no less than Mary was.

## *Go Deeper:*
Luke 1:47, 48
Matthew 1:18, 20, 21
Isaiah 7:14
Luke 1:35-38
Matthew 5
Matthew 20:16
Matthew 19:30
Matthew 8:20:19
Psalm 37:4-5
Psalm 104
Isaiah 40
Job 38, 40-41

***Minute by Minute:***
Was it difficult for you to speak aloud the above confession? Did it stick in your throat at all? If so, you are not alone. Complete surrender to God's will is a *simple* thing, but not an *easy* one. It may be that you are looking back at what you think you must give up instead of forward at what you will gain. The greatness of His plan for you far outshines anything you may leave behind.

Delighting yourself in the Lord is the remedy. Psalm 37:4 exhorts us, *Delight yourself in the Lord; and He will give you the desires of your heart.* Put down all else and by an act of your will, delight yourself in the Lord. Read Psalm 104, Isaiah 40, and Job 38, 40 and 41, meditating on the wonder of His greatness, knowing that it is this same God who desires to live in your heart and guide your life.

Follow this simple plan until you have had a personal revelation of who He is and who He wants to be in your life and then return to the above confession.

## *Reflections on Miriam*[19]        Week 50
## *A Rejoicing Spirit*

> *My soul exalts the Lord,*
> *and my spirit has rejoiced in God my Savior,*
> *For He has regard for the humble state of His bondslave;*
> Luke 1:47, 48

What did this young girl do, what was her response to the overwhelming message of the angel? And what lessons can we take away from what we know of her?

1. *Live a life of preparedness.*
   When we hear God calling us, through the written Word, a still small voice within, or a Word so loud and clear it stops us in our tracks, will we be prepared? In season and out, if we have made a decision for Jesus Christ and received the Holy Spirit, we should be in a state of constant readiness. Be in the word of God daily; stay in fellowship with the Father; be attuned to the voice of the Holy Spirit.
2. *Step out on the plan you know.*
   Miriam was not waiting for an angel to appear in order to proceed with her life. She lived a godly life (we can be certain of that from the angelic salutation) and she proceeded with the plan she *knew*, espoused to a good man, according to her tradition. But she was prepared to *alter* her plan, according to the revealed will of God, through His word.
3. *Know the treasure of God within you.*
   We must daily think as an expectant mother who takes great care with her body, her whole focus on what is growing inside her, preparing with excellence for the day when the child will be released into the world, given an opportunity to make an impact.
4. *Practice birthing the Holy Spirit into your world.*
   Ours is to be a daily process of birthing, of bringing the Good News of Jesus Christ into a lost and dying world. If we are to ful-

fill the Great Commission (Mark 16:15), we must each go into all the world we know, surrendering ourselves to the process.
5. **Heed the message.**

*For with God nothing is ever impossible and no word from God shall be without power or impossible of fulfillment.*
Luke 1:37 AMP

We need not feel worthy, nor even up to the task. We need only be available and surrendered to the power of God, to do it in us, through us and for us. Mary surrendered to the process of God's will. She did not cause it and she had no conscious part in its unfolding. She did what she knew by way of following the traditions surrounding pregnancy. She knew the law entitled Joseph a legal recourse to her pregnancy, but she trusted in the word of God, regardless of the circumstances. We can do the same.

6. **Turn your life over to the plan of God.**
Say with Miriam, *behold, the handmaid of the Lord; be it done unto me according to thy word.* (Luke 1:38) She referred to herself as a bondslave, not as one forced into servitude, but one who willingly surrenders all they are and all they have to another. This servitude of spirit, soul and body is a whole life choice, definitely not one of convenience, but one of dedication to the will of another.
7. **Exalt the Lord.**
Her life and plan totally altered, her life's direction changed for eternity, Miriam's response was to praise God for using her. (Luke 1:46-55) Can we do any less?

Today, during this season of preparedness, once again let us examine ourselves for our readiness to receive and to continue to receive the presence of the Holy Spirit within us. Let us rededicate ourselves, even as this young woman did 2000 years ago, to altering our lives and direction in conformance to the will of God. Let us be ever mindful of the precious Presence we carry within us, and be prepared to release that Presence into our needy world.

Miriam had God in her — so do we! We are no less chosen as sacred vessels than she was. Let us renew our willingness to surrender to that awesome honor, not just in this season but from this day forward.

***

*Confession:*
*My soul exalts the Lord, and my spirit has rejoiced in God my Savior, for He has regard for the humble state of His bondslave.* (Luke 1:47, 48) Along with Mary, I yield myself fully to fulfilling God's plan for my life as a demonstration of His glory in the earth.

*Go Deeper:*
Luke 1:47, 48
Mark 16:15
Isaiah 55:11
Luke 1:38
Luke 1:46-55
Matthew 25:1-13

*Minute by Minute:*
Review the first of the seven suggestions above. Living a life of preparedness is the key to all the rest. Do not be as the five foolish virgins in Matthew 25, who scurried to make ready at the sound of the bridegroom's approach. Instead, do as the five prudent virgins, and be prepared, lamp filled with oil and wick trimmed, awaiting the sound of His call.

Are you now living such a life? If not, what is holding you back? What would you need to change, remove or implement in order to be in a state of constant readiness? Be specific. Then put your plan into effect.

# *Hearts Are Open*            Week 50

*"Behold, I say to you, lift up your eyes, and look on the fields,*
*that they are white for harvest.*
*I sent you to reap that for which you have not labored,*
*and you have entered into their labor."*
John 4:35b, 38 NAS

*"Then He said to His disciples, 'The harvest is plentiful,*
*but the workers are few...'*
*'And as you go, preach, saying, "The kingdom of heaven*
*is at hand."*
*Heal the sick, raise the dead, cleanse the lepers,*
*cast out demons; freely you received, freely give.'"*
Matthew 9:37; 10:7, 8 NAS

Read these scriptures over several times. They are familiar passages, but really get them down inside before we go on.

There are some tough questions to be answered by each of us, and we need to be grounded in an understanding of our Blood bought righteousness before God, and in the above Scriptures, before we can answer them without getting offended. Do not read any further until that has been done. If it means taking a few days to get grounded, that's fine.

We need to get tough about sharing the Gospel. We must squarely face our own issues with what Jesus has to say in our foundation Scriptures. We must ask ourselves if we are selling out, playing it safe. Are we falling short in the name of sensitivity, in the name of political correctness? Are we holding back in order to "keep the door open?" You say, Look, I don't want to lose the relationship. What would I be able to accomplish then? Each of these, and more, is an excuse we have used for not sharing the Gospel, but are they valid excuses? I wonder, is any excuse a valid one?

I am not referring to sledgehammer Christianity! Everyone avoids the rabid dog approach. The idea is not to drive people away but to draw them in, to allow the Holy Spirit to shine *through* us. It

## The Bible Minute

is God Who attracts people to Himself, not us. Be a willing vessel and be attuned to the voice of the Holy Spirit urging you to approach someone. Then allow Him to do the work.

We are in a *prime time*, a season of ripeness right now for sharing the love of God with others. Perhaps you don't have the gift of evangelism, and just thinking about reaching out to the unsaved makes your palms clammy. The love of God is not only to be shared with the unsaved, unchurched sinners of the world. There are millions right in the Body of Christ who are suffering from a lack of knowledge or understanding. (Hosea 4:6). Many have gone through the motions of making Jesus their Lord, praying the "sinner's prayer," but never had anyone disciple them, taking them by the hand and walking with them for a time.

There are many who love the Lord with their whole heart and soul, but have no idea of the power of the Holy Spirit dwelling in them. It is critical to witness to the Christian just as it is to the unsaved. We feel that's only for pastors, but the Bible is very clear that we are the salt of the earth, we are the light of world, we are sent out to be the eyes and ears, the hands and feet, the *mouth* of God in the world.

It is so much easier to play it safe. I'll pray for them, in faith you say. And of course you must, but that is just not enough — plain and simple. Doing is the breath of faith, the fruit of the tree of faith. James 1:22, says that it is not enough to hear, or even hear and meditate, on the word; but we must be doers of the word. In James 2:17, we are exhorted, *Even so faith, if it has no works, is dead, by itself.* We must step out on the knowledge we possess.

Did Jesus play it safe? What a ridiculous question — of course not. Then we cannot either. He plainly told us in John 14:12 & 13, *Truly, truly, I say to you, he who believes in Me, the works that I do shall he do also; and greater than these shall he do; because I go to the Father.* But let's not stop there; let's ask *WHY*? And then read on, *If you ask Me anything in My name, I will do it.* There it is, we have not only been commanded to go out and do, but we have been given the means, and moreover, we have been empowered.

We have no valid excuse! We have been commanded to go into all the world and preach the gospel to **all** creation, (Mark 16:15), and more, (see verse 17 & 18). I have a personal suspicion, which I have not yet found in Scripture, that when we stand before the throne and are asked to give an account of every thought, word and deed from the time of our rebirth, that we will also be shown the consequence, of each, but also of *all that we did not do*.

If that should be the case, I would perhaps be shown unspeakable suffering that I had the Word of Life available to quell. I would perhaps be shown souls in the pit of hell for all eternity, without God, to whom I had been given the opportunity to speak the Word of Life — and did not because I might offend. And then, perhaps I would be shown all the damned souls suffering because I was not willing to come alongside with a healing Word for the suffering Christian brother or sister who was called to reach *them* — and so they never knew. Can I carry that with me into eternity — I pray I do not need to!

Now is the time to get tough with ourselves, and then to go before the Lord, the God of mercy and grace, who calls us to come before Him in time of need (Hebrews 4:16). Ask for forgiveness for each time you stood back and did not offer a word, for each time you took the safe stance, and then move forward in the power of the Holy Spirit to fulfill the Great Commission.

Now is the time; this is the season; hearts are soft and people have questions. We have the answers. Move out into your world with the answers on your lips.

Blessings!

***

## *Confession:*

I will start on a new path today, one that knows no self-consciousness. I will step out boldly on the Word that I know. I will listen at all times for the leading of the Holy Spirit. I will speak to those He brings across my path whatever He gives me to speak, in certainty that I am called to labor in the Master's fields.

***Go Deeper:***
John 4:35b, 38
Matthew 9:3; 10:7, 8
Hosea 4:6
James 1:22
James 2:17
John 14:12 & 13
Mark 16:15, 17-18
Hebrews 4:16

***Minute by Minute:***
    Make a list of those within your circle, family, friends, coworkers, for whom you regularly pray and intercede. Then list what you would like each of them to know to enrich their lives, today and for eternity. Now, consider stepping out of your comfort zone and being the one to tell them. What better time than this? Hearts are open!

# The Spirit Led Life  Week 51

*We have not ceased to pray for you…*
*that you may be filled with the knowledge of His will*
*in all spiritual wisdom*
*and understanding, so that you will walk in a manner*
*worthy of the Lord,*
*to please Him in all respects, bearing fruit in every good work*
*and increasing in the knowledge of God*
Colossians 1:9-10 NAS

I am sure that walking *in a manner worthy of the Lord* is something each of us desires. But in order to conduct our lives in this way, we must rely on something or someone other than our own puny wisdom and our own weak will.

Walking in the Spirit is the answer. If you have been following along with us, you know we talk about practicing the presence of God, maintaining divine focus and establishing divine connection. When our focus is on our heavenly Father, when our eyes are on Him at all times and in all circumstances, we will also be open to His leading by the Holy Spirit. This divine connection opens up a two way communication, in which we continually share our love, our joy in Him, our wants, needs and desires with God, all the while learning to be attentive to His voice.

The Holy Spirit is depicted in the New Testament by the Greek word *parakletos*. It denotes a legal advisor, pleader, proxy, advocate, helper, a counselor, and a representative. The literal translation, and my favorite, is *one who is called (kaleo) to come and walk alongside (para)*. Now that is indeed a comforting picture!

Of course we know that the Holy Spirit is closer even than that, as close as our next breath in fact (John 14:17). So let's make a quality decision that beginning today we will listen for His voice,

- in the Word of God, personalizing it for us and bringing it to our remembrance in times of need (John 14:26),
- in gentle leading, prompting throughout the day, and

- in major revelations.

God is speaking to us at all times and in all situations. Whether we are open to His leading depends on the atmosphere we cultivate. Actively still the clamor and the voices of the world. Then, according to Psalm 46:10, still your own soul.

\*\*\*

## *Confession:*
I commit right now to developing a greater awareness of the One who walks alongside me, and to listen expectantly for His voice throughout the day.

## *Go Deeper:*
Colossians 1:9-10
John 14:17
John 14:26
Psalm 46:10

## *Minute by Minute:*
Begin by keeping a chronicle and referring to it regularly. All too often, when our prayers are answered we miss it because we have neglected to wait and watch expectantly. If you have been listening all along, commit today to an even deeper listening and a quick to do it response. Then consider stepping out and helping a brother or sister in the faith with what you have learned.

# Friends Forever    Week 51

> *He made known His ways to Moses,*
> *His acts to the sons of Israel.*
> Psalm 103:7 NAS

Two Old Testament patriarchs, Abraham and Moses, share the great distinction of being called friends of God.

Abraham displayed his faith in God, cutting covenant with Him, and God called Him friend. Abraham enjoyed such closeness with God that He was very much in the inner circle when it came to the decision of the destruction of Sodom and Gomorrah. (Genesis 18:16-33)

Moses spoke face to face with God in such profound harmony that his countenance reflected the very glory of God. (Exodus 34:31) While Moses' behavior at Meribah cost him entrance into the Promised Land (Numbers 20:8-13), it did not lose him friendship with God. In fact, so intimate is their friendship that none but God knows where he is buried. (Deuteronomy 34:6)

It is important to know that what gained these two men friendship with God was *not* their behavior, for both fell short in that regard. It was their willingness to take God at His Word, not only to believe it, but then to act upon it. They are set apart from others in the Old Testament whom God loved and called to greatness by their designation as friends.

Knowing God as Friend takes us to a place of not only witnessing His acts, but gives us entrance into knowledge of His ways, the secrets of the inner circle. (Psalm 103:7) God tells us, through Isaiah, that His thoughts are not our thoughts, and our ways are not His ways. (Isaiah 55:8-11). Many have taken this to mean that we are left without understanding. But Jesus gives us entrance to friendship with Him and, along with it, knowledge of the ways of God. (John 15:12-17)

Nothing has changed today. There is a deep intimacy in true friendship and when we accept the invitation to make Jesus our personal Savior, we are drawn into that inner circle and we become friends of God simply by accepting and believing. Isn't it about time we started acting more like friends than pitiful outsiders?

Isn't it time we started sharing His invitation with the world? There's an end time harvest out there, just waiting to be brought in from the fields and there's great Good News to share. The world is no longer able to discern even the acts of God and it is up to us to make known God's invitation to friendship and knowledge of His ways.

***

*Confession:*
I share deep and intimate friendship with God. I have His mind (1 Corinthians 2:16) and I know His ways. I will go into the world sharing His love and inviting new friendships.

*Go Deeper:*
Psalm 103:7
Genesis 18:16-33
Exodus 34:31
Numbers 20:8-13
Deuteronomy 34:6
Isaiah 55:8-11
John 15:12-17
1 Corinthians 2:16
Hosea 4:6

*Minute by Minute:*
If you have made Jesus Christ your personal Lord and Savior, you have been given access to intimacy with Him. If you have not been experiencing this closeness, it may be lack of knowledge (Hosea 4:6) and unclear understanding of your position.

You cannot earn intimacy with God based on your exemplary behavior. It is your willingness to take God at His Word, not only to believe it, but then to act upon it. It is by faith that you will enter in.

Consider spending time studying the lives of Moses and Abraham. Then look at David, who was far from perfect but was nonetheless a man after God's heart, and Joseph, the prideful little brother who saved all of Israel from starvation because God was with him. They were not perfect but they had in common that they believed and acted on what they believed.

There is a lost and hurting world out there just waiting for what we have been given and who is to share it with them if not us? So step into that intimacy that is offered and then step out into the world and share the Good News.

# Why Me? **Week 52**
# Well Equipped

*And Moses said to God, 'Who am I that I should go to Pharaoh, and that I should bring forth the sons of Israel out of Egypt?' And He said, 'I will be with you. And this shall be the sign to you that I have sent you: When you have brought forth the people out of Egypt, you shall serve God upon this mountain'. And Moses said to God, 'Behold, when I come to the sons of Israel, and shall say to them, The God of your fathers has sent me to you, and they shall say to me, '"What is His name?"' What shall I say to them?' And God said to Moses, 'I AM THAT I AM.'*
Exodus 3:11-14 NKJV

Is there something you believe God is calling you to do? Are you finding reasons why you cannot possibly do it? Are you disputing it with God? If that is the case, you are in good company. Even Moses, God's friend, to whom God revealed His ways (Psalm 103:7), began by trying to convince God he was the wrong man for the project.

If Moses' experience strikes a familiar chord, here are a few considerations, which will help you through it.

### 1. *God knows us better than we know ourselves.*

We are not the ones to determine whether we are right for the job. At best, we have only limited vision and perspective. Godly perspective is what is called for in determining placement in the kingdom.

### 2. *When God calls, He equips.*

How many NASA astronauts, upon entering the space program, run out to *Astronauts 'R Us* and begin to equip themselves for the mission? Do you suppose they call their wives and say, *better get going packing up the freeze dried PB&J for a long trip — and don't forget my toothbrush and jammies...?* Ludicrous, of course, but accurate.

God no more expects us to equip ourselves for what He asks of us, than NASA expects it of their astronauts. NASA wants the absolute best for the program, and no one person can provide that. Only the assembled NASA team can do that. God wants the absolute best for His program and only He can provide it. Rely on that!

### 3. *Dependence is the key.*

From the time we are barely walking, society teaches us that independence is the ultimate goal. Needing no one, self-sufficient, self-directed, self-motivated, self-centered, society would call us successful. But when God calls us, He is not interested in what we *can* do; He is interested in what we *cannot* do. He is looking for those who are without resource and know it, for those who will say *yes* and then expect instruction from the Holy Spirit. A wonderful example is how God used the very unlikely Gideon, whom God called a *mighty man of valor*, in Judges 6-8.

### 4. *Grace is the gift.*

According to Merriam Webster, *grace is unmerited, divine assistance given humans for their regeneration or sanctification; approval; favor; privilege*. Grace is unmerited favor. It cannot be earned, so there is no price we can hope to pay for it. It is a pure gift. Grace is the favor necessary to accomplish what God has asked. It is God's Name going before us. Do not make the mistake of attempting anything ordained by God without the necessary grace!

### 5. *The Holy Spirit is the power.*

Your own paltry power can barely propel you out of bed in the morning so how can you expect it to accomplish the divine? No, this will take the power of God in and on the flesh of man, to do the will of God in these critical last days. You would never pull out the wooden oars to row the Queen Mary across the Atlantic — ridiculous! You would use the humungous engines provided for the job. Why then do we consistently set out to do God's work in our own power?

## 6. *Your part is surrender and submission.*

That just doesn't seem right you might be saying. You mean all I have to do is say *yes* and surrender? How could that possibly work? Take another look at Moses. There are indications that Moses could not speak well. (Exodus 4:10, 11) Some Bible scholars have even speculated that the text indicates an actual speech impediment, a stutter perhaps.

What's more, the last place Moses would want to go was back to Egypt where he was wanted for murder. Having actually been a part of Pharaoh's household, it is not likely that his crime would have been forgotten. He clearly could not rely on the favor of man. His only hope was in surrender and submission to God and *His* power to fulfill *His* plan.

\*\*\*

### *Confession:*

By the world's standards, I feel unworthy to be called by God. But I will learn from Moses' protests. God is the Author of the plan and my part is but to make myself available.

### *Go Deeper:*
Exodus 3:11-14
Psalm 103:7
Judges 6, 7 & 8
Exodus 4:10, 11

### *Minute by Minute:*

*Needing no one, self-sufficient, self-directed, self-motivated, self-centered — these are the qualities the world prizes, the traits deemed necessary for success.* Contrast that with the very different expectations of the *upside down* kingdom of God as presented in the Sermon on the Mount in Matthew 5-7.

God is interested in what we *cannot* do. It is essential that we are aware of who we are *without* God so that we can truly understand who we are *with* Him. We must be aware that our resources are inconsequential when it comes to what is required for kingdom work.

Study the example of Gideon in Judges 6-8 noting how God maneuvered his resources so that Gideon would fulfill his calling in God's power, not his own. Now, note any parallels between Gideon's experience and your own. How often do you become ensnared by measuring yourself according to the world's standards? For the next 24 hours, become aware of, and chronicle, how often you assess yourself by world rather than Kingdom standards.

# *Why Me?*        Week 52
# *The Fire of God and You!*

> *And the light of Israel shall be as a fire,*
> *and His Holy One as a flame;*
> *and it shall burn and devour his thorns and his briers in one day.*
> Isaiah 10:17 NKJV

> *And the angel of the Lord appeared to him*
> *in a blazing fire from the midst of a bush,*
> *and he looked, and behold, the bush was burning with fire,*
> *yet the bush was not consumed.*
> Exodus 3:2 NAS

Review Part 1 of this message, *Well Equipped* and then look once more at Exodus 3, the account of Moses' encounter with God at Mount Horeb. What has been revealed to us concerning the nature of the fire and the burning bush itself?

### 1. The bush was entirely engulfed but not consumed.

The fire of God as it applies to His servants, to His holy (set apart) ones is not a consuming fire, though He certainly has shown Himself as such to those who would dare to stand against Him. (Deuteronomy 4:24; Deuteronomy 9:3)

### 2. The bush was on fire for a purpose.

The fire of God burning in our spirits drives us forward to accomplish what He has called us to, in the same way that the fire in the bellies of the great furnaces of ocean vessels drives them powerfully forward to their destination. Desire was not enough to fuel these giants; nor even the best of plans, charts and maps, interpreted by the greatest masters of the sea. No, it took fire to make the charted course a reality.

***3. The bush indicated holy ground.***

In order to grasp this, we must have a clear biblical understanding of the concept of *holy*. Holy, in its simplest form, means set apart from the ordinary for a specific purpose, usually in the sense of indicating the presence of God. It applies to people as well as to objects and places. Sanctification is the process of being made holy. Following directly from this is another use of the word holy, to be perfect or spiritually pure. Of course where God is present we expect perfection and purity. It also means filled with superhuman power, awe-inspiring. It makes sense doesn't it, once you grasp its simplest meaning?

Wherever the fire of God burns, the ground is holy, set apart for His purpose. His purpose was to draw Moses' attention in a very forceful way and indicate to him that the power of God was present. Do you have the fire of God burning in your spirit? Is God speaking to you personally from that place? Are you on fire for a purpose? Are you on fire at all?

Perhaps you have long feared the fire of God, thinking it would strike you and burn you to a cinder leaving no recognizable remains. How many times have you felt the Spirit of God stirring and calling in that still small voice — and yet allowing you to turn the other way? Has it now perhaps become a burning insistence?

We have all known Christians we referred to as *on fire*. If we take a close look, we will see that they remain recognizable, aflame but not destroyed, not burnt up and most importantly, not burned out. Only when the fire of God strikes us, unquenched by our fear, can we truly do what we are called to do and not burn out — one of those characteristics of the upside down kingdom. Give to get, love those who despise you, do good to those who desire to harm you, die to come to new life, be on fire and not burn out — upside down principles of the kingdom.

When I AM THAT I AM sends you (Exodus 3:14 KJV), the fire will burn strong and true and your strength will burn strong and true as well. Your sign will be to serve God upon the mountain, just as it was for Moses. You will know it is not you, but the Lord your God who sends you, who strengthens you with His fire, who empowers you, and who calls you to give glory to His Name!

Some years ago in a Bible school class in which we were studying some great evangelists and preachers, it was noted that many of these faith giants were "quirky." The instructor reminded us that when we give our lives completely to the Lord, inviting Him into our hearts, while He gives us a brand new spirit, He does not change our personalities. He uses them. Be assured that if you decide to answer your own burning call, in all of your uniqueness, God will not incinerate you. He will set you apart, empower you and use you to fulfill the prayer He Himself gave us, *Thy Kingdom come, Thy will be done on earth as it is in Heaven.* (Matthew 6:10)

*\*\*\**

*Confession:*
At the call of the Lord, I will say with Isaiah, *Here am I. Send me.* (Isaiah 6:8) God does not require my ability but He does require my total availability. He will do the rest.

*Go Deeper:*
Isaiah 10:17
Deuteronomy 4:24
Deuteronomy 9:3
Exodus 3:14
Matthew 6:10
Isaiah 6:8

*Minute by Minute:*
Samuel Chadwick observed in his classic book <u>The Way to Pentecost</u>,[20] *Destitute of the Fire of God, nothing else counts; possessing Fire, nothing else matters.*

Is this in line with the biblical account of Moses' encounter with God in the burning bush? How did Moses' experience change him, along with his destiny? How did he have to alter his thinking in order to step out in God's plan? Why do you think God chose the burning bush scenario to reveal Himself and His plan to Moses? What role did the Fire of God play?

Do you have the fire of God burning in your spirit? Is God speaking to you personally from that place? Are you on fire for a purpose? Are you on fire at all?

Have you already had your own personal experience with the Fire of God? If so, how has it changed you and your self-perception? How has it changed the direction of your life?

If you have not yet experienced the Fire of God, assuming that each of us needs it to carry out His work in the world, how can you position yourself on a day to day basis for just such an experience?

# *Final Decision*

I would be remiss if I closed without offering one more opportunity to confess Jesus as your personal Lord and Savior. No other event in my own life has had the same powerful impact as the decision I made in the early morning hours of a spring day in 1993. Not only did my eternal future change that day, but the course of my life shifted drastically. Since then I have come to the full knowledge that we can only hope to realize our full significance in our willingness to make Jesus Christ the Lord of our lives.

> *Jesus answered him, I assure you, most solemnly I tell you,*
> *that unless a person is born again (anew, from above),*
> *he cannot ever see (know, be acquainted with, and experience)*
> *the kingdom of God.*
> John 3:3 AMP

In John 3, Jesus told Nicodemus that it was necessary for him to be born again from above. But why? Romans 3:23 says that *all have sinned and fall short of the glory of God* but that if we confess with our mouths and believe with our hearts that God raised Jesus from the dead, then we are saved. (Romans 10:9)

But what is this *saved* and is it something that we really need to be — or are we already? You may be thinking, *but I've gone to church all my life. I'm a good, honest, loving, law-abiding person. Isn't that enough? Aren't I saved?*

We were fashioned in the image and likeness of the Creator, by Him and for Him, to be joined with Him in perfect bliss for all of eternity. To be in His image, it was necessary for us to be endowed with His characteristics, all but the divinity; which was His alone. One of those characteristics is choice, free will. Free will without divinity — well, you can see the risk. And sure enough, it wasn't long before man, the crown of God's creation, made the consummate bad choice and handed over his inheritance to the enemy.

The Greek word that is translated as salvation is *soteria*. Soteria is the culmination of God's plan to reverse the curse of that bad choice back in the garden and bring us back to Him. It is a wonderful word and an understanding of the Greek will make it much clearer to us. Soteria is both material and temporal deliverance, material and present, as well as spiritual and eternal. It is a word that suggests *all* the blessing of God. In other words, it means blessing on earth and eternity in heaven.

Though it is available to anyone who wants it, it does not come without a price — complete surrender. God wants nothing less than your whole heart, and in return, the immeasurable gift of eternity with Him is yours. If that is what you want, really want, with all your heart, pray this prayer, or one like it, and begin the greatest adventure imaginable.

*Lord, I confess that I have been on the wrong road, one of my own making. Lord Jesus, I confess that too often I have done things my way, attempting to create my own path to Heaven. I have diluted your crystal clear word, to make it seem more palatable. Now Lord, I give up my own way and repent for each wrong footstep I have taken.*

*I confess now with my mouth that You stepped from heaven into the earth and took on human form, and You died for me, paying the penalty for my wrong doing. You were raised from the dead and ever live as my staunchest Sponsor, Supporter, and Backer before the Throne.*

*Lord Jesus, I confess your name aloud as my One and only Lord and Savior. I ask You to come into my heart and be my personal*

*Redeemer, the Lord of my life and my Best Friend. I am now and forever Your own and You are mine. In Jesus' name – Amen*

If you have never confessed Jesus as Lord, congratulations, you are now born again! Your future is assured. It is not necessary that you pray these exact words, only that the words come from your heart. If Jesus is already the Lord of your life, there can be no better confession than the renewal of that vow.

Now the adventure begins in earnest. From the moment I made the decision to surrender my all to Jesus Christ, my life became exciting, challenging and oh so fulfilling!

Welcome to the Body of Christ!

# *In Closing*

*'For I know the plans that I have for you,'*
*declares the Lord, plans for welfare*
*and not for calamity to give you a future and a hope.*
Jeremiah 29:11 NAS

God has a plan and a purpose for your life, specifically designed for you, one that fits you like a glove! While each of us is called to that plan, and equipped according to our calling, many of us are still working through the process of discerning what our particular calling is. In the meantime, there is one thing we can know with absolute certainty. We are all called to make a difference!

*How can I make a difference? I'm not a teacher, a preacher or an evangelist. I'm not even sure I would know how to pray for someone and I never seem to know what to say when friends are going through tough times.*

But we're not talking about skill, talent, advanced degrees or eloquence. This is about presence, compassion and sensitivity, about being a walking example of the life-giving love of God.

*And hope maketh not ashamed;*
*because the love of God is shed abroad in our hearts*
*by the Holy Ghost which is given unto us.*
Romans 5:5 KJV

Even a cursory reading of Scripture illustrates that God is clearly not looking for *ability*, but for *availability*. Determine to be available and your heavenly Father will supply whatever ability is needed. All He asks of you is your heartfelt *Yes* in response to His call. Say with Isaiah, *Here I am. Send me.* (Isaiah 6:8) He does not require your *assistance*, but your *assent* is essential.

The needs of our brothers and sisters in this life can be met most often with a willing ear far better than an eloquent tongue. Perhaps a casserole accompanied by a simple note, *I'm praying for you* is exactly what is called for. Send an e-card, offer to do the laundry, or pick the kids up from school. It is simply a matter of whatever you can do to make a difference in your world. Can you cook? Can you babysit? Can you drive someone to the doctor? Can you mow a lawn, invite someone for coffee…?

If you don't know what to say to someone who is suffering, say just that. *I can't imagine what it's like for you, and I don't know what to say, but I'm thinking about you and praying for you.* People know you cannot fix their problems and probably don't want you to try, but most, in the dark times of the soul, do want to know that they are in your heart. You *can* do that!

There can be no better way to evidence the love of God to a hurting world than to provide a living example of it. That is the sure way to draw people to a personal relationship with Jesus Christ. After all, that's what evangelism truly is. Show them what it looks like and it will draw them in like a magnet. Then simply give them the Word of life. (See John 1:1, 14 and John 14:6)

Now consider taking it to another level. At the start of each new day when you are having your quiet time with the Father, ask Him to direct suffering people across your path and to anoint you to make a difference in each life. You can be assured that He will answer prayers such as these!

This is the time; the opportunities exist for our finest hour as Christians. We are in the last of the last days in the midst of the final end-time harvest Jesus spoke of in John 4:35-38 and Matthew 13:37-39. The greatest harvest of souls in all of human history is slated for this hour on God's time clock. But each of us will need to be in position according to God's plan, prepared to witness, to evidence a relationship with Jesus Christ, the only Savior of our souls.

Be obedient to God's call and experience a life of excitement, joy and fulfillment beyond your imaginings. Fill up on the Word, keeping your Holy Spirit connection strong, and step into God's plan for you. Resolve this day, and every day, to walk in the love of God, actively seeking ways to evidence the life-giving love that has been shed abroad in your heart. Make a difference!

To God be the glory!
Karin

# *Endnotes*

***Proper Goodbyes***
[1] *Today with Marilyn & Sarah*, a daily television broadcast sponsored by Marilyn Hickey Ministries (http://www.marilynandsarah.org/)
[2] Laura C. Schlesinger, *Bad Childhood—Good Life: How to Blossom and Thrive in Spite of an Unhappy Childhood*, (New York, NY: HarperCollins Publishers, 2006)
[3] *Mission Accomplished – Strategic Life Planning* is available in hard copy or a downloadable eBook through Karin's website at www.solushunz.com

***A Peaceful Life***
[4] Brother Lawrence, *The Practice of the Presence of God, Brother Lawrence's Conversations and Letters*, Light Heart Edition, http://www.practicegodspresence.com (May 27, 2010)

***Complete Transfusion***
[5] M.R. DeHaan, M.D., *The Chemistry of the Blood* (Grand Rapids Michigan: Zondervan Publishing House, 1943/1981), p.25

***The Survey Shows***
[6] *The Christian Counseling Connection*, The American Association of Christian Counselors. This article appeared in 2005, Issue 1. Other statistics drawn from www.galluppoll.com.

### *Be Still — The Lord Almighty*
7  YHWH/Yahweh/Jehovah, God whose Name is too awesome to be spoken; The completely self-existing One, always present, never changing, the I AM God. (See Exodus 3:14-15)
Jehovah Rapha, Healer; the One who makes bitter experiences sweet
Jehovah M'Kaddesh, Your Sanctifier
Jehovah Nissi, your Victory, your Banner
Jehovah Shalom, your Peace
Jehovah Tsidkenu, your Righteousness
Jehovah Rohi, your Shepherd
Jehovah Shammah, your Helper, who will never leave, never forsake you (Deuteronomy 31:6, 8; Hebrews 13:5).

### *Altered Sight*
8  Fasting is associated with preparation, humbling, re-focusing, putting down the flesh nature, pointing up areas of need, also in conjunction with prayer and with worship. For further study, see Matthew 6:17, 18; Isaiah 58:6; Joel 2:12; Luke 2:37; Acts 13:2; Acts 14:23; Daniel 9:3.

### *Journey to Promise — Without a Vision*
9  Karin S. Syren, *Mission Accomplished, A Handbook for Visionaries*, 2006, is available in eBook form for download at the Karin's website at www.solushunz.com.

### *Father, Forgive Them...*
10  *Pay It Forward Movement*, http://www.payitforwardmovement.com/ (May 25, 2010)
11  http://payitforward.warnerbros.com/Pay_It_Forward/

### *Hope Realized*
12  Originally published 2/8/06 at the birth of my second grandchild.

### *What Do You Have Faith For?*
13  "Endometriosis is a condition where tissue similar to the lining of the uterus (the endometrial stroma and glands, which should only be located inside the uterus) is found elsewhere in the body.

Endometriosis lesions can be found anywhere in the pelvic cavity: on the ovaries, the fallopian tubes, and on the pelvic sidewall. Other common sites include the uterosacral ligaments, the cul-de-sac, the Pouch of Douglas, and in the rectal-vaginal septum.

The most common symptom of endometriosis is pelvic pain. The pain often correlates to the menstrual cycle, but a woman with endometriosis may also experience pain that doesn't correlate to her cycle. For many women, the pain of endometriosis is so severe and debilitating that it impacts their lives in significant ways.

Endometriosis can also cause scar tissue and adhesions to develop that can distort a woman's internal anatomy. In advanced stages, internal organs may fuse together, causing a condition known as a 'frozen pelvis.'"
*Endometriosis*, http://www.endometriois.org/endometriosis.html (May 25, 2010)

## *Common Opportunities*
[14] Dick Eastman, "Intimacy and Spiritual Breakthrough," Kingdom Dynamics article, Jack W. Hayford, exec. ed., *The New Spirit Filled Life Bible*, (Thomas Nelson Bibles, A Division of Thomas Nelson, Inc. 2002) 807. Dick Eastman is the international president of Every Home for Christ, Colorado Springs, CO., http://www.ehc.org.

## *Nuggets from the Proverbs — Walk in the Light*
[15] For a detailed explanation, see the Karin's book, <u>Mission Accomplished, A Handbook for Visionaries</u>, which outlines the entire strategic planning program. It is available through her website at www.Solushunz.com

## *A Great Calm Occurred*
[16] Lit., *A great calm occurred.*
[17] *Sea of Galilee*, http://www.bibleplaces.com/seagalilee.htm (May 25, 2010)

### Reflections on Joseph – Man in the Shadows
[18] Kenneth E. Hagin, personal ministry prayer, *Rhema Word of Faith* magazine (July, 2001), a publication of Kenneth Hagin Ministries, https://www.rhema.org/

### Reflections on Miriam
[19] *Miriam* is the Hebrew for Mary

### Why Me? The Fire of God and You!
[20] Samuel Chadwick, *The Way to Pentecost*, (Original publication, Berne, Indiana, Light and Hope Publications,1937). Digital Edition 08/14/98, Holiness Data Ministry. No evidence of a current copyright for the printed book has been found. http://www.jesus.org.uk/vault/library/chadwick.shtml (MY 25, 2010)

LaVergne, TN USA
12 July 2010
189205LV00001B/89/P